MADAME ELISABETH

After a most successful excursion into the seventeenth century with *The Nun*, Margaret Trouncer returns to the Versailles of the eighteenth century. Her loving study of Louis XVI's sister, the saintly Madame Elisabeth, is set against a background of bejewelled inanity. We see the members of a vanished aristocracy spinning elegantly to destruction, ironically heedless of impending doom, as they dance gavottes at Queen Marie-Antoinette's parties in the lantern-lit gardens of Petit Trianon, watch the first balloon flight, or sneer during the trial of the Cardinal de Rohan in the Necklace Affair which heralded the Revolution.

Springing from this foetid atmosphere, Madame Elisabeth, the lily of the French Court, was one of those women who make goodness attractive. The Prince de Bourbon-Parme said she had "a rare moral elegance". Before the Revolution, we see her, devoted to the poor, an ardent botanist, a fearless horsewoman who could hunt for eleven hours at a stretch and then dance till three in the morning: and yet, this did not prevent her from rising early to visit the Carmelite nuns whom she longed to join. An engaging letter-writer, she wrote amusingly to the little group of ladies-in-waiting, to whom she was the perfect friend, leaving a kiss where there had been a wound.

In prison, at the end, this model of sisterly devotion was the only friend left to the tragic Marie-Antoinette and her family before they all perished under the guillotine.

Catholics hope that the cause for her Beatification will soon be introduced at Rome.

Other works by MARGARET TROUNCER

Courtesan of Paradise (*Translated into Swedish*)
(Book Guild Recommendation)
The Pompadour
Go, Lovely Rose
Why So Pale?
The Smiling Madonna
Oriflamme
She Walks in Beauty
Madame Récamier
The Bride's Tale
The Nun (*Translated into four languages*)

DECLARATION

If I have inadvertently referred to Madame Elisabeth as a saint, I in no wise anticipate the final Judgment of the Church, to whose decrees I bow with filial love.

MARGARET TROUNCER

ACKNOWLEDGMENTS

I want to thank my friend Mademoiselle Agnès Joly, of the Bibliothèque de Versailles, for allowing me to use her paper on the Dauphin. I am very grateful to Mademoiselle Chantrell of Château de Montreuil, Versailles, for her permission to reproduce the portrait of Madame Elisabeth de France by Madame Labille-Guyard.

CONTENTS

Introduction   *Page* 13

Part I

"CLOUD-CAPPED PALACES"

Chapter I   Domestic felicity at Court   17

  II   A Versailles childhood   29

  III   In which Elisabeth falls in love with the Carmelite
Order and meets Marie-Antoinette   38

  IV   A royal schoolroom at Versailles   49

  V   Marie-Antoinette   58

  VI   Trials and pleasures of early girlhood   70

  VII   A visit to Carmel   80

  VIII   Elisabeth surveys her new apartment   88

  IX   Elisabeth's friends   99

  X   Elisabeth stays at Petit Trianon, and meets the Queen's
friends   102

  XI   In which Bombon makes his appearance at Court and
Elisabeth becomes Châtelaine of Montreuil   116

  XII   The Russian Visit and the Chantilly house-party   133

  XIII   A bad winter, and balloons   148

  XIV   The Model village at Petit Trianon, and the Necklace
Affair   164

  XV   Louise de Condé, and last days at Versailles   172

Part II

"THE REFINER AND PURIFIER OF SILVER"

XVI	Farewell, Versailles . . .	*Page* 185
XVII	The palace of the Tuileries	192
XVIII	The horizon darkens	197
XIX	Nuns and priests in hiding	208
XX	The flight to Varennes	216
XXI	Caught	224
XXII	After Varennes	236
XXIII	The fatal year	242

Part III

THE CHALICE

XXIV	The Temple prison	255
XXV	The September Massacres and the King's death	263
XXVI	After the King's death	275
XXVII	The Queen's tragedy	281
XXVIII	Last days together	293
XXIX	The Crucible	299
	Appendix	319

INTRODUCTION

In this delicious book, we live in two worlds; we watch, as it were, two tapestries. The first is a delicate *petit-point*, vaporous, misty, stitched in pastel tints, scattered with Redouté roses, turbulent with ostrich feather head-dresses, billowing panniers and untethered balloons.

And in the background of this tambour frame, the figure of a young girl, floating in her garden of Montreuil. Although living in all the luxury and sin of the end of the eighteenth century, we realize that she took no part in the scandals; she was untouched by contact with the vices of Versailles. An aureole of holiness shielded her during her short life, till the dreadful end.

And then we gaze at this white-robed figure, blown by an ill wind on to the other arras, painted like "Macbeth" in black and red—sombre, dramatic. Instead of roses, we see blood trickling slowly into the gutter after the Princesse de Lamballe has been publicly slaughtered by viragos who included her kitchen-maid. Instead of glittering rapiers at Trianon, we see the blade of the guillotine, the blade falling with a sharp thud on the swan-like neck of Elisabeth, this sister of Kings.

Margaret Trouncer has accomplished a profoundly deep and true work of art. Although many interesting books may appear this year, I feel confident that *Madame Elisabeth* will stand out as a shining star among them all. Once again, the author has shown her vast knowledge of history and her profound understanding of the French nation.

AGNES DE STOECKL

Coppins Cottage,
Iver.

PART I

"Cloud-Capped Palaces"

CHAPTER I

Domestic felicity at Court

WHEN the Dauphin, dying of galloping consumption at Fontainebleau, held his frail baby daughter Elisabeth in his arms for the last time, he gazed at her and then whispered: "What goodness in her eyes!"

They say that Providence matches the need of a corrupt century with a suitable saint. In pre-Revolution France, in these marshes of sexual vice, a spotless lily sprang, a royal Fleur-de-Lys, who was to redeem her age. The great Dominican preacher Lacordaire said that it is the mark of great hearts to meet the need of their age. Just as lust was the chief vice of eighteenth-century France, darkening the pages of its history, until the culminating horror of the Marquis de Sade, so chasteness and pure love, incarnate in the members of a small élite, like Madame Elisabeth and the Princesse de Condé, saved that century from utter cataclysm.

The de Goncourt brothers said that men had sunk so low, that they prided themselves on "leaving a wound where they had dropped a kiss". Madame Elisabeth prided herself on leaving a kiss where there had been a wound. The sure key to her heart was to be lonely and unhappy. She was "in love" with nobody but God, and all her short life, she loved and gave: big gifts like husbands and dowries to her women friends, loyalty to disagreeable aunts and unpopular sisters-in-law, gaiety to frivolous brothers who would have been put off by piety, and who needed to be enticed to virtue, training in self-discipline to a niece, pensions to widows, jobs to the workless, food and warmth to the sick and poor, milk to village babies, devotion till death to her brother's family in prison. She gave little things, like amusing letters to neglected people, Sèvres porcelain to her impecunious friends, a gold-embroidered ball-gown to one girl at court, riding lessons to another.

Like a spring bubbling up from the ground, she was a "giver".

What a contrast with a man like the Duc de Richelieu, for instance! The very antipodes—a taker, a robber, a murderer of lives. Richelieu, the Casanova of his day, even worse than Louis XV, one day took it into his head to steal, by trickery, the affections of the wife of Michelin, a maker of mirror-glass. She was a pretty, innocent, fair-haired thing of eighteen whom he had coveted at daily Mass. He got her into his house, by sending a faked order for a mirror from a duchess. When Madame Michelin realised that she was dishonoured, she suffered such moral tortures, that she fell ill and eventually died. Shortly after, Richelieu from his carriage saw a man in deep mourning. He called him in. It was Michelin; he had buried his wife two days ago. The duke, an epicure for unusual sensations, made him get in and sit next to him, to hear him weep. . . .

Richelieu . . . Madame Elisabeth. . . .

.   .   .   .   .

Even her body buried against the wall of the Parc Monceau, brings its own redeeming virtue, to that park to which the Duc d'Orléans once enticed a young girl, raped her and then had her corpse thrown into the Seine.

Whereas the crimes of a Richelieu are recorded in many memoirs, the annals of pure married happiness are rare indeed. Its portrayal lends itself to subtle derision. We are far more apt to be arrested by the notorious Tillys and Lanzuns, the arch seducers, than to seek out the quiet lives which distil so delicate a fragrance in the secret pages of French history. And yet, Elisabeth's parents were only two among many adoring young husbands and wives. Again the de Goncourts tell us the most touching story, as if to cancel out the terrifying Richelieu anecdote: "A woman condemned by her physicians had only several days to live. Her husband sensed that she read her death in his sadness and in the tears which he tried to hide from her. He goes to buy a diamond necklace for 48,000 livres, brings it to the dying woman, speaks to her of the day when she will put it on, of the court ball at which she will display it; and while making the necklace glitter on her bed, he causes hope, convalescence, cure, life, the future, to shine in her soul. He lulled and soothed her agony in a dream! And that husband, the Marquis de Choiseul, was poor: he had pledged an estate to buy those diamonds which, by a clause in his marriage contract, were destined to come back to his wife's family."

From such a conjugal love sprang Elisabeth princess of France.

A person of felicitous character is often born of saintly parents, the fruit of happy love. In a court where fifteen out of twenty men lived apart from their wives, Elisabeth's father and mother distinguished themselves, and indeed incurred ridicule, by being models of fidelity. The Dauphin, Louis XV's only son, was a handsome young man, to judge by Roslin's portrait.[1] We can still see him at Versailles. Here he is, in full military rig, gorgeous high-plumed helmet and white curled wig. The eyebrows are a little sardonic, the whole poise of the body indicates movement and dash, quite different from Carmontelle's later portrait, when trouble and frustration had aged him.

His beloved first wife, the Infanta Marie Thérèse, had died in childbed in 1746. The Dauphin was only sixteen when they had married in March 1745, and it was at their wedding ball, in the Galerie des Glaces, that the future Marquise de Pompadour, in charming fancy-dress, had thrown her cap so successfully at Louis XV. The Dauphin Louis had adored his wife, even though she called him *hibou*—owl. Writing on a drum from the camp of Fontenoy, he had exclaimed delightedly to a friend: "I can hardly believe it's true that I am so soon to be a father!" When Marie Thérèse died, "he was like an inconsolable child".

For reasons of state, his father made him marry again. Fifteen-year-old Marie-Josèphe de Saxe, to judge by Nattier's ravishing picture of her in court dress of cherry-embroidered damask, had a queenly air, falcon-wide eyes, and a most intelligent expression. La Tour's pastel of her in the Louvre, shows a really lovely woman, with large, expressive, intelligent eyes set in a well-shaped face. Her powdered hair is close cut, with a small posy of flowers in front. (Her hair was, in fact, unfashionably red, and her spinster sister-in-law, Madame Adélaïde, seething with envy, did little else but remind the bridegroom of this

[1] For much information on the Dauphin, I am indebted to Mademoiselle Agnès Joly of Versailles.

fact.) La Tour's pastel shows her delightful taste in dress, with all those eighteenth-century details of fan, diamond bracelet, flounced lace sleeves, ruched blue ribbons, and coral bows, which were so flattering and feminine. Before she came to Versailles, Louis XV had written to the Maréchal de Richelieu to tell Madame de Brancas to give her a bath: (which confirms one in the horrid suspicion that the poor departed Infanta, for all her Spanish brocades and diamonds, had perhaps neglected her ablutions!) The new Dauphine gave every promise of being a good Queen. Wearing a skirt which weighed sixty pounds and a bodice like a cuirass, she received the congratulations of the courtiers for hours on end without flinching or showing any sign of fatigue.

Alas, on her wedding night, this child of fifteen had need of all her fortitude and tact. When she was left alone with her bridegroom, she noticed that he looked around the bridal chamber and gazed very mournfully at some furniture which had been in his beloved Infanta's room. He turned his face away, clenching his teeth to master his sobs. The fate of the marriage hung by a thread. At length he collapsed by her side. She looked so kind and understanding, that the tears he had been trying to blink away all day, at last poured down his cheeks. Leashing hurt pride, she tried to comfort him.

More tears for both of them, during their official entry into Paris, when beggars clung to the doors of their coach, crying: "We don't want your money, we want bread."

But even after she had steered him through the quicksands of that honeymoon, when any other girl's self-assurance would have been broken for life, he continued to show his aversion for her. She began to wonder if the Infanta's pompous funeral trappings had not affected his mind, for in those days the apartments and coaches of mourning princes were heavily draped in black, and even the mirrors were covered. Or did he take after his father, who like many voluptuaries showed such a morbid taste for death and corpses? The Dauphin and his five peculiar spinster sisters would walk round their rooms, murmuring sombrely: "We are dead." They played cards by the light of funeral tapers, still muttering: "We are dead." The bride sat in a corner, bravely trying to smile, bravely trying to put up a façade to hide her horror and fear. The five sisters were not very reassuring. It was now hard to recognise them in Nattier's glowing canvases. Madame Louise, who was to become a Carmelite nun, was slightly deformed; Madame Adélaïde, domineering, restless and a blue-stocking; Madame Victoire immersed in the pleasures of a table whose Lenten menu was renowned throughout Europe; Madame Sophie, trotting so quickly that she looked like a hare, was so timid that she only became friendly during thunderstorms, when she would clutch people's hands almost passionately. The only human creature of the lot was sad, sweet Madame Henriette. Rumour had it that she was dying of love for her cousin, the Duc de Chartres. Indeed very soon, she fell into a decline and died. Her corpse, fully rouged and powdered, dressed in huge satin panniers, was propped up and driven in a coach to Paris. She alone of the five sisters had understood the anguish of the young bride. She did all she could to bring the newly married pair together and she succeeded. Had it not been for her, the marriage would have foundered altogether.

The Dauphine triumped at last when her husband caught smallpox, and, in spite of protests on all sides, she insisted on nursing him herself. She did this so successfully, that an onlooker, a stranger to ceremonial, said to the doctor: "That is an excellent nurse you have there. Never get rid of her." Regardless of infection, she kissed her husband. That heroic action won his heart for ever.

When he recovered, they became the most openly devoted couple at Versailles. The courtiers tittered behind their muffs and fans, as they watched them walking arm in arm on the terrace just outside their ground-floor suite in the south wing, overlooking the Orangery. The courtiers would have laughed still more, had they known about the union of their souls. Each day they recited the Great Office of the Paris Breviary together. After his death, she wrote to the Bishop of Verdun: "I have just finished saying Matins, which we never missed reciting together. I thought I was again in the great closet, walking up and down with him. I heard him read the lessons. Sweet illusion, but cruel when it ceased."

He assisted at the parish services at Notre Dame de Versailles and sang with the faithful in that sonorous voice of his which he had

trained so carefully. The philosophers treated him as a bigot, a *dévot*—
which since "Tartufe" was a term of derision. But this was not true:
this prince who read Locke on his death-bed, had a broad, tolerant
mind. He did not live in ascetic seclusion at court: his apartments were
decorated with sumptuous art and he had composed his library with
fine taste. He took part in all the court festivities and ceremonies, in
spite of keeping a very strict personal rule of life. Although the duty
of his state obliged him to go to bed fairly late, he used to rise very
early in the morning, and prepare by prayer and study to play his
part in the King's councils. He gave orders to his servants that they were
to get him out of bed forcibly, at the time prescribed. This was all the
more meritorious, for a tendency to plumpness in childhood pre-
disposed him to indolence and indifference.

The Dauphin and his wife were as one mind. Together they
shared in Queen Marie Leczinska's devotion to the Sacred Heart of
Christ. Regardless of courtiers who nicknamed them the "Cordi-
cules", they joined the Sacred Heart confraternity of their parish. The
members had to apply themselves to sincere forgiveness of their
enemies, to conquest of their antipathies, and cordiality to "unkindred"
spirits. Excellent preparation for the trials which awaited them with the
triumphant advent of the Pompadour! The Dauphin is said to have
stuck out his tongue at her and nicknamed her "Pompon", but, after a
while, not wishing to be estranged from his father, he conquered his
disgust and treated her with outward courtesy.

They had eight children in all, three of whom were to be the last
three Bourbon Kings of France, the Duc de Berry who became
Louis XVI, the Comte de Provence who became Louis XVIII, and
the Comte d'Artois who became Charles X. Their seventh child,
Madame Clotilde, was beatified very soon after her death. Madame
Elisabeth was their eighth and last child. Louis XV nicknamed her
Madame Dernière.

The young couple's married life was almost idyllic: reading together, gardening, enjoying music—(the young Mozart played for
them very shortly before Madame Elisabeth's birth). The Dauphin
sang, played the spinet, the violin and the organ. Dufort de Cheverny
wrote of him: "I have seen him gay in his home life, but of a restrained

gaiety, *et du meilleur ton*. On one of the Cordon Bleu procession days, there had been a performance of Sedaine's play 'The peasant and his lord', in which the peasant clamoured for his wig because his lord was going to call. The Dauphin acted it so delightfully, that he made everybody go into fits of laughter by the verve with which he interpreted the part, without, however, giving cause for ridicule."

In a century when a wife only made herself ridiculous by showing jealousy, the Dauphine had several altercations with her husband, who proved his consanguinity with Louis XV by indulging in several minor flirtations. (The temptations were so great.) But these transitory little affairs did nothing to mar their essential harmony of heart and mind.

He had given up hunting after accidentally shooting his squire. He could never forgive himself for having caused a man's death.

Both he and his wife were extremely charitable to the poor, and in this, above all else, Elisabeth was to resemble her parents. He would often tell his children's tutors to take them to the houses of the poor: "They must learn to weep. A Prince who has never shed any tears cannot be good." Beggars were always sure of a good reception at those ground-floor windows. Wishing to give all his children a lesson on the equality of all Christian souls before God, the Dauphin would have the baptismal register brought from the parish church of Notre Dame, where his children had all been christened: "Look, my children, look at your names written after the name of a pauper. The only thing that can establish any difference between you is virtue."

Nurtured in such a family, Elisabeth said later that she had been overwhelmed with graces from her earliest childhood. Living so ascetic a life, it is surprising that the Dauphine managed to rear any children at all. A fortnight before Elisabeth's birth in 1764, she mentions in a letter to a friend that the Holy Week services, which she loved, were tiring her horribly. The following year, in Lent, she wrote to her brother: ". . . I'm dying of hunger; it's past nine o'clock, and I have only a salad and several asparagus heads cooked in water, inside me." She had a great devotion to the Feast of the Holy Cross which fell on May 3rd, and in 1764, she had hoped to celebrate that day. She wrote to her confessor: "But I am not sure from one day to the next, of being in a state to do so." And strangely enough, on Thursday, May 3rd, 1764, her child Elisabeth was born at two o'clock in the morning. She was baptised by the Archbishop of Rheims—Rheims the Cathedral of angels and lilies, the sanctuary of coronations. She was given the names of Elisabeth-Philippine-Marie-Helène and styled *Madame*. She was so frail that they trembled for her life, and she was only saved by the care of her devoted wet-nurse, Marie-Thérèse Hecquet. Even infants were martyrs to court etiquette, for they were rudely awakened at stated times to be changed, whether they needed it or not. If, later, they needed changing, they were left for hours untended by their army of menials, if it did not chance to be the correct hour. It's no wonder that the infant mortality at Versailles was so high.

Alas, the Dauphin did not live to bring up his daughter. He had been very thin for some time. It may have been grief at his eldest son's death, or some secret sorrow, but he fell seriously ill in 1765. There is a supernatural explanation of this illness, which has no proved historical foundation. It appears that the Queen, who dearly loved her son, and who called him "her consolation", had been privately informed of a grave danger attacking his virtue. She had asked God to recall her son to Himself, rather than allow him to succumb. (Later, when she saw that her prayer was heard, how poignantly she was to regret her heroism!) In August of that year, after catching a chill in camp, where he always treated his soldiers as friends, he started coughing blood and suffering from dysentery. Horace Walpole, who saw him at Versailles on October 3rd, said he looked like a spectre, and gave him three months to live. When he got to Fontainebleau, where the court always spent the autumn, he was obliged to take to his bed. Fontainebleau was impossible to warm at all, and rats scampered about all night. It was there that his eighteen-month-old Elisabeth was brought to him as he lay dying, and he whispered: "What goodness in her eyes."

From Fontainebleau, he wrote to a friend that his soul was always gay, although exasperated by what its yoke-fellow the body made it suffer. Gaiety was one of the chief gifts he bestowed on his daughter. With despair in her heart, the Dauphine pinned his travelling crucifix on the bed curtains and then left him alone to prepare for his end. All the court came to see him receive Extreme Unction. His sweet serene expression contrasted deeply with the tear-stained faces of the sobbing courtiers. When the Dauphine came in again, she was struck by the contentment, the joy and beatitude shining in his eyes. He held out his hand to her, saying: "I am overwhelmed with joy. I would never have thought that receiving these last Sacraments would frighten so little, and be so consoling. You couldn't believe it." Though he appeared very gay with the King and Queen, from time to time he cast a glance at his crucifix, which had now been placed on his bed. He looked at it with a joy which shone out in spite of himself. The King said to him: "I'm told that the Parisians were at the doors of Saint Geneviève at five o'clock this morning, in spite of the desperate cold. The Dragoons of your own regiment have kept a fast and given alms." The Dauphin replied: "Alas, six months ago, plenty of people detested me. I had deserved it no more than the love which they show me at present." His wife turned him so that he could lie on his side, for he was suffering from a painful tumour. He apologised to his father for turning his back on him. When he fell into a fitful half sleep, he betrayed his sufferings by groans. After a while he woke up, and catching sight of some princes and princesses of the blood royal, and a few ambassadors, he murmured apologetically: "I am regaling you with quite a little agony!" Again, his wife left him alone.

Though the separation of husband and wife before the end was quite in the tradition of the eighteenth century, the Dauphin felt its poignancy. The next morning, he betrayed his delight on seeing his wife again: "What, is it yourself? Eh, good morning, *mon petit cœur*. How glad I am to see you! I thought you were lost. . . . How I love you!" After a terrible attack of coughing, he cried out, when he got his breath again, "Go away, my dear Pepa, go away, it's too cruel to bear." But towards evening, they allowed his old friend Nicolay to come in; he took his hand and pressed it on his heart, whispering: "You won't leave me?" For several hours he could still talk, and even cracked jokes. On November 20th, towards six in the morning, he lost consciousness and died peacefully at eight o'clock. He was only thirty-six.

The Cardinal de Luynes said: "There is no Trappist monk who would not envy the way Monsieur le Dauphin has died."

His widow Marie-Josèphe, who would now never be Queen of France, wrote to her confessor: "I know that one can only invoke the saints whom the Church has canonised, but I don't think I do wrong, when, passing in front of his portrait, I beg him to remember me before God. I talk to it, that portrait, as I used to talk to him when he was alive." She found it almost impossible to overcome her grief. He had cared for her soul's progress, and she for his, for they had made a pact to correct each other's faults.

His funeral took place in that cathedral of Sens, through which Saint Louis had passed bearing the Crown of Thorns. The day after, the broken-hearted widow cut off the hair which her husband had so greatly loved, and gave up the use of rouge. She moved to an apartment nearer her father-in-law's staircase, and for a short while, rejoiced in the trust he showed her. But everything continued to speak to her of her departed husband. One day, in the following February, walking through Queen Marie Leczinska's apartment, she caught sight of Alexis Belle's radiant picture of her mother-in-law holding the Dauphin as a very plump, overfed little boy. Elisabeth, who was toddling by her side, called out: "Papa, Papa." The Dauphine looked down at the child, who, from being a frail waif, was now almost as plump as her father had been. (Indeed, Horace Walpole, seeing "the little Madame's pap dinner", had written to a friend in England that the Dauphin's little girl was "as round and as fat as a pudding".) Her mother, remembering some of the anecdotes about her husband as a child, secretly thought that his daughter resembled him, for she was very tempestuous and would stamp her feet with rage when thwarted or when her waiting women did not serve her quickly enough. Louis had once given the Bishop of Mirepoix a big smack for contradicting him. He'd ordered his tutor to make the wind stop howling, and he'd said to the Comtesse de Noailles: "Will we always see you with the clothes of a fifteen-year-old, the face of a thirty-five-year-old, and the manners of a person of eighty?" . . . "But Monsieur, what can one do to please you?" one of his attendants asked in desperation. To which had come the dry answer: "Change." The child Elisabeth was as proud as Lucifer. Quite unlike her gracious little sister Clotilde, who would always embrace the people presented to her, Elisabeth would simply hold out her podgy little hand to be kissed. The small nose promised to be a forceful aquiline beak, and her lower lip, even now, jutted out in forceful fashion. The Dauphine did not bend down to caress her child. That was not at all in the tradition of the epoch before Rousseau. Instead, she left her to chase her pug along the Galerie des Glaces, and to play with the ass which was being led to her own private apartments to be milked.

The Dauphine, looking up at Roslin's picture of her husband, recalled how his tutor had scolded him for what he called his "exaggerated prosternations" at Mass, and told him not to adore the Blessed Sacrament like a monk. How little they knew him! He had always been so gay in his home life. The Dauphine gazed out of the windows at the park in the February twilight. She glanced towards the south wing, where they had been so happy together, and recalled his passion for gardening. She must see that Elisabeth had a little plot of her own, for the child seemed to love flowers just as much as her father had done. Perhaps her aunts, Mesdames Tantes, who cultivated jasmine, clematis and shrubs in wooden tubs on their balconies, would encourage that taste. She must speak to the gardener at Trianon, and tell him to give the child some seeds in March, and a tiny rake.

Alas, by March 13th, 1767, fifteen months after her husband, she was dead. Poor Clotilde screamed with wretchedness. A cortège of desolate peasants attended her coffin to Sens, where she was buried, as she had wished, by her husband's side.

The five surviving orphans were bereft indeed. So much did they lack affection, that the little Duc de Berry, the future Louis XVI, sobbed aloud in a children's game: "Whom could I possibly love here, where nobody loves me?" Their aunts, Mesdames Tantes, were absorbed in narrow-minded piety, back-biting, creature comforts, the pleasures of the table and the telling of risqué stories. Their grandmother, Queen Marie Leczinska, who was to be with them only a year more, had been so crushed throughout her life, that she had faded away into a dim, resigned nonentity, very strict on the minutiae of etiquette and ceremonial. When her own daughter, Madame Louise, wanted to see her for a longer time than usual, and in private, she refused, saying: "But there are some customs at court to which even natural feelings must bow." Her grand-children were brought in to her every day to kiss her hand. They would give horrified glances at the skull on her table, which she nick-named "*Ma chère Mignonne*".[1] Elisabeth would try not to overtopple as she made her curtsey in her wide panniers. After the Queen's death, in fact shockingly soon after, the King became absorbed in Madame du Barry. Madame de Marsan, the governess of the two little girls, felt sorry for them. On Elisabeth's fifth birthday, on the Feast of the Holy Cross, she showed her the two treasures which her mother had left her in her will: an ivory statue of the Virgin which had been in the Dauphin's oratory, and a relic of the True Cross in a crystal reliquary. She tried to explain to the child a little of the preciousness of such bequests. The child looked up at her with those big blue eyes, and the governess recalled what her father had said about her on his death-bed. She heaved a sign, and thought to herself: "I wish that were true."

The child was a sorry handful.

---

[1] The skull of Ninon de Lenclos.

CHAPTER II

A Versailles childhood

THE trouble with the child was that she ran so quickly, it was impossible to catch her. Madame de Marsan the governess really could not compromise her dignity and her legs any more by chasing her through Louis XIV's Labyrinth. Probably Elisabeth would be hiding behind a statue, calling "Cuckoo!" She would throw her ball into the marble basins of the park, just for the sheer pleasure of watching the pages fish it out with a long pole. But her great aim in life was to be rowed in the gondolas by some of the King's Venetian gondoliers. Water had an irresistible attraction for her, and for her tiresome pug, who was her constant companion and fellow truant—the same little pug which she is holding in Drouais' picture.[1]

The child was undisciplined, impertinent, haughty. She made one look ridiculous. Madame de Marsan, feeling she had no hold on her, grew almost to dislike her, for she had to contend with an iron will in a very small person. The governess took refuge in favouring the elder sister, Clotilde, who, although so plump that she was nick-named "Gros-Madame", had, according to Horace Walpole, "a glorious face". Without being a prig, *that* child was almost perfect. Madame de Marsan made the great mistake of constantly holding her up to Elisabeth as a model, and this only made things much worse.

One May evening, the governess was sitting with Clotilde near the Bassin de Latone, whilst the setting sun caressed the golden statues of Ceres, Flora and Bacchus. Flora was offering a bouquet to the passing courtiers, a bouquet which, in those days, was painted in life-like tints. Elisabeth, as usual, had lost her pug and was hunting for him in the Labyrinth, where he had an assignation with Madame de Choiseul's toy spaniel. In the distance, a duchess was taking the evening air, her green taffeta parasol held over her head by a gorgeously dressed little black servant. Madame de Marsan turned to the page in the King's red,

[1] Lépicié also painted her embracing a spaniel. (Collection Cognacq-Jay.)

white and blue livery and commanded: "Find Madame Elisabeth, and bring her back at once."

The young scamp was quite pleased to leave such stuffy company, and exercise his long legs. He was tired of standing and listening to old Madame de Maintenon's maxims being read aloud to "Gros-Madame". Being a page had its boring moments. His grandfather, in Auvergne, who had been at the court of Louis XIV, was always quoting Madame de Sévigné's *mot* about Versailles. "Yes, it is an enchanted place, but the Enchanter must be there." He personally found the gardens too much like state apartments, and preferred pranking in the taverns of Versailles with his friends. *Grand-père* used to tell him about the flower beds of the Grand Trianon, planted with orange trees, jasmine, narcissus and tuberose: "Yes, my child, I have seen the King and all his courtiers forced to leave the garden because the scent was too much for them."

"Cuckoo," sounded a little voice. Suddenly, Madame Elisabeth de France appeared, her white Valenciennes lace pinny drenched with water and her cap askew. The page gave a low bow. "Madame, I have been ordered to bring you home." Her face fell and she said petulantly: "I am never allowed out of sight for one moment, and there are so many things I want to watch here. I want to go to the menagerie and see the lynx, and the tiger and the rhinoceros and the pelican. Do you know, the lion is always escorted by his friend, the mad-cap dog, and they are inseparable. Lucky lion, having someone to play with."

"Poor little girl," thought the page. She rattled on: "When I am older, *Grand-papa Roi* will take me for a night party on the Canal, and I will listen to the violins, and watch the English yachts." The page said enthusiastically: "Madame, you will see the miniature frigate, and the great galley all glistening with gold and fleurs-de-lys and shells and sea gods. It's heavenly to float on the water in the middle of the night. You see, Madame, you've got a great deal to look forward to."

She sighed. "But it's *now* that I'd like to be happy. There's never much that I'm allowed to do. Everything seems forbidden. I'm always being reminded that I must behave like a princess, and Madame de Marsan is always praising my sister. If only I could see a little more of my brothers."

The page interposed: "But Madame, I thought you saw them yesterday in the riding school?"

Again the child's face fell. "That was not very pleasant. I wanted to ride too, and Madame de Marsan wouldn't let me, so I walked off in a huff, without saying good-bye to anybody. And when I got home I had to do two whole pages of lines."

"What were your lines, Madame?"

"I had to write, as best I could: 'Jesus Christ who was God was obedient.' I make great resolutions to be as good as my sister, but I keep forgetting."

At last the pug appeared, looking as crestfallen and damp as his mistress. "I'm afraid he's been sick; I smacked him yesterday, and when my sister scolded me, I gave him all my pudding to console him, and it was too much for him."

The page enticed the princess homewards, listening to her chatter about her brothers. She seemed absolutely devoted to the youngest, the Comte d'Artois. "I think he's like Prince Charming, so slender and tall, with his nice little white curled wig. What fun he and I will have together when I come out of the nursery! He promised me that we should go hunting together. He's got such a kind heart. Do you know what he did the other morning? He was chattering to the man who was polishing his floor, and when he heard that he was earning a very small wage, and had a wife and five children to feed, he ran to his private treasure chest, and gave him a whole month's pocket money!"

"Ah," laughed the page, "that explains what happened last night when Monsieur le Comte d'Artois said he could not afford to take part in the lottery; he said he had a wife and five children to feed!"

At length he brought her back to Madame de Marsan, who was beginning to grow anxious. She scolded her charge for her long absence and unkempt appearance. Elisabeth started howling: "There's no one to play with. I'm very lonely. I'd rather be an orphan at St. Cyr than an orphan here! At least the girls there have each other to play with!"

The governess had a brilliant inspiration. She hesitated a moment, and then said, "If you are very good this evening, and go to bed without slipping away or giving any trouble to your maids, I will take you to St. Cyr at the end of the week. Yes, I will take you to St. Cyr. Why didn't I think of it before?"

.   .   .   .   .

Mesdames Tantes applauded this idea of going to St. Cyr. (They, poor creatures, had been stuffed away by Cardinal Fleury, to the far-away abbey of Fontevrault and kept there for years without seeing their parents. And one day, a nun punished Sophie by locking her up in a dark house over the mortuary, and she had never been the same child since.) Yes, by all means take the little girls to St. Cyr. So, one bright May morning, attended by their pages, Clotilde and Elisabeth walked down the pink marble steps by the Orangery, for at the bottom, on the road leading to St. Cyr, stood their great coach with its postilions and out-riders.

Marie Louise de Rohan-Soubise, the widow of the Comte de Marsan, Prince de Lorraine, was, when one comes to think of it, a strangely unsuitable choice as governess for the royal children. Madame de Pompadour hated her because she represented the cream of piety. Mercy, the Austrian ambassador, was to warn Marie-Antoinette against this outwardly amiable and honeyed woman, because she was vindictive and dangerous. She probably owed her position at court to the fact that Louis XV liked her father for his beautiful manners, and because he flattered his mistresses. Her brother had a frenzied taste for women and lived a scandalous existence in Paris with Opera dancers. Her niece, to whom she eventually handed over her charge of Madame Elisabeth, was the Princesse de Guémenée. She had a lover, lived apart from her husband and was finally involved in the most scandalous bankruptcy of the reign. Her cousin, the Cardinal de Rohan, was responsible for the Necklace Affair, and it was owing to Madame de Marsan's machinations and intrigues that he was eventually created Grand Almoner of France, much to the disgust of Marie-Antoinette. It was a Rohan who had had young Monsieur de Voltaire thrashed by his six lackeys. Madame de Marsan lived for the glory of her House and its advancement. All the biographies say she was "*très*

Rohan and très Lorraine", and like all the de Rohans, she insisted in passing in front of dukes at court, because she claimed descent from the Kings of Brittany and Navarre. Madame de Marsan's enemies at court whispered that she had been madly in love with a Monsieur de Bissi, who was killed just before their wedding. It seems she had consoled herself in later life by becoming the mistress of Le Monnier, the botany master and physician of the royal children. A secret door connected their houses at Montreuil. The Duc de Richelieu says that, in order to satisfy her fancy without offending Heaven and smirching her family honour, she had married Le Monnier *"du pied gauche"*. It is significant that she was a great friend of the Duc de Vauguyon, who listened outside Marie-Antoinettte's bed-chamber door. Marie-Antoinette wrote to her mother about the governess' influence on Madame Clotilde: "Her dear little friend had totally overpowered her. We are almost rid of this famous governess."

That morning as she drove to St. Cyr with her charges, she improved the shining hour by telling them that for some years now, the Ladies of St. Cyr had enjoyed the privilege of an Office and Mass of the Sacred Heart. "And when your honoured Grandmother was beginning to despair of ever having a son, she decided to begin a novena or nine-days' prayer to the Sacred Heart of Our Lord, to obtain a Dauphin for France."

"And so my father was born," cried Elisabeth gleefully.

At length the seventeenth-century red brick building designed by Mansart came into sight. All the bells were pealing. The footman leapt off his seat and let down the footboard. At the front door were the Ladies of Saint Louis, soberly dressed in that harmonious costume which Louis XIV himself had helped to design on a miniature doll. Their gowns were of beautiful thin black stuff, with a white collar, their slippers were of marocain and their bronzed gloves were lined with white. They wore black taffeta bonnets, ruched with white gauze round the face, the whole covered with a white veil coming very low. A silver fleur-de-lys crucifix adorned their bosoms. All the young *demoiselles* were twittering with excitement, for since the tumultuous hey-day of Racine and Madame Guyon, when the young ladies had oscillated so dangerously twixt the Scylla of play-acting

C

and the Charybdis of mysticism (both painfully smothered), their house had become rather a backwater. Certainly St. Cyr was very much out of favour with the courtiers, who felt little sympathy for an education which produced the reasonable, resigned mediocre women destined to moulder away in the provinces. However, despite their unmodishness, here were the *demoiselles*, dressed in brown and very well corseted, as Madame de Maintenon had wished them to be, with their white linen head-dresses edged with lace, and more lace at neck and wrist. They all curtsied very low, as the royal ladies greeted them graciously. One tender-hearted *dame* longed to pick up that little bundle of suppressed mischief holding a pug, but of course their beloved foundress had forbidden the nuns to hug their pupils, let alone royal princesses. (Madame de Maintenon's own mother had only carressed her twice in her whole life.) The superior led them into the vestibule, with its brick floor and grey and gold woodwork, just like a charming drawing-room. This long room with its book cupboards in soft pastel colours, warm and peaceful in the sunlight, had all the grace of seventeenth-century France. It looked on to the courtyards and some old trees. Whilst Madame Clotilde was taken to the room where Madame de Maintenon had died, with its little blue bed and its crucifix—a room which was kept as a kind of chapel by the adoring nuns—Elisabeth, on being asked what she would like to do, surprisingly chose a visit to the kitchens: "I've never seen a kitchen." This was greatly to the liking of her pug, who soon won the respectful attentions of the chef and his young minions. The chef was preparing a great festal repast for the royal guests. (Too late in the season to concoct *vol au vent d'huitres à la Maintenon*, too sad to have *beignets à la Dauphine*, indiscreet to make *pets de nonne*, immoral to suggest *asperges à la Pompadour*, so he had decided on *écrevisses cardinalisées de Monsieur le Prince*, prepared in champagne and served in a silver dish, a few vine-fed Paris snails, and *quenelles de carpe* done with artichokes. And to flatter that old *dévote*, the governess, *poires à la Bourdaloue*.)

Elisabeth was allowed to stir a vanilla sauce. This made her feel quite hungry, for like a true daughter of the Bourbons, she had a good healthy appetite, and was to write to a friend: "I love a good dinner." Then she played with the spice boxes, helped to turn the spit, put her little arms up to the elbows in the flour-bin, and had to be cleaned up by an understanding nun. Seeing some pastry, she cut out a royal Fleur-de-Lys and presented it to the chef, with a mixture of hauteur and grace which nearly upset his equilibrium.

Tiring of all this, she suddenly announced that she would like to play a game of hide-and-seek. The manuscript memoirs of the royal house of St. Cyr tell us that, whilst Madame Clotilde was holding reasonable and sensible conversations, Madame Elisabeth was playing and dancing. "But of all the amusements which pleased her most, and which she desired more passionately than anything else, was hide-and-seek (*cligne musette*). Usually she chose for this game the tallest *demoiselles*, as much to appear grown up as to make a strong rampart against those who were looking for her; she wrapped herself around their clothes and their persons, enchanted that they should seek her a long time, and thinking herself safe, although she herself would give many devices for finding her, by discreet sorties which finally led to her discovery."

The rest of the day was spent in listening to the classes, in receiving the best pupils and going to Benediction in the chapel. Madame de Marsan, who felt a little tired, seized the opportunity of a quarter of an hour's repose in the superior's room. Talking about her charges, she spent most of the time praising the elder one. The superior enquired: "And how are you progressing with Madame Elisabeth? I heard she was refusing to learn to read, as she said princesses were always surrounded by people who could do their tasks for them."

"Oh, that little hurdle was safely overcome. When she was ill, Madame Clotilde insisted on nursing her, and so, by winning her affections, she was able to persuade her into learning her alphabet. I think that now they are very much attached to one another, in spite of the difference in age. I must confess that this is a load off my mind. I am not as young as I was, and these children are a great responsibility. In fact, I had meant to ask you to recommend an assistant."

The superior was delighted. "What about one of our old pupils, the Baronne de Mackau? She has a delightful daughter who is eventually coming to us. Angélique is two years older than your Madame

Elisabeth. Since her widowhood, Madame de Mackau has been living in reduced circumstances at Strasbourg. I think you would find her invaluable. She is imbued with all our principles of education, she has a high moral character, and is firm yet kind." The superior did not add that she thought Angélique, who has been called "*la beauté des beautés et l'ange des anges*", would be a delightful friend for the lonely toddler, whose naughtiness probably sprang from an unsatisfied craving for affection.

When Angélique de Mackau came to Versailles with her mother, she and Madame Elisabeth looked at one another for a long time, after the manner of young children, and then started playing blind man's buff. The friendship thus begun, was to continue to the end of Elisabeth's life. Angélique was indeed a beautiful child, with large expressive eyes, well-cut features and pretty curls. The picture of her as a young woman is most attractive. She was a good little girl too, and Madame de Marsan soon realised that she could use her as a bait to make her idle pupil do some work. When Elisabeth made an effort with her deplorable spelling (her childhood letters have no punctuation and no capitals), she was rewarded by playtime with Angélique. Soon Elisabeth persuaded Madame de Marsan to let her new friend stay on at Versailles and share her education, instead of going to St. Cyr. Louis XV gladly consented, and Madame de Guémenée promised to see to her dowry when she was of marriageable age. The prudent Baronne de Mackau had a suitable husband in reserve—the charming Marquis de Bombelles, twenty years older than her daughter and a very amusing person, with a good diplomatic career ahead of him. As it was, Angélique innocently adored him already, so that was all to the good. The Baronne was very ambitious for her daughter, for she wrote to the Marquis de Bombelles pointing out the benefits that might fall to their lot if the friendship between Angélique and Elisabeth were encouraged. A wise mother could not begin to lay her plans too early, particularly in a court where the morals were not of the highest. There was no denying that the entourage of His Most Christian Majesty left much to be desired. This new creature, the du Barry, whose name was linked with a Parisian brothel, had been given an apartment so very soon after the Queen's death: no wonder Mesdames Tantes were scandalised. What would Monsieur the Dauphin have said, had he been alive?

The youngest of Mesdames Tantes, Madame Louise, the greediest, the haughtiest, the most intriguing of the lot, and the only one who in the end wholly reformed her character and achieved holiness, was secretly planning to become a Carmelite nun and offer her life in expiation for her father's sins. She was very fond of her little niece, Elisabeth, and believed that one day she would probably have a Carmelite vocation herself. "Humph," retorted Madame de Marsan, in whom she confided this pious hope, "you would not have thought so last week, Madame, when we took her to the Clothing ceremony of a novice at the Holy Child Convent."

"Why, what happened?"

"Madame Elisabeth stamped her feet with rage, because she wanted to wear a nun's habit, and none could be found to fit her. Her temper is terrible."

"I thought things had improved lately. Since her sister nursed her through her illness, I've noticed she has softened considerably, even her voice has become less raucous. Who knows? Yes, she might one day become a nun!"

"Heaven help the other nuns," cried Madame de Marsan.

CHAPTER III

In which Elisabeth falls in love with the Carmelite Order and meets Marie-Antoinette

LOUIS XV was devoted to Mesdames Tantes, his daughters, and nicknamed them "Rags, Sow, Crackling and Poor Silk". Madame de Pompadour used to say he would never have found any torture cruel enough for the man who might try to seduce any one of them. But this King, who had not learnt to rule his passions, never married off these daughters who were quickly going to seed in his vast palace. The eldest, deep-voiced Adélaïde, whom Nattier has painted so charmingly in her fur-trimmed, red velvet gown, was beautiful for a short time. A young nobleman had fallen in love with her, and she had given him a snuff box. When her father heard of this, he was absolutely furious, and sent the young man packing. Terribly thwarted, Adélaïde took refuge in playing every musical instrument under the sun—the bagpipes, the guitar, the viol, the Jew's harp and the hunting horn. A little clock-maker (who scribbled his name on a window pane) used to try and please her by bringing her new instruments from Paris. During her brother's lifetime, they had all enjoyed delightful musical evenings together, for the Dauphin, as well as having a deep bass voice, had played the organ, the harpsichord and the violin. This enterprising clock-maker was none other than Beaumarchais, who wrote "Le Mariage de Figaro" and "Le Barbier de Séville" out of the plenitude of his experiences as a court parasite. Adélaïde soon lost her looks entirely, and indeed became quite hideous. It is very chastening to compare the early portraits with the later ones by Heinsius and Madame Labille-Guyard. The Duc de Genevois said: "She is frightful. Her eyes are popping out of her head, her lips very thick, her skin grey, and she has a rough, vindictive expression." The Comte de Maurienne says: "Adélaïde is horrible. Victoire, big and fat." Towards the end,

Adélaïde, according to Madame de Boigne, wore a violet dress on her tall thin body, a *bonnet à papillons*, and had only two big teeth left. She would have been a great princess, if only she had married. She had shown heroism as a child, when she had tried to run away from home with the little boy who kept the donkey, in order to beat the English and bring their King captive to her father's feet. But now there was nothing but malice left. Unlike her dead sister Henriette, she had done all she could to keep the Dauphin away from his second wife, Marie-Josèphe de Saxe, continually twitting her about her unfashionable auburn hair. Gradually she too became a stickler for the minutiae of etiquette. She rated her chaplain soundly for saying "Dominus Vobiscum" with excessive light-heartedness, and she snapped at her reader Madame Campan, because one day, when she was taking her muff upstairs, she actually had the impertinence to put her fingers inside it. Yes, the Hebe, the Flora of the early days of the reign, had turned into a viperish Medusa. Her disapproval of her father's latest infatuation had not improved her temper. Totally uneducated, she could not take refuge in literature. The great consolation of her life, however, was her position as the eldest of the sisters. She knew everything that went on in their entourage, (or at least she thought she did,) and she prided herself that they would never have taken a decisive step without consulting her.

At that time, they all lived on the ground floor near the *Parterre du Nord*. Every day they received a visit from their nieces who came across from the *Parterre du Midi*; the royal children lived on the ground floor which had a view of the gardens and park, and overlooked the Orangery. Twice a day, the King visited his daughter. First thing in the morning, he would always bring his coffee, which he made himself, to Madame Adélaïde's room. She rang the bell to warn Madame Victoire, who in her turn warned Sophie (or had warned Sophie, during her lifetime), and Sophie rang for Louise whose suite of rooms was the furthest away, and she always arrived last, puffing and panting. Madame Campan tells us that the princesses put on gold-embroidered skirts over their enormous panniers, tied long detachable trains around their waists and concealed the disorder of their appearance by great cloaks of black taffeta which muffled them up to their chins. In the evening, their squires, ladies, gentlemen ushers, and pages carrying great torches, accompanied them to the King for a moment as he was taking his boots off after hunting.

One morning, early in 1770, for some reason or other, the morning visit of the two young nieces coincided with that of the King. His debaucheries had not affected his handsome face, and he had a noble air. In fact even his expression of *ennui* was not wholly without charm. Horace Walpole said he "has great sweetness in his countenance". The daughters were standing in the way that naughty Horace Walpole has described in one of his letters: "The four Mesdames, who are clumsy plump old wenches, with a bad likeness to their father, stand in a bed-chamber in a row, with black cloaks and knotting[1] bags, looking good-humoured, not knowing what to say, and wriggling as if they wanted to make water. . . ."

The children curtsied. The King took Elisabeth on his knee. "*Eh bien*," he said, "have you learnt how to spell yet?" Elisabeth relapsed into a broad and ingratiating grin.

"Grand-papa," she replied, "that has never been my *forte*, but I have other talents. Ask Aunt Louise."

Louise was the great horsewoman of the family (her last words on her death-bed were "To Paradise, quickly, quickly, at the gallop!"). "Yes," she said, "I think Elisabeth would make a good horsewoman if only she could go to the riding school with her brothers." At this point, Madame de Marsan interposed: "If your Majesty would permit, Madame Elisabeth could recite to him La Fontaine's poem about the old cat and the young mouse. Or perhaps your Majesty would prefer Florian's poem about the dove and her nursling?"

The King glanced at the governess from under his heavy-lidded eyes, and said, with his usual courtesy: "No, Madame de Marsan, I think I should like to see Madame pretend to be a young mouse."

It must be admitted that Elisabeth recited the fable in the most adorably engaging manner, acting the part of the frightened, wheedling mouse and the worldly wise old cat to perfection.

[1] *Parfilage.*

"A very inexperienced young mouse
Thought she could soften an old cat's heart by imploring
 his clemency
And by reasoning with Raminogrobis.
'Let me live: a mouse
Of my size, who costs so little to feed,
Could she be a burden to this household?
In your opinion, would I make
The host and hostess and everybody else hungry?
I feed myself with a grain of wheat:
A nut makes me quite round.
At the moment I am thin; wait a little.
Keep this meal in reserve for Messieurs your children. . . .' "

After she had been applauded, there was a commotion outside the door, as if the sedan chairs of the princes were being brought by their lackeys. (The galleries were overcrowded, and the stairs overflowed with merchants selling their wares, so the princes of the blood hardly ever walked in the palace.) The three young brothers came in and made their bows. Madame de Marsan nearly gave a gasp of horror, for the Comte d'Artois still had his hat on his head! But before anything could be said, he twiddled on his red heel in front of his grandfather and said: "Grand-papa, do you like my new hat?"

"Yes, very fine. You will have to wear it at the next ball." The Comte d'Artois turned triumphantly to his two brothers and laughed. "You see, I told you so! I've won my wager! They dared me to come into your presence with my hat on." They all laughed. The King said: "Your sister has been regaling us with a fine bit of miming. She would make an excellent actress. I love her when she does La Fontaine's little mouse." The Duc de Berry, the future Louis XVI, picked up his sister and said: "Elisabeth, don't you think it's ridiculous to make animals talk as if they were human beings?"

"Oh no," she said, with her roguish look, "you see they can say what human beings daren't." "The silky puss," chortled the King, concealing a yawn. They all laughed at Elisabeth's shrewdness, all except the Comte de Provence, a perfectly horrid boy, fat, clumsy, with sulky, sensuous features and an underhand glance. He thought himself greatly superior to his brother, the future king, and indeed was to spend the rest of his life before the Revolution, plotting to overthrow him. And this very morning of all mornings, he was destined to hear news which was not to his liking, nor to the liking of Mesdames Tantes. The King announced, "I have arranged that the archduchess Marie-Antoinette of Austria, is to come to France in mid-May, and the marriage will be in the Chapel Royal at Versailles." The future bridegroom took the news sullenly. He was beginning to wonder whether the wedding festivities would interrupt a day's sport. It is notorious that on his wedding day, and at the outbreak of the Revolution, he wrote in his private diary one shattering little word: "Nothing." Moreover he had his own private reasons against being forced to provide heirs to the throne. He suffered from a form of impotence which only the surgeon's knife could cure, and he was afraid.

The Comte d'Artois at that time was falling in love with the Princesse Louise de Condé, who was still at her convent school. If only he had been allowed to marry her, perhaps the course of French history might have been different. He gazed indifferently at his elder brother, on the brink of matrimony.

Madame Victoire, dragging her thoughts back from a certain orange-flower conserve, concocted by the dear nuns of Poissy, thought she should break the silence of consternation which had fallen upon the company.

"Papa, could you tell us what the archduchess looks like?"

"I have it on the best authority, her colouring is so superb that she will never have to wear rouge. She holds her head very proudly and walks like a young goddess. She is a wonderfully graceful dancer."

Elisabeth rushed over to Madame Louise, her favourite aunt. "Perhaps you will take her out hunting, Aunt Louise, and perhaps I will come too, when I am a little older." Madame Louise did not reply. A shrewd observer might have noticed that she looked out of the window towards the woods, where she had enjoyed so many good hunts, with a look of intense regret. The King glanced at his daughter, then at the great gilded clock, and hurried away to the meet.

Madame Louise said in a whisper to her beloved niece Elisabeth: "Come along for a moment to my room. I have a present for you."

When they were alone, the princess took the child in her arms, as if she were saying farewell. Then, reaching out to her prie-Dieu, she took from it the Breviary of the Divine Office for the Paris diocese, bound in red morocco and engraved with the Arms of the late Dauphin, her brother. "When you've learnt to read, I want you to have your father's own Office book. He used it every day, and I have marked with a silk ribbon one of my favourite passages, which you must read to yourself if you feel too sad because you are an orphan." And she read aloud to her those admirable lines from the book of Isaias, which the Dauphin had chosen as if he had foreseen that one day his daughter would need consolation: "Behold I will bring upon her as it were a river of peace, and as an overflowing torrent the glory of the Gentiles, which you shall suck; you shall be carried at the breasts, and upon the knees they shall caress you.

"As one whom the mother caresseth, so will I comfort you: and you shall be comforted in Jerusalem."

.   .   .   .   .

One morning, very early, Madame Louise ran away to be a Carmelite.

A few weeks before that momentous day, the poorest Carmelite convent in the kingdom, the Carmel of St. Denis, unable to bear its poverty any longer, had started a novena of prayer to ask God for a rich postulant, who would rescue them from near-starvation. On the last day of the novena, they received a formal application, under pledge of great secrecy, from the King's youngest daughter, Madame Louise de France. She slipped away without having told her sisters. (For this, Madame Adélaïde never forgave her.) When she reached the convent, she entered the enclosure, and, once safely on the other side of the grille, she showed the King's written permission to her squires, pages and ladies-in-waiting and ordered them to leave her. They returned to Versailles in dismay.

The sisters who had remained behind were acrimoniously discussing Marie-Antoinette, whose marriage, they knew, had been engineered by the odious Pompadour. "I suppose Mother's pearls and diamonds will be given to this little Austrian thing. Ah, well, there is this to be said for the du Barry, she does not interfere in affairs of State." And all three of them thought somewhat bitterly of how their father had placed more trust in the counsels of his mistresses, than in that of their poor dead mother. Cardinal Fleury had told Louis XV to use his wife only for the purpose of breeding children. The King had taken that advice to the letter, and moreover had spared no pains to make his wife as unhappy as possible. He had given his permission for Louise to enter Carmel, knowing, without being told, that she was offering herself up on his behalf, to save his soul. It was so many years now since he had received the Sacraments.

"Madame, Madame," cried Madame Campan, rushing in without ceremony: "Madame Louise has gone to Carmel, she is not coming back."

Madame Adélaïde nearly died from a paroxysm of rage.

When the news was broken to Elisabeth, she did not weep, but begged Madame de Marsan to take her to Carmel as soon as possible, where she could see her aunt inside the enclosure. Princesses of the blood royal are always allowed in. In the carriage, on the way, it was her sister Clotilde who told her all she knew about this great Order. "They have rough brown habits and sandals. They sleep on hard boards in icy cold cells. In spite of wearing hair shirts and iron chains and taking the discipline, they are very gay, like all nuns in very austere Orders, because they have given everything to God. They leave their foreheads uncovered, to symbolise that liberty of spirit which Saint Teresa wanted for her nuns. Our great-great-grandfather, Louis XIV, was loved by a court lady, called Louise, Duchesse de la Vallière, who went to pray for him for long years in the Carmel of the Rue d'Enfer in Paris."

"Why did he especially need praying for so hard?" asked Elisabeth.

"Sh," said Madame de Marsan, with her finger to her lips.

The governess had just had a good long gossip with Madame Campan, the reader of Mesdames Tantes, who told her that Madame Louise must have been preparing herself for some time in secret, for she had slept on bare boards and worn a hair shirt under her gorgeous brocade court dresses.

"I should like to be a Carmelite," said Elisabeth after a long silence.

Once at St. Denis, she had a good long talk alone with her aunt. "What do you find the hardest to bear in here, Tante Louise?"

"You must call me Sœur Thérèse de Saint-Augustin now. The thing I find the hardest is walking down stairs alone, without a squire.

The child replied gravely: "Well, I'd better get into training quite soon, for I want to come here too. Is there anything else I can learn?"

"Oh, plenty. I've been put in the kitchen, and do you know what I did the first time I was told to wash up? I filled a wooden tub with water, and threw everything in at once, even the great iron saucepans. The kitchen sisters were in despair, but I don't see how we can have a chance to practise washing-up at home. However, you can always find some little mortifications; for example, trying very hard at your lessons, your handwriting, which is deplorable, and your grammar and spelling, which make me fear that you are illiterate. But it will be you, *ma petite Reine*, who will give me the veil on my clothing day."

"Oh, no, *Ma Tante*, it must be the Dauphine Marie-Antoinette. She will not feel her loss as I do."

Madame Louise had a special tenderness for her little niece. Before her feast day in November, she wrote to a priest friend of hers, asking him to pray for the child. "She has, by God's Grace, a firm determination to belong to Him; but I know only too well the world she lives in; the purest virtues need most firm support therein."

When the King came to visit his daughter, he talked to her alone in her cell, and behaved with endearing simplicity with the eager nuns. The gargantuan feast he provided for them and for his suite on that day must have demolished many a Carmelite entrail, unused to anything richer than black bread. Before leaving them, he made a characteristically funereal remark. Glancing out of the barred window, towards the great Abbey of St. Denis which loomed over the convent, he said, almost with relish, "That is where I will finish up."

(Twenty-two years later, on October the 16th, 1792, his rotting corpse was dragged out of its tomb by a howling mob.)

.   .   .   .   .

In early May, the palace of Versailles was swarming with carpenters, upholsterers and actors. Great festivities were planned for the wedding. "What a pity I'm too little to go to the ball and the banquet!" wailed Elisabeth.

"If you're very good, I shall let you stay up to watch the fireworks," said Madame de Marsan, whose notorious cousin the Cardinal de Rohan had already greeted Marie-Antoinette on her first appearance on French soil.

On the 16th of May, 1770, at ten o'clock in the morning, the children heard a sound of distant cheering and the beating of drums. Coaches sped through the gilded grille and passed between lines of French and Swiss guards presenting arms. With an airy grace, the young golden-haired Dauphine stepped out into the sunlight of the Cour de Marbre. She was received at the entrance by Louis XV holding Elisabeth and Clotilde. Madame de Marsan, in her usual fashion, tried to push Madame Clotilde forward, but Marie-Antoinette, with the independence which characterised her, at once picked on the wild, shy little six-year-old child. In fact, she lost her heart to her from that very moment, thus seriously annoying Madame de Marsan. This preference was one of the causes of a life-long enmity between the two. Madame de Marsan was everything that Marie-Antoinette could not stand—an overweening snob, fussily self-important, a blue-stocking and a stickler for etiquette. Moreover, with a young girl's unfailing intuition—and she was only fifteen—she sensed the hollow-ness and hypocrisy behind the façade, and immediately distrusted her honeyed looks.

Elisabeth heard distant echoes of the great day, and of how radiant the young bride had looked in her great silver brocade panniers, exciting a murmur of admiration among the courtiers assembled on wooden stands put up in the state apartments. The Dauphin, in his cloth of gold, had looked awkward and clumsy: he seemed entirely lacking in that ardour befitting a bridegroom. Another tit-bit was passed on by a lady-in-waiting of Mesdames Tantes. When the bride had signed the register with unformed handwriting, her pen had made a great blot of ink! From that moment onwards, Elisabeth had a fellow feeling for her.

Alas, the fireworks were not as good as they had hoped. They had been drenched by a thunderstorm, which appeared to some people very much like an evil omen.

(When the young couple made their state visit to Paris a few days later, there was a terrible accident with the crowds in the Place Louis XV in which more than twelve hundred people were crushed in a stampede. A young Parisian notary had lain for hours under a heap of wounded or dead people. He had been so overcome by this ghastly experience, that until the day of his death, sixty-six years later, he could no longer lie down, but always slept upright in an armchair. The victims were buried in the common grave of the Madeleine cemetery. Just over twenty years later, the royal bride and bridegroom were to lie there among the victims of the Revolution. Marie-Antoinette was never to forget the screams of horror and anguish coming from the crowds.)

At the great ball, held on the wedding night, there was an unseemly quarrel about etiquette. Many of the nobility had remained away on purpose, because they did not wish the representatives of the House of Lorraine to have precedence over the French dukes and princes. Madame de Marsan, allied as she was with the House of Lorraine, took this as another personal affront.

In the meantime, the weather had cleared. Warmly wrapped up in a shawl, Elisabeth slipped out of bed and pressed her nose against the window panes. Two hundred thousand people from Paris and its vicinity quite filled the immense gardens. They danced to the sound of orchestras installed in the groves. A procession of the King's oarsmen, dressed in white, with red and blue scarves, danced in these glades, thus encouraging everyone else to do likewise. As night fell, the crowd, held back by the Swiss guards, surrounded the scaffoldings for the fireworks, some of which were on the terrace in front of the royal children's apartment. Madame de Marsan had had the bedchamber candles snuffed, but each time a firework splashed up into golden rain, the room was filled with light. The applause sounded very near. Elisabeth cried: "Oh, look, look! Here's a turning sun, carrying the Arms of France. And look, they're going to start the illuminations now, at the very end of the Grand Canal, on the right of St. Cyr. I can just glimpse the Temple of the Sun. Oh, let's go into the next room, so that we can see the Canal a little better." The child gazed at the flotilla of gondolas covered with lanterns, being oared slowly on the waters to the sound of the brass bands of the French Guards. Gradually, the illuminations came nearer to the palace. Louis XV was watching from a grilled window of the Galerie des Glaces: he did not want to go into the gardens to catch cold. He caught sight of his mistress, Madame du Barry, at another window, and wished he were not prevented from being alone with her. A hundred and sixty thousand little lamps lit up the yews in arcades and garlands. The outlines of the château began to stand out. It was the greatest illumination at Versailles since the time of Louis XIV.

After a while, Madame de Marsan said somewhat impatiently: "Now I really insist: you must come to bed. All these goings on and gallivantings will spoil your studies."

All this fuss about a little Austrian wasn't going to be allowed to upset the routine of *her* schoolroom.

CHAPTER IV

A royal schoolroom at Versailles

THE bridegroom continued to look indifferent for a long time after his wedding. When the superintendent of the Queen's household, the Duchesse de Noailles, discovered that the Duc de Vauguyon was listening at the bedroom door, she went straight to the King and threatened to resign unless he were stopped. The poor little Dauphine, who had been brought up with such high religious principles, had the company of Madame du Barry foisted upon her at every turn. At first, she took refuge with Mesdames Tantes, who were sweet to her to begin with, in order to be sure of winning her allegiance, and to see that she adopted the correct attitude to the du Barry creature. Even Mercy, the Austrian ambassador, noticed her pathetic, forlorn air, when she turned to her dog for company. At that time, she could not take refuge in all the hard work involved in being the most fashionably dressed woman of Europe, for the Mistress of the Wardrobe was pious and sick, and neglected her duties so much that the Dauphine looked very untidy and got scolding letters from her mother about it. When Madame de Marsan could be circumvented, the Dauphine had a good romp with her new sister Elisabeth. In spite of the difference in age, the two seemed to have taken to each other from the start. They both felt rather lost and unwanted, and they were both still little tomboys, and remained so, even when the Dauphine became Queen, as is shown in the following anecdote, which Rouget de l'Isle, the future author of the Marseillaise, told one of his friends: "I was fifteen years of age and was on holiday with a lady who was a relation of mine, who had her lodgings in the château de Versailles. All of a sudden, I heard the door of the apartment in which I was, being struck in a certain manner, and my relation, very much upset, said to me: 'Ah, *Dieu*, my child, hide quickly, here's the Queen!' And at the same time she pushed me into the next room, quickly pulling the curtains over me. And indeed, Marie-Antoinette and Elisabeth came in, and soon, freed from the yoke of etiquette, they began to jump, to run and to chase one another; the young woman was as mad and as gay as a young girl. I, curious, trying to part the curtains, made a noise and was surprised in my hiding place. My relation was covered with confusion for having allowed a stranger to surprise the Queen's games. Marie-Antoinette reassured him and left me charmed with her grace and her affability."

Marie-Antoinette took Elisabeth to the Carmelite Convent of St. Denis, although she herself did not rave about Mère Thérèse de Saint Augustin; she called her "the biggest little intriguer in Europe".

Madame du Deffand also speaks of Marie-Antoinette taking Elisabeth and Clotilde with her to visit the Comte de Caraman and his fine garden in the Faubourg St. Germain. His eight children were in attendance, for he cosseted flowers and babies with the same devotion. His ten-year-old daughter, dressed up as a little peasant girl, presented bouquets to Marie-Antoinette. She came home full of ideas for a garden of her own.

On Sunday evenings, Madame de Marsan arranged concerts, recitations and the acting of proverbs in the apartments of the royal children. Marie-Antoinette used to sing, in her delightful true voice.

In the midst of all these new excitements, lessons had to be done, but now it was so much easier, since Angélique de Mackau was always with Elisabeth to spur her on to keener competition.

At Montreuil, in those days a hamlet not far from Versailles, Madame de Marsan possessed a pretty house and garden, which she handed over to Madame de Mackau. This place, which was next to the magnificent estate of Madame de Guémenée, quite soon became the headquarters of Elisabeth and her friends. They were all delighted to go there for the day and escape from Versailles with its etiquette, its squires and its pages. Madame de Mackau, whom Elisabeth nicknamed "Mère Poule", found it hard work to maintain a semblance of discipline in her happy little brood. There existed in the archives of an old Versailles family, now extinct, a legend which is so charming that it deserves to be recorded here. Not far from the house of Madame de

Mackau, at the end of the Rue Champ la Garde, in a wretched hovel, there lived the widow of a château workman. Madame de Mackau came nearly every day to bring her some food or little treats. This poor woman had not only lost her husband but two of her children, and now her ten-year-old daughter had fallen ill of a very serious complaint. The doctor told Madame de Mackau that this disease was contagious and she must not let any of her young girls go to the house. "Now, you understand quite clearly, my dears, I absolutely forbid any of you, not only to go into the cottage, but even into the lane close by."

One morning, Elisabeth, who was picking flowers near the property of Madame de Guémenée, noticed the poor widow who seemed beside herself with grief. She ran to the princess and kneeling, cried out with joined hands: "Good princess, my beloved daughter is going to die . . . you alone who are of the blood royal can save her by touching her. . . . She is my whole life, I have only her. Good princess, save her." Forgetting Madame de Mackau's strict injunctions, Elisabeth followed the mother into her cottage, where they found the daughter lying motionless and white on her bed. For a moment she thought she must be dead. Without fear or hesitation, she took the little hands in hers and ardently begged God to leave the child to its mother. At that precise moment she felt the hands twitch in her own. She bent down and kissed her burning brow, and immediately the child opened her eyes and smiled at her. The mother burst into tears, fell on her knees, laughing and crying at the same time: "Thank you, God has listened to you. My child is saved."

When Elisabeth slipped out again, she fell straight into the arms of Madame de Mackau, who was in a terrible state. She segregated her from her companions for a week. (We will hear later what happened to this child.)

In 1771, Madame de Marsan, who was really beginning to feel that the intellectual demands of her charges were growing beyond her, asked an old friend to help her out. This was the daughter of Madame Geoffrin, the Marquise de la Ferté-Imbault, who, many years ago, had launched the future Pompadour in her own drawing-room. Madame de la Ferté-Imbault had lost her only child, a daughter of thirteen, and grief had made her grow deaf. She took refuge in fashionable dissipation, but all in the best of taste. She had a kind of clamorous gaiety, "which promised to last indefinitely, because it was founded on nothing". Her many friends nicknamed her "Marquise Carillon". She had a great reputation for eccentricity, which, of course, was all the mode, and she was still very pretty, with very black eyebrows. She spent her life in country house visiting, and caused so much merriment wherever she went, that no-one would have suspected that she had been trained by some of the great intellects of her century, and that she had read very deeply and widely, even browsing in the writings of Seneca and Cicero. After hearing that she had made selections from Plutarch's Lives and extracts from the ancient philosophers, suitable for the young, Madame de Marsan decided to ask her to come and stay at the château and give the young princesses an hour's lesson every evening, from eight till nine.

In the days when the Pompadour was in favour, she had not been able to persuade Madame de la Ferté-Imbault to come and stay at Versailles. She pleaded ill-health, but in reality the Marquis de Ségur says she probably did not want to be beholden to a little woman she had formerly patronised. It is easy to picture her having a gossip with Madame de Marsan before the arrival of her pupils. They were talking about the house-parties given in the old days by the Duc and Duchesse de Luynes at the Château of Dampierre. These gatherings, contrary to expectation, were very merry. "Oh yes, my hosts amused me, and I repaid them in kind. So many ecclesiastics, you know. Priests of good morals have a certain pure and youthful gaiety which they always keep; I love that gaiety, I feel a kinship to it. . . . Would you believe it, from morning till night, we made all the high clerics dance, even the Cardinal de la Rochefecauld and the Cardinal de la Roche-Aymon, who baptised your little Madame Elisabeth. I even used to call the Archbishop of Paris, Christophe de Beaumont, '*mon petit chat*'. One day, they played me such a funny practical joke; they introduced me to a lot of their vicar-generals, and, as I was making my respectful curtsies to them, they all burst into fits of laughter. They weren't vicar-generals at all, but valets in disguise. The dear duke used to say I must be a Jansenist, for I had no lover. As for the duchess, she was overflowing with a good naïve merriment '*qui me faisait du bien à l'estomac*' whenever I was unhappy."

"*Chère Marquise*," gushed Madame de Marsan into her ear-trumpet, "I believe you bring happiness wherever you go."

"Eh? What? Happiness? That is what King Stanilas used to say at Lunéville, when his house-parties were enlivened by the Chevalier de Boufflers and the Abbé Porquet. His Majesty used to call me *sa chère folle*. Oh yes, I know how to cure my *ennui*, not so much by renouncing rouge but by dividing my time between the Holy Water stoup and the writing desk."

Madame de Marsan laughed and shouted: "You mustn't make yourself out to be a *dévote*. I shall never forget the time the jealous ladies at the Temple tried to make you kiss the Prince de Conti's hand and you bit it."

"Eh? What? Prince de Conti? Ha, ha, ha. You should have seen the faces of the ladies! And the Prince himself thought I had rabies!"

Madame de Marsan looked at the clock. "I think I will ring for the princesses. Don't be anxious if Madame Elisabeth appears very wild at first."

"Wild? Have no fear, I am used to difficult children. I shall never forget the gratitude of the little Prince de Condé when I befriended him. He was so shy. Before they come, *chère amie*, you *are* looking into the question of a little increase in payment for me, aren't you?" (The King was notoriously mean.)

"Have no fear, all will be well, *ma chère*."

Madame de la Ferté-Imbault fell in love at once with this naughty Elisabeth, who, from infancy, had so greatly intimidated her nurses and nappy-changers by her explosions of wrath. Before very long, the Marquise Carillon had so captivated her interest that, when she was idle or naughty at her other lessons, they only had to threaten that she would be deprived of her philosophy lesson in the evening, and she would behave at once.

Madame de Mackau loved to watch the self-important little air with which Elisabeth would say, "I am now going to have my lesson in philosophy." She too had grown to love the child. "I suppose you love philosophy because Monsieur the Dauphin your father did."

"Oh, I didn't know that! Yes, I want to be like him in everything. What a pity I can't read quickly enough yet. I want to be able to say the Divine Office like he did, from his Breviary that Tante Louise gave me before she left for Carmel."

Madame de Mackau too had made a success of her task, where Madame de Marsan had not fully succeeded. When Elisabeth mis-behaved, she looked very pained. Gradually she taught her habits of self-control, most necessary in a royal personage. Moreover, herself not very well endowed with this world's goods, she led her charge into ways of thrift which were to stand her in good stead when she had a household of her own, and was obliged to keep accounts and save for her many benefactions and charities.

At the same time, Signor Goldini was summoned seven months before the wedding of Madame Clotilde with the Prince of Piémont to give the girls Italian lessons. He wrote of Elisabeth: "This young princess, lively, gay and amiable, was more of an age to amuse herself than to apply herself. I have assisted at some Latin lessons which they were giving her, and I have noticed that she had good dispositions to learn, but she did not like to linger on small difficulties. She wanted to turn her occupation into an amusement and I tried to give my lessons in the form of agreeable conversation."

About that time, the Comte de Provence got married to a Princess of the House of Savoy, plain and disagreeable, who was to become one of Marie-Antoinette's most relentless enemies. She was a bit of a prude, and when her lady-in-waiting wanted to apply her rouge for her, she cried: "Fie, fie, Madame, do you take my face for a wig stand?" Only when her husband told her to conform to the usage of the court, did she say: "Madame, put plenty of rouge on, because then I would please my husband better." When Elisabeth was old enough to see her sister-in-law's faults and to realise what a trouble-maker she was in the royal circle, she never showed her feelings. She was a naturally tactful girl, and it was because she kept the peace wherever she went that she was nicknamed the angel of the royal family.

The Comte d'Artois was Elisabeth's favourite brother, because there was something chivalrous and elegant about him, and he was so gay and devil-may-care. He was already in love with Princesse Louise de Condé. Louise was to become one of Elisabeth's greatest friends, in spite of being seven years older than she was. Her mother, a Rohan-Soubise who had been a rapturously happy wife, died when the child was three. When her father began an illicit association with the Princesse de Monaco, he sent the child to the convent of Beaumont-Les-Tours, where her great-Aunt was the Abbess. This lovely woman had declined the hand of Louis XV; she locked herself up in a high turret the day he called at the convent. Louise de Condé distinguished herself at the Office of Compline by shaking the hour glass, and crying out, "I've had enough!" She had a few happy years there—watching the exotic birds, playing in the hot houses and orangeries, and basking in the Abbess's affection. She used to call her Mamma—a word she loved. In April 1770, when she was only thirteen, she was presented at court, where she was nicknamed Hébé-Bourbon, for she was tall and lovely, with fine eyes. She and Elisabeth had much in common. They enjoyed reading, hunting, drawing and playing the harpsichord, and both loved to visit the poor. A little shepherdess in the Chantilly hospice said as Louise passed by, "Do kiss me, Mademoiselle." It was probably her vocation as a Benedictine nun which drew her to Elisabeth when she grew older, though that vocation had been nurtured by a frustrated love affair.

As quite young girls, Elisabeth and Louise shared the fashionable taste for the pastoral pleasures of the day. Louise invited the two sisters to her château at Vanves, which her father had given her, and which she helped to build up again with her own hands, donning a big apron and wielding a trowel among the workmen. At last, when all was ready, Louise organised a rustic fiesta. She disguised herself as a farmer's wife and received Elisabeth and Clotilde whilst churning the butter. The children were given gifts of a lamb, a bird's nest and bouquets of wild flowers. They were led to a temple, and, to the sound of delicious music, the three princesses wrote their names in a magnificent book, vowing eternal friendship. What a pity Louise de Condé did not marry the Comte d'Artois. What a good sister-in-law she would have made, what an asset to the court circle and what a good friend to Marie-Antoinette. But alas, Louis XV was a man of long rancours, and in May 1773 the Comte d'Artois was betrothed against his will to Marie-

Thérèse de Savoie, the sister of Madame de Provence. She was very plain, small-minded and disagreeable, and he was soon unfaithful to her with the actress Duthé: the cruel "*mot*" went round Paris that Monsieur le Comte d'Artois, after an attack of indigestion caused by "*biscuit de Savoie*", had taken "*du thé*". All this was such a blow to the pride of Louise de Condé, that she grew to love solitude and began to see the world for what it was really worth, though the great grief of her whole life did not come till several years later.

A few days after Elisabeth's tenth birthday, on May the 10th, 1774, Louis XV died. Some days previously, whilst staying at Petit Trianon with the du Barry, he had suddenly been seized with violent shivering. His physicians wanted him to go to bed at Petit Trianon, but he said, "One can die nowhere else but at Versailles." Mesdames Tantes at once came to nurse him. The following morning, somebody looked at him closely and noticed that there were red blotches on his face. He had caught the dreaded smallpox. The French were behind all other nations in Christendom in the matter of inoculation. It was a terrible and disgusting death. He rotted visibly before everyone's eyes. The stench was so noxious, that fifty people who had merely passed through the Galerie des Glaces, caught the pestilence, and several died. There was the usual tra-là-là about dismissing the mistress, receiving the Last Sacraments, begging forgiveness in public for the scandal he had caused—all probably with the *arrière pensée* that, if he recovered again, as he had done twice before, he could return to his sins.

At last this cold-hearted lecher was in the pitiless clutch of man's last enemy. He was at the mercy of *something*. No longer would hapless little girls be at his mercy, nor would love-sick women who had succumbed to the charm of his husky voice and his princely manner, live to know bitter weeping and regret. When one ponders on the immense amount of ill he wrought, it is difficult to resist the temptation of weighing the rights and wrongs of the case. He said himself that the only woman he had ever loved had been the Duchesse de Châteauroux. If only he had married her, instead of being forced into marriage, at the age of fifteen, with a princess of twenty-three, who, even according to her own father, was one of the most boring people he had ever known! Being a Slav, there was that touch of the bizarre in Marie Leczinska, which was the worst thing in the world for a man like Louis XV.

He died in the afternoon. Marie-Antoinette and Louis XVI heard a sound like distant thunder. The doors burst open: it was the courtiers come to pay homage to them.

"Your grand-father is dead," announced Madame de Marsan to her two charges. "And now, we must all get ready to leave at once."

The carriages had been waiting in the courtyards for some time. For fear of infection, everybody rushed downstairs and left the palace before the body was cold. When the gentleman of the bedchamber ordered the physician-in-ordinary to proceed with the usual autopsy, he replied politely: "May I point out, Sir, that in that case, it is your privilege to hold the head?" The gentleman of the bedchamber said no more about the matter. Even when the King was safely in his leaden coffin, he inspired his cortège with such a fear of infection, that he was buried with indecent haste and no pomp at all. He was no longer "the Well-Beloved".

CHAPTER V

Marie-Antoinette

IN 1774, Rose Bertin, the Queen's new dressmaker, appeared at Versailles. She was the despair of the mistress of the robes, because, when she sent in her enormous bills, she would not specify individual items. This camouflaging of highway robbery, was, in the end, to deplete the finances quite seriously, and constantly to make the Queen exceed her dress allowance. The ladies-in-waiting simply detested Rose Bertin—she was so familiar and haughty, a terrible snob and an autocrat. When the Princesse de Lamballe meekly suggested that she would like to have a dress made in such and such a way, the Bertin got so enraged that she told her to go elsewhere for her clothes. Madame de Lamballe had to appeal tearfully to the Queen, and beg her to plead her cause with the dressmaker.

The Queen's determination about receiving Rose Bertin as she wished, was only one other indication of her desire to shake off the shackles of etiquette. Quite early in the reign, Marie-Antoinette started doing this. Her public *lever* in the morning had been such an ordeal. Her chemise could only be handed to her by the lady of the highest rank then in the room. If, at that precise moment, somebody of higher rank came in, the chemise had to be handed on to her, and the Queen would stand naked and shivering, whilst her attendant stripped off her many-buttoned court gloves. If it were the Comtesse d'Artois, she maliciously took care to upset the Queen's head-dress as she put the chemise over her head. Even if the Queen asked for a glass of water, it had to be brought to her on a gilded tray with a covered jug and a covered cup by a certain page, who would hand it to a certain lady, who would then hand it to another lady.

Marie-Antoinette at last lost patience. She caused great scandal when she shortened the ordeal of her toilette. She would slip away through the little door on the left of her great bed, to her private apartments—small, low rooms overlooking sunless courtyards, where Rose Bertin would be waiting for her with all the latest Parisian novelties. The chairs were strewn with charmingly striped gauzed ribbons, the new heliotrope taffeta, the white taffeta embroidered with heartsease and speedwell, the white "mousseline" with the white satin stripe, the pale mauve-pink slipper satin embroidered with spangles stitched in with yellow thread, not to speak of her favourite black velvet pouf for her head, or some bouquets of flowers and ostrich feathers for a new head-dress. The ladies-in-waiting angrily refused to be present at these feminine confabulations; they would not put up with the impertinence of the creature who had to be cut short and kept at a distance. The Baroness d'Oberkirch, when she came to France, could not bear her. Eventually, however, much to the delight of the ladies, the dressmaker got involved in a nasty scandal. One Easter Day, in the Salon de la Guerre, Rose Bertin caught sight of Demoiselle Picot, whom she detested. She was one of her old shop girls, who had had the audacity to leave her for a rival house, and who, in so doing, had taken away valuable clientèle. The Bertin looked at her fixedly with an air of contempt and spat at her neck near the left shoulder, saying, "I promised you this, I am keeping my word." Demoiselle Picot swooned away, whilst everyone, in a great flutter, called for eau-de-Cologne. Rose Bertin sailed off and afterwards protested that she had never done it. "What, I commit so low an indecency near the Queen's apartments?!" A lawsuit ensued, which kept the court in fits of laughter for a long time.

Now that Marie-Antoinette was Queen, Madame de Marsan was more careful not to thwart her in her desire to see Elisabeth. It is very probable that it was Marie-Antoinette's guidance which helped Elisabeth to cultivate her now exquisite taste. In all her portraits and miniatures, Elisabeth always looks charming, but particularly so in the portrait by Madame Labille-Guyard, which can be seen at Versailles to-day. She wears one of the poufs invented by Rose Bertin, which made her fortune and which are supposed to betray the soul of a whole generation. She looks *"très grande dame"*, reserved, with a little air of worldly wisdom; altogether highly finished. Every era in history sets its own fashion in faces. The Regency trollops were all cast in the same mould, red-cheeked, brazen and bold-eyed. Louis XV's court ladies admired mythological grandeur. They were Hebes, Floras and Minervas, and, as somebody has so wittily said, they were in the habit of giving eagles drinks out of golden cups brimming with white wine. Later, the beloved Carmontelle, who could only draw in profile, caught the elegance of bearing of all that vanished era. But in this great portrait of Madame Elisabeth, we see that woman has become a thinking personality, instead of a plaything or a domino in a carnival. She should have been surrounded by all her favourite emblems, her books, palette, writing desk—for she became a great letter-writer— her embroidery frame, her purse for alms, her plant pots for her botanical studies, and, in the distance, her horses.

The Comte de Provence, who was a great connoisseur of clothes, praised his sister's taste in dress. Her appearance must have resembled in some way, Madame de Sabran, whose great speciality was complete simplicity, which, however, was very deceptive, for if one examined more closely, one saw that no detail had been overlooked.

On June the 11th, 1775, Louis XVI was crowned at Rheims. According to the ancient tradition of France, the Queen remained in the background, but she was given a seat in a tribune. Moreau's engraving shows her surrounded by her sisters-in-law and her ladies, resplendent in a toilette, no doubt created for the occasion by Rose Bertin. Who knows, had there been no Salic law in France, and had Marie-Antoinette received the grace of Sacring and Anointing, as do our Queens, she might have acquired more sense of responsibility towards her people.

At the most solemn moment, the Queen left the tribune to hide her tears. Mercy says: "This sensibility had such an effect on the King that for the rest of the day, he looked at his august spouse with such adoration that it was impossible to describe." The ceremonies in the Church were interrupted at the moment of the Coronation by the most touching acclamations, and Marie-Antoinette wrote to her mother: "I could not resist it, my tears began to flow in spite of myself."

How enchanting is that engraving of Moreau, the tiers of seats, the great lustres filled with lighted candles. We are told about the orchestra of a hundred musicians, and the throne on the dais draped with violet velvet and studded with fleurs-de-lys. There were tapestries over the pillars to hide the "horrid Gothic architecture of barbarous ages". The Queen and the princesses appeared in their tribunes at seven in the morning; soon, a march, played by trumpets, drums and oboes, announced that the King's procession was coming from the archbishop's palace. Everyone rose from their seats. The King appeared in his long robe of silver cloth. All the holders of ancient names were there. Golden-crowned dukes wore marvellous cloth-of-gold jackets and ducal cloaks of violet cloth bordered and lined with ermine. Elisabeth noticed that her favourite brother, the Comte d'Artois, was behaving very irreverently, and, in fact, in quite an unseemly way, laughing and chattering. As Monsieur de Nolhac has said, he did not know that he would come back himself in fifty years' time, and that the last coronation of Rheims cathedral would be for him. The holy phial was brought from the Abbey of St. Rémy by the Grand Prior in a gilded coach drawn by a white horse with silver trappings. The King was led to the altar, the archbishop put on his spurs and girded him for a moment with his sword. Then they both prostrated themselves side by side on a violet square while the choir sang the litanies. The anointings followed and then the investitures with the tunic, the dalmatic, the cloak, the gloves, the ring, the silver sceptre and the hand of justice. Twelve dukes summoned to their master held the crown of Charlemagne above his head. A burst of thrilling music from the organ, and the archbishop at last placed the crown on Louis XVI's brow. Alas, he was said to have murmured: *"Elle me gêne"*—"It's uncomfortable!" This was when the Queen retired, overcome with emotion. When she returned, the crowds cheered and clapped. The King was solemnly enthroned. Then the dukes embraced him and acclaimed the eternity of the monarchy. "May the King live for ever." The fanfares burst out. The great west doors were opened, the crowds rushed in, crying out and filling the naves. When the archbishop intoned the Mass, little symbolic birds were let loose in the high arches, while heralds scattered coronation medals. Outside, the bells pealed and the guns boomed.

This awesome pageantry, hallowed by long centuries of French history, made a deep impression on Elisabeth. Forever afterwards, not only did she regard Louis XVI as her dearly beloved brother, but as the King to whom she must be loyal in all her conversations at court. If only all the other members of the royal family had imitated her example!

On August the 13th of that year, 1775, Elisabeth made her first Communion in the chapel of Versailles, the housel cloth being held for her by Madame de Marsan and the Princesse de Guémenée. As with most great souls, this act marked a solemn turning point in her life. At that altar, she became imbued with moral courage and learnt the secret of inward happiness. Very soon, she was to need all her fortitude, for, at the end of August, her sister left France for ever to marry the Prince de Piémont. Madame Clotilde later became Queen of Sardinia. In those days, when a royal princess left her father's house, she very rarely met any of the members of her family again. Elisabeth was in a terrible state of despair and grief. There is a lovely childhood picture of Clotilde and the Comte d'Artois which was exhibited many years ago at the Bibliothèque de Versailles. It shows her seated on a goat, and the expression on her face is the sweetest imaginable. In losing her, Elisabeth felt twice orphaned. Marie-Antoinette had to tear Elisabeth away from the last embrace. She wrote the following letter to her mother, the Empress Maria Theresa: "I am enchanted with my sister Elisabeth, on the occasion of the departure of her sister and in several other circumstances, she shows charming sensibility and right feeling. When one is so perceptive at eleven, that is very precious. I will see her more now that she will be in the hands of Madame de Guémenée."

Madame de Marsan took this opportunity to hand in her resignation to the King, and her place was taken by an equally unsuitable person, her niece, the Princesse de Guémenée. She had a delightful house near Versailles, in a hamlet called Montreuil, which, in those days, was in rural surroundings. She lived very luxuriously, entertained lavishly, never paid her debts, and, in the evening, her drawing-room, according to Marie-Antoinette's brother, became a veritable gambling hell. He was horrified to see what company his sister kept. As Imbert de Saint-Amand says about the game of *faro*: "All begins charmingly, and then, in a hot room, charged with an electric atmosphere, the facial expressions change and evil instincts are aroused. The winner cannot hide a repugnant joy, the loser is in a terrible state." The Emperor Joseph II said to Mercy, "At bottom my sister does not like gaming." The Princesse de Guémenée was very fond of little dogs and said they brought her into touch with the invisible world. Needless to say, she did not approve of the way in which Madame Elisabeth had been brought up. She thought her aunt had been too severe, and as for Madame de Mackau's plan of education, that was altogether too pious, too unassuming. She made up her mind to bring the child out into society a little more, to make her go to dances (Elisabeth, who said in one of her letters that she never had been fond of dancing). She tried to foster in her an interest in clothes, to become sophisticated in her appearance and manner. For a child of only eleven years old, Elisabeth put up a quiet but firm resistance. Angélique de Mackau says that there were ructions between the two. She was very mature for her age and knew what she wanted.

If Elisabeth was in any danger, it was from her association with the frivolous young Queen, for she now saw her much more often. In 1776, from the age of twelve, she was admitted to the family suppers, which took place in the Comtesse de Provence's apartment, looking over the rue de la Surintendance. The Comtesse de Provence would bring some little birds she had snared herself and concoct a soup which was supposed to be her *spécialité*. The other members of the family brought their own contributions which they warmed up in chafing dishes, all this with much laughter. In fact, anybody passing in the street at the time would have heard loud guffaws, for the King was always in a very good humour. On hunting days, the hunters were put at a special table where they were most lavishly provided for. The Queen saw to it personally that they had everything they needed, and she would have special choice tit-bits sent to them. The room in which the court ladies were entertained, was hung with brocades of fire and gold. The Duc de Croÿ, who had been an habitué of Louis XV's suppers (where he had even kept the abstinence days much to the edification of others), now returned to sup with Louis XVI. When he saw the King's bedchamber in passing, he recalled the terrible spectacle of Extreme Unction when the late King had died in the middle of that very room, in a little crimson bed. But, no, no, no, one must not think of death. Corpses were not allowed to stay a moment at Versailles. Indeed, it was against etiquette to die there at all, and one only did so accidentally. The Duc de Croÿ speaks about these intimate little supper parties: "The King, as was his wont, tried to chuckle and snigger about people . . . I would very much have liked to see him behave with better breeding, but he did all this with so much kindness and affability, that you could not help loving him. . . . The King was at his best, very gay, chatting, playing pranks, but really very amiable." The only time Louis XVI really became rather a bore, was when he talked endlessly of the day's hunting. The Queen, who had already had a meal before she came, sometimes did not eat at all, but sat at the table doing her embroidery. Many of the nobles did not sup, but just had a bite at the buffet. Gastronomy never rose to greater heights than it did in those early years of the reign. The delicious food of the *petits appartements* had become proverbial. Mesdames Tantes, now safely stuffed away at the Pompadour's old château of Bellevue, greatly disapproved of mixing the sexes at these supper parties, not realising that the company of women had a civilising influence on the men. On the days when Louis XVI supped alone with his hunters, anecdotes used to become more and more *risqué*, though the King never failed to put a stop to them if there were some young noblemen present for whose morals he felt responsible.

We have various tributes to Elisabeth's looks in those early days. Horace Walpole said she was "very pretty and genteel", which meant *distinguée*. Madame de Mackau said she was "as fresh as a rose", and always amiable. Madame Guénard says that, though she was not a perfect beauty, there was much charm and dignity in her whole person. She had chestnut-coloured hair. Although she had the Bourbon nose, it was much more refined than the other noses of her illustrious house. She had a glance which was full of sensibility and melancholy, and that inexpressible sweetness which belongs only to blue eyes. She had a beautiful complexion of lilies and roses, was slightly plump and not very tall. Madame Vigée Le Brun, who painted her, said her great freshness was remarkable: in all, "she had the charm of a pretty shepherdess". A page, the Comte Félix d'Hézecques, who wrote of her at twenty-two, also notices the freshness and lovely carnation tints of her complexion, and her serene air.

It was a great relief to Marie-Antoinette when Mesdames Tantes left Versailles for Bellevue. They had only been kind to her at the beginning, because they wanted to make quite sure of her allegiance. As matters turned out, they did a great deal to harm her marriage in its most intimate aspect, by stupidly repeating to all and sundry any childhood confidences she had made, thereby embarrassing their nephew even more than he was already. And now, from a distance, they criticised the Queen for everything she did, and their venomed darts found their way to the filthy pamphleteers of the Paris streets. They jeered at the plumes of her head-dresses, which they called horse trappings, at her sisterly friendship with the gay Comte d'Artois, at her getting up early one morning to watch the sunrise, though Madame Victoire, it must be said, had done the same thing. They disapproved of her going to the races, of her playing cards, of the adoring young men who surrounded her, of her women friends, of her driving into Paris in a sledge, going disguised to Opera balls, playing cards for thirty-six hours on end. It was from the château de Bellevue that the whisper began that Comte Axel Fersen was her lover. It must be remembered that the Comtesse de Boigne, who mentions this as a matter of course, was the daughter of a lady-in-waiting to Mesdames Tantes at Bellevue.

Calumny! When Beaumarchais in the "Barbier de Séville" speaks of its insidious power, he must have been thinking of Marie-Antoinette.

Saint Philip Neri, once hearing a woman in Rome confess that she had spoken ill of her neighbours, gave her one of his eccentric penances. He told her to scatter a handful of feathers in the street and then return to him. When she did so, he ordered her to go back and bring him all the feathers she had scattered. When she returned in despair, having been unable to obey, he said: "And so are the words of calumny. They can never be taken back."

These frustrated old maids had carried their art to perfection. It was as if the unhappy young Queen lived in a glass house. Every tiny action, almost every sigh, would be reported by their stool pigeons, and thence trickle into Paris and subsequently all over the kingdom. And when,

E

tired of living on show, continuously in the public eye, even dressing and undressing in public, Marie-Antoinette began to furnish the dark little rooms of her private suite, their wrath knew no bounds. "And what do you think she has done with the oratory of poor dear Mamma? She has transformed it into a *lieu à l'anglaise*."

"Well, didn't you know that she even had one behind her tribune at the Coronation?"

Had they only seen the Queen's pathetic letter to Mercy about that time (1776)! "I never cease to think of the strangeness of my situation, the way the King neglects me. I am afraid of being bored, and I am afraid of myself. To escape this obsession I need movement and noise." Before his death, Louis XV tried to probe into the strangeness of her marital situation. Accompanied by the court physician, he took the Dauphine outside to the *Tapis Vert*, where no-one could overhear them, and put her through a most embarrassing catechising. The cure for her husband's impotence would have been surgical intervention, but he lost his courage on the fatal day, and nothing was done for a long time. Had they lived completely apart, Marie-Antoinette's nervous system might not have been shaken, but she was continually in the ambiguous position of being neither bride nor maiden. After many years of this, the strain began to tell. She had migraines, attacks of weeping, and violent fevers which Mercy called the vapours. It is remarkable that she kept her marriage vows as she did, for she was surrounded by a court of ardent and unscrupulous men who created an atmosphere of desire around her. She probably did not realize what was happening to herself, for she had no-one to whom she could turn for advice. Her mother was continually making her lose her belief in her own good looks, and then nagging her about her sterility and giving her hints about how to be attractive to the King, without realising that it did not depend on her. Hence, the Queen's great affection for her women friends. A very happily married woman has no close women friends. The Comte de Reiset says it was the fashion at the time for a woman to have an inseparable woman friend to whom she wrote a little note every morning and with whom she would rush about the rest of the day. This is exactly what Marie-Antoinette did, for she had no artistic or intellectual interests on which to fall back.

Mesdames Tantes had plenty of disagreeable things to say about the Princesse de Lamballe and Gabrielle de Polignac, when they appeared upon the scene.

Indeed, the Queen was incurably frivolous. With her intimates, she could not talk of serious things. She always asked for news of the theatre, always said "Was there a great crowd there?". Someone would bow low and reply, "Madame, there was not so much as a cat," which meant the audience was composed of financiers, provincials and other members of the middle classes. Here is her programme for the early part of 1777. On January the 30th, from midnight till four the next morning, she was at party at the Palais Royal, and then went through a corridor to assist at the Opera ball. On February the 6th she repeated the process, returning to Versailles at six in the morning. On the 9th of February, Opera ball; 10th of February she gave a ball, which lasted from five until nine; after supper she went to Paris to the Opera ball, where she stayed till six in the morning.

Making allowances for the fact that she was often unjustly criticised, and constantly watched and spied on by all her relations-in-law, her servants and courtiers, and their servants and courtiers, her fundamental mistake lay in not realising that the French need to look up to a Queen. Rivarol said about her that she was always more conscious of the charm of her sex than of her position, she forgot that she had been made to live and die on a real throne; "too much did she desire that fictitious and fugitive empire which is given to ordinary women by beauty and which makes them queens of a moment". Monseigneur Beauchesne, without giving any positive proof, in his life of Madame Elisabeth says: "Madame Elisabeth was pained to see that the Queen showed herself too easily, going to Paris without any ceremonial, and on beautiful summer evenings, allowing herself to be surrounded by the people walking on the terrace of the garden of Versailles. Madame Elisabeth was persuaded that the success acquired by the woman, took away something from the prestige of the Queen, and that familiarity brought a lessening of respect. When Kings remained invisible, the popular imagination saw them as supernatural beings."

She made two great mistakes at the beginning of her time at Versailles. The first one, indeed, was talked of fifteen years later and it really was not her fault. When she was receiving mourning visits after Louis XV's death, she welcomed to perfection the tottering old dowagers dripping with crêpe, who were making their curtsies. Odd as some of these ladies were, she did not flicker an eyelid. Unfortunately, one of her own young ladies-in-waiting, the Marquise de Clermont-Tonnerre, tired of having to stand for so long, took advantage of being behind the wide panniers of the other ladies and sat down on the floor. And there, alas! she attracted attention by her exuberant cheerfulness, her mimicries, her pulling of skirts and playing all kinds of tricks on the others. Unfortunately, the Queen noticed this, and the contrast was so great, that she had to put up her fan to hide her smiles. Afterwards, as far down as Auvergne, the rumour spread that the Queen had burst out laughing under the very noses of the duchesses and sixty-year-old princesses. The arrogant little Austrian—how dare she . . .

This reputation for mockery was not altogether unfounded. Her unhappy tendency for ridiculing others, which had made her so many enemies, was to be developed by her entourage, which was the most malicious, slandering clique in any court that ever was. Madame Vigée Le Brun says that one day, when she was painting her, the Baron de Breteuil came in to chatter with the Queen, and the whole visit was devoted to speaking ill of all the women he knew. People will forgive much, but they will not forgive a woman for making them appear ridiculous.

Whatever Elisabeth thought privately, she was admirably loyal to her sister-in-law. There is an incident, indeed, which shows the two young things, drawn together in understanding, when Madame Adélaïde was furious with Madame Elisabeth for not telling her that she was going to be inoculated against smallpox. Elisabeth wrote to Marie-Antoinette, telling her how she had soothed down her aunt. One gathers, by the tone of her letter, that the Queen understood only too well. Elisabeth must have been horrified to see the way the Savoie sisters-in-law treated the Queen, one of them going so far as to say to her one day, "You may be Queen of France, but you will never be Queen of the French." The Comtesse de Provence was particularly odious and cunning in her malice. She would dress very simply on purpose and refuse to go to festivities, to give the nation the impression that she was a serious-minded kind of person, a great contrast to the thistledown Austrian. She was, of course, hand in glove with her husband, who wanted to be King, and who hired an army of pamphleteers to spread rumours about Marie-Antoinette in Paris. It was under his aegis that rhymes about her lovers appeared. And whilst he was secretly spewing up all this venom, he would smother her with hypocritical attentions. One day, having broken her fan, he sent her another with the following little poem:

> In the midst of extreme heat,
> Happy to amuse your leisures,
> My care is to bring the zephyrs to you;
> The little winged gods of love will come of their own accord.

CHAPTER VI

Trials and pleasures of early girlhood

IT was as well that, in the middle of all these family agitations, sensed beneath the façade of perfect good breeding, Elisabeth had her childhood friend, Angélique de Mackau. The princess who never fell in love, soon became the delighted onlooker at a happy idyll. From early childhood, the beautiful Angélique had been in love with the Marquis de Bombelles, a man twenty years older than herself. Having watched her, step by step from early infancy, he now fell in love with this accomplished young girl, whose enchanting character and perfect education were so highly praised by Comte Fleury. One fine day, he fell ill at Madame de Mackau's house at Montreuil, and she nursed him like a mother. The child's visits charmed the convalescence of the diplomat, and they went for long rambles together in the Princesse de Guémenée's park at Montreuil. Quite soon, encouraged by his own sister, he lost his heart completely. Underneath Angélique's apparent childishness, he glimpsed a gentle, reasonable, affectionate nature. Her lovely face expressed the soul within. Her features were refined and her eyes had a pure and frank expression. Madame de Mackau did not discourage their friendship, for she had plans of her own; she even reminded them of the days when they had played together when Angélique was a toddler and she used to call him her husband. Angélique was to write to him later: "I assure you that I have always loved you since that time, and reason, which follows on after childhood, instead of destroying the tender friendship which I had for you, only increased it. No, it is not a dream, I can unveil my heart to you with assurance. Since my destiny will be united to yours . . . your age has never frightened me, it is rather for you to be frightened of mine."

Or again: "As you say so well, the heart has no age. Mine will always be united to yours, and the desire that I have of pleasing you, will make up to you for the faults which you may find in me. I am convinced that you will always be the same with me, I judge you by myself. I know that when two people live continually together, they cannot always be making love, but tender and constant friendship will follow after this, and the one is just as good as the other."

In those days, of course, one's Mamma saw one's love-letters, and Madame de Mackau adds to this one: "She unveils her soul and lets it speak freely; I did not want to interfere in this, nor correct a single word. . . . This little girl loves the affirmative, and I should not be astonished if, at the altar, she were to say 'Yes, yes'."

There was really something adorable about that Angélique, who lived only for love. "I am pleased that you have marked with a black line all the *I want*'s of husbands; they are very disagreeable for a woman. Your prayers will always be orders for me, and I shall only be too delighted to please you. But I must confess that I will never do a thing willingly, whenever you have said 'I want', and there is only this nasty word which could put me a little out of temper." It is not surprising that when the Marquis received this letter of mingled tenderness and folly, he wept and laughed at the same time.

That park belonging to the Princesse de Guémenée at Montreuil, so charming a place, full of rare shrubs and trees—if only its ghosts could speak to us! Madame de Sabran walking in it during a torch-light evening party, thought of her beloved Chevalier de Boufflers, far away in Africa. Marie-Antoinette walked there, and probably thought of Comte Axel Fersen. Angélique de Mackau, the dearest and most intimate friend of Elisabeth, became betrothed in its green shade to the man she was to adore for the rest of her short life. It is strange that, though Elisabeth watched human love in all its sweetness, and some years later was to receive the confidences of the Princesse Louise de Condé when she fell in love with the Marquis de Gervaisais, she herself never had the slightest wish to marry. During a visit of the Emperor Joseph II to France, there was much talk that he might be coming for Elisabeth's hand. Fortunately it came to nothing—he was a most unlikeable person. Marie-Antoinette had said how important it was not to remain a spinster at a place like Versailles, but there was not the slightest tinge of the spinster mentality about Elisabeth, not a suspicion of small-mindedness, envy or bitterness. She cannot have been devoid of temperament, with such ancestors as hers. She was a Bourbon through and through, with Polish, Spanish and Italian blood coursing in her veins; and yet, she seems like a pure lily in a quiet garden. From the day of her first Communion, the love of God took possession of her heart, and nothing else seemed very much worth while. A very old lady at Versailles once said: "There really was something very different about the *jeunes filles* of the past, something angelic, almost celestial. They inspired respect wherever they went." It seems as if wonderful sisters are a speciality of France. It was Elisabeth's vocation to be the perfect sister, aunt and sister-in-law, bringing consolation to four lives which would have foundered in despairing grief without her. And to fulfil this vocation, she remained unmarried. She took Angélique and her Marquis under her protection. Despite the timidity which paralysed her in the presence of her brother, Elisabeth reminded the King that he had once promised to establish her friend. He kept that promise: the young bride received a dowry of five thousand francs, a pension of a thousand *écus*, and a place as her lady-in-waiting, for which she would receive her remuneration, even when in residence abroad with her husband. The marriage was celebrated on January the 23rd, 1778, in the Church of Saint Louis of Versailles. Over the Marquis' spirited comments on his wedding day, a chaste veil must be drawn.

Elisabeth had made one condition to the marriage, and that was that her "*petit ange*", as she called her, should remain with her until their joint education was completed. Very sadly, in the following February, Monsieur de Bombelles had to rejoin his post at Ratisbonne, leaving his young wife behind with Madame de Mackau and the princess. And here a slight shadow darkens the picture. Prodded no doubt by her intriguing mother, Angélique now began to pester her princess to give her husband the post of ambassador at Constantinople, and to urge her to ask the King to pay his debts. How many times in the history of Louis XVI does this happen, and how greatly it must have contributed to emptying the treasury.

Angélique wrote the most delightful letters to her husband, so we learn what was happening at Versailles. She speaks of a carnival party which sounded most amusing. ". . . we acted a play which we'd make up; you can imagine how fine that was! And then Mamma put on a coat, undid her hair and doffed an old hat. Madame de Sorans clothed herself in a voluminous green taffeta, which wrapped her head and body, and they sang a dialogue of a drunkard and a penitent which comes from St. Cyr. Mamma, in acting the part of the drunkard, had such a funny appearance, everyone laughed so hard you couldn't hear her any more. You can imagine that evening was very happy for Madame Elisabeth. . . ."

In the previous year, Madame de Mackau had written to her future son-in-law: "Moreover you have to realise, my dear friend, that it would be very much in your own interest to allow her to cement and cultivate the tender friendship that this princess has for her, which is unparallcled and which can only be very useful to you, whether she stays in France or goes elsewhere."

Elisabeth gave the young bride a little room at the Château of Versailles and personally superintended the furnishing of it with tapestry armchairs which she ordered to be brought up. Every morning the two friends would meet. Often Elisabeth had her breakfast carried to Angélique's room, and they would sit by the window together and talk about the absent Marquis.

We get another glimpse into the young feminine society of the time. A certain very poor but very austere Madame de Causans, a widow highly respected by the King, had received the mission of supervising the young princess's household, whilst only holding the title of lady-in-waiting. She lived in Paris with three of her daughters, in a small flat in the Rue de Grenelle. As she had no dowry to give them, these girls would never be able to marry and had therefore become canonesses of the Chapter of St. Louis of Metz. The statutes of the Chapter obliged them to spend eight months of the year in the Convent. It was not exactly as strict as a religious Order, for the notorious Diane de Polignac herself was a canoness and the royal family used to call her "*Ma Mère*". It was more like a glorified kind of club, where dowerless daughters could live with dignity among other girls of their own rank. Taine tells us that many of these ladies were very richly dressed and even wore panniers under their habits in choir, and fine furs and jewels. There were some houses where the poor members nearly starved to death in the common refectory, while the richer girls had private meals served to them by their own servants in their cells. It is all on a par with the Portuguese Abbess urging her nuns to be hospitable to the young French soldiers returning from the American War of Independence, because such conduct would fit them for their vocation.

It is easy to read between the lines that the three daughters of Madame de Causans had no vocation, and were secretly pining away for court festivities. When their mother was on duty at Versailles, she bundled them away into her little flat in the château, and there they remained indoors all day, under the eagle eye of an elderly servant, forbidden to take any exercise. When Elisabeth heard of this, she begged their mother to allow them to come to her apartments, but Madame de Causans was adamant in her refusal. Would it not be cruel, she argued, to let her girls catch a glimpse of a world which would never be theirs? One day though, Elisabeth circumvented her. Her friends were playing at *"ombres chinoises"*, or *"silhouettes"*, in her drawing-room. Elisabeth was directing operations behind the scenes, and her ladies were called upon in turns to guess the name of the persons who passed behind the cloth. The Marquise de Causans was in the audience:[1] "Madame Elisabeth secretly gave one of her women strict orders to bring her the young person at once, without allowing her to change her dress. Mademoiselle de Causans, whose heart was beating madly, crossed the apartment, rather embarrassed by the simplicity of her get-up. All of a sudden, a door half opened; Madame Elisabeth appeared, arranged the head-dress of the young girl, draped a muslin on her gown, taught her quickly the attitudes to take, and then returned to the drawing-room. Soon, a charming silhouette was outlined on the backcloth, passed back and forth, making court curtsies with a perfect knowledge of etiquette. The onlookers, much puzzled, searched in vain for the name of this charming apparition. Alone, Madame de Causans had recognised the figure and features of her daughter, but how could she suppose that she would be behind the backcloth, defying her most rigorous commands? . . . There followed several moments of hesitation. At last the mother, offended, but

[1] Related by Vicomte de Causans, and quoted by Comtesse d'Armaillé.

entranced, guessed, got up and cried, addressing herself to the princess:
'Ah, Madame, what a betrayal!' Everyone was delighted; and the
future nun, presented in this way to the court, took away the memory
of this pretty scene which she loved to recall to her young sister."

Very soon, Elisabeth became very friendly with one of the de
Causans girls, Louise. In 1784, by personal deprivations, she was able
to give her a dowry which enabled her to marry Monsieur de Raigecourt. In the meantime, she continued to have lessons with Angélique
de Bombelles, for she soon realised that she had not been properly
educated. She made a particular study of botany under the aegis of
Le Monnier, the famous botanist. In the days before Louis XVI gave
Petit Trianon to Marie-Antoinette, its garden was a botanist's paradise,
full of glasshouses, packed with rare orchids and other plants which
the French navy had brought to Louis XV from all parts of the world.
With the new reign, many an old courtier deplored the loss of these
treasures and their transfer to the Jardin des Plantes in Paris. Before
their disappearance, Elisabeth had loved the damp, warm atmosphere
of the hot-houses, the fantastic vegetation and bizarre flowers.

> "All things counter, original, spare, strange;
>   Whatever is fickle, freckled (who knows how?)"

"The violet of wounds, the apoplectic reds, the mauve bells
bursting forth at the end of long curly stalks, the varnished leaves
which looked as if they had been cut out from gold-beaters' skin,
the shaggy surfaces of strange stems, the nepenthes with their
drooping green pipes, covered with fine hairs; and on the roofs, on
their cut and dried up roots, the Brazilian orchids hurled their scin-
tillating rockets into the air." And then the whole world of ferns, and
cruel carnivorous plants. The collection of shrubs and rare trees at
Petit Trianon has always been renowned. In the spring, it must have
been a delight to watch the Chinese apple trees, the almond blossom,
the hawthorn, the Judas trees, the ashes, cedars and chestnuts. Very
soon Marie-Antoinette ordered thousands of bulbs from Holland,
particularly hyacinths and tulips.

There is an amusing little private note to the head gardener from the

Dutch bulb owner, saying he is in despair to realise that the order had come from the Queen; he thought it was from a private individual. Would the gardener kindly send him back the bill and he would triple his charges.

Le Monnier had a great collection of pressed flowers in albums and boxes of rare minerals. He was also something of a herbalist. He was a great believer in the healing properties of herbs, and when he was ruined by the Revolution, he was able to open a little herbalist's shop in Versailles. He and his royal pupil often went on botanical expeditions in the woods around. One day, Elisabeth met a poor woman gleaning dry sticks in the Bois de Satory, which is on the left as you go to St. Cyr. Elisabeth gave her all the money that she had in her purse, thus saving the woman and her family from starvation.

She also saw a great deal of her mathematical master Mauduit, one of the best professors of mathematics in the capital. He kept a very ingenious table of logarithms devised by the princess. It is strange that, with her taste for mathematics, she never became an accomplished musician. In vain did Angélique de Bombelles try to teach her to play the harpsichord in time, but it was no use, and one day when they tried to play a concerto for four hands, for the Comte d'Artois, the performance was a failure. The Marquis de Bombelles was asked to choose a good harpsichord for her in Portugal. Unmusical herself, however, and probably taking no interest in the fashionable enthusiasm for Glück and Piccini, she wanted her musical friends to enjoy themselves. Angélique de Bombelles wrote to her husband: "By the way, Madame Elisabeth took away that harp about which I spoke to you, which had given me so much pleasure. I said to her what the holy man Job said to the Lord when he took away his worldly goods, and I have heard since that she had given it to your sister. Imagine my wrath! At last, having undergone these trials, there appeared the prettiest harp which has ever been since the world began. Having shared my griefs, I hope that you will share my joy."

Van Blarenberghe was her drawing-master. The Duke of Buccleuch possesses an imposing sea-scape painted by Madame Elisabeth, though, to be sure, it looks as if the drawing-master has had more hand in its creation than the pupil. It is a pity that the matchless Redouté, who taught Marie-Antoinette how to paint roses, did not give Elisabeth some lessons too, for then she could have combined her love of drawing and botany. She wrote one day to Madame de Causans: "For three days I am calling out for M.B. (Van Blarenberghe) and he does not come; I am dying with fear that he is dead. When I say that I have been waiting for him for three days, you must count as if it were yesterday. I am going to begin a little drawing for the ladies of St. Cyr; it is charming. I have not said to B. (Marquise de Bombelles) that it is for them, for I think that would have put her into a bad temper."

In the inner library at Versailles, there is still a tiny etching of hers on the wall.

It was really the fashionable thing to draw and paint a little. Madame de Sabran, one recalls, was always surrounded by paints, palettes and unfinished canvases which she hid between the mattresses. Roussel d'Epinal, who accompanied the Duke of Bedford in his visit to the Tuileries Palace, after the insurrection of August the 10th, saw in Madame Elisabeth's apartments all the tools with which she always loved to surround herself—compasses, mathematical instruments and so on: "What surprised Bedford was the richness of the instruments. The rulers were of ivory, ornamented with gold; the compasses of gilded silver and the other things of precious workmanship. . . . Near the window, overlooking the garden, was placed another table covered with paint brushes and colours. . . . Lord Bedford, who was something of a connoisseur in painting, assured the others that her talent was far above the ordinary. They looked at a small painting in body colour, representing a parade on the boulevard with eighteen little figures very distinctly painted in that square, with a house and landscape in the distance. The finish of it was all the more precious because everything had been painted on the back of a playing card."

The page, Comte Félix d'Hézecques, said: "The last oil painting which I saw her do in Paris was a great canvas representing a landscape with a great waterfall. When she was virtually a prisoner at the Tuileries, her paintbox helped her to wander out into the countryside she loved so much and paint plains and woods and country roads with horsemen on them."

Elisabeth was also a very talented needlewoman, and she and Marie-Antoinette worked at many beautiful pieces of embroidery together, a few of which are still kept as treasured relics in French châteaux. One of her ladies once said to her: "It is really a pity that Madame is so able." "And why?" asked the princess. "Because this would be such a suitable gift to poor girls. Their talent would enable them to earn their living and that of their family." "It is perhaps for that reason that God has given it me," she replied. "Who knows? One day perhaps I may make use of it to feed myself and my family."

During the Princesse de Guémenée's term of office, there had been several squalls, and Elisabeth said that she could really only see the Marquis de Bombelles by hiding behind a door. On May the 17th, 1778, Madame de Guémenée resigned her post in order to devote herself to Madame Royale, and another even more unsuitable person was placed at the head of Elisabeth's household. This was the Comtesse Diane de Polignac, the sister-in-law of the Gabrielle de Polignac who was to become one of the Queen's most intimate friends. She was "scandal personified". Horace Walpole spoke of her terrible morals. On November the 15th, 1781, he wrote: "The theme is a delightful episode of a Mademoiselle Diane de Polignac, a friend of the favourite Duchess, who was *dame* to Madame Elisabeth, and who was so very pious and had so bemethodised her mistress, that they feared the Princess would follow her aunt Louise into a convent, and they would have dismissed the saint, if the Queen would have consented, and if the saint had not, one *beau matin*, had the misfortune to have a little one."

Diane de Polignac was in the clique where women never lived with their own husbands, but always had lovers. Her own sister-in-law's association with the Comte de Vaudreuil was notorious. It is impossible to see what made for her enormous success at court. Her biting tongue kept her enemies at bay. She soon became so powerful that many people became afraid to cross her path. She was ugly, ill shaped, almost hump-backed, dressed in a slovenly manner, making no attempt to have recourse to artifice. And yet, she was the life and soul of every party. She concealed her avid grasping nature under the modish sensibility. She blushed like a school-girl and trembled at nothings. She would weep for a trifle and wrote touching little verses to her friends. The only thing which makes one suspect that she had some redeeming quality, was that she was a great friend of the exquisite Madame de Sabran, whom she often entertained in her house at Montreuil, and to whom she wrote touching verses on the sorrow of parting from her.

When Diane de Polignac and her brother accompanied Madame de Sabran to Switzerland, she was impervious to the grandeur of the scenery.

Nicolas has said of her: "This Diane, heedless, with casual manners, good-natured and frank, has always been a little familiar with the boys."

After this short thumbnail sketch, it is reasonable to suppose that she was not ideally suited to Madame Elisabeth. But the princess, young as she was, kept her in her place, just as she had kept the Princesse de Guémenée at a distance. She was very polite to her, but never allowed her to encroach one inch on her private life and occupations. Diane de Polignac took her revenge in a subterranean way. She criticised her looks and appearance and made fun of her clothes. Indeed, one fine day, she went too far and shocked the Princesse de Wurtenberg when she visited France under the name of Comtesse du Nord. Her friend the Baronne d'Oberkirch reports: "After these visits I went to see Madame la Comtesse du Nord in her suite. I found her very shocked by an indiscreet remark by the lady-in-waiting Comtesse Diane de Polignac at Madame Elisabeth's expense. Madame la Grande Duchesse having visited the princess, the Comtesse Diane was charged to show her out again, as is correct, to the precincts of the apartment. Madame la Comtesse du Nord was loud in her praises of the graces, the amiability and the charming face of Madame Elisabeth.—'Yes,' replied Madame de Polignac, 'she has some beauty, but plumpness spoils all.' This remark was doubly tactless, for if there was anything to criticise in my princess, it was just this plumpness, which her tall well-made figure concealed so happily. As one can imagine, this remark displeased her, so she left the Comtesse, saying to her rather dryly, 'I couldn't have found Madame Elisabeth better looking than I did, Madame, and I have not been struck with the fault of which you speak.'"

CHAPTER VII

A visit to Carmel

Elisabeth's niece, Louise Thérèse Charlotte de France, in the memoir which she wrote on their captivity during the Revolution, said: "Since the age of 15, she had given herself to God, and thought of nothing else but her salvation." One of her greatest friends, one whom she is said greatly to have resembled, the Princesse Louise de Condé, became a Benedictine nun and founded the Convent of the Rue Monsieur. "Birds of a feather flock together." There is, to this very day, a tradition among the French Carmelites that Elisabeth had all the marks of a true vocation and a very great attraction for everything that pertained to Carmelite life. Sometimes she must have been tempted to imitate her aunt and leave very early one morning, to disappear behind the black iron grille at St. Denis. But with all the élan and dash of her nature, Elisabeth had such a foundation of quiet prudence and good sense, that she would not have done things in that way. A later letter to Mademoiselle Marie de Causans, written before she began her own novitiate, is most revealing: ". . . to begin with, *mon cœur*, one cannot know if a vocation is really the work of God, unless, with the desire to follow his will, one has, however, allowed oneself to fight the attraction in good faith". She warns Marie against "a transitory fervour which gets a grip of a heart which is attached to no earthly object, and thinks it will save itself from the danger of forming an attachment which Heaven would not approve, by consecrating itself to God". She speaks of the desire which the heart has of forming a bond which will fill it entirely. Then she says how bodily mortifications cost so little, one can get accustomed to them, but it is not the same with the mortifications of the spirit and heart. She begs her young friend not to dismiss the troubles of her novitiate as if they were temptations, but to weigh them up, lest, when she has taken her final vows, they make for her life's unhappiness. Also, she warns her against forming a Utopian picture of the convent which she is entering, and urges her to realise beforehand that she will meet people there who will be difficult to put up with, even people who will scandalise her. "Happy is he who can live only for God and with God." All this has an autobiographical tone, as if she too had weighed a vocation in the balance.

She often went to see her white-cloaked aunt, Mère Thérèse de St. Augustin, at St. Denis. It is so easy to picture her in her aunt's cell in that Carmel, which, before her arrival, had been so poor that the baker refused to give the nuns credit any longer.

A Carmelite cell! The walls are whitewashed, the floor is of cold red brick, the bed a bare board with a straw palliasse on top. When this palliasse is new, it is so domed that, unless you first jump on it hard, you are apt to fall out of bed. On the wall, a great bare wooden cross without a figure on it. On the floor, an earthenware jug and basin, and a small wooden stool on which the Carmelite sits to write her letters or to do her needlework. As this extremely ancient Order seeks to foster the eremitical life, the Carmelite is in her cell alone for long stretches of time, and though that, of course, means that she is freer from the trials of nuns who live in community, like the Visitation sisters, she has, at first, to get used to the intense cold of winter. There is only the light of one tallow candle; no curtain at the window, only a board. But as Thomas à Kempis has said, the monastic cell becomes sweeter, the longer one lives in it, for there, gradually, day by day, to the humble listening heart, the presence of God reveals itself.

And what of the trials, the aridities, the spiritual desert, the Dark Night of the Soul? Through this "cloud of unknowing", St. John of the Cross is the guide, detaching the soul from spiritual gluttony, making her love God for His own sake and not for the sweetness which He sends. It is a virile, strengthening doctrine which forms courageous nuns. Their great Saint Teresa of Avila has said: "His Majesty greatly loveth the courageous soul." Night and morning there is one hour's mental prayer in choir, there is the long fast and abstinence, from September to Easter, which is, alas, the undoing of so many modern constitutions, and there are the recreations which surpass those of all other Orders for gaiety. Yes, that Teresian gaiety appealed to

F

Elisabeth, for all her letters to her friends sparkle with a robust good humour, almost a "*bonhomie*". It is an Order in which the body, the intellect and the aesthetic sense find no satisfaction whatever. The Office is sung on one dreary, monotonous note, and the chapel is very bare indeed. It all reminds one of Thomas à Kempis—"Naked follow the naked Christ". Madame Louise was longing for her niece to come and join her. She longed to see her safe from the entourage of the court, with its sins, its unkind sarcasms, its pleasures which were but ashes. Oh Versailles which now had no place for the old, for did not the Queen herself say she could not understand why people over thirty had the audacity to come to court, and, if she saw guests dancing badly at one of her balls, she never asked them again.

"What would you like to do before you go home to-day, *mon cœur*?" the Carmelite said to her niece. Elisabeth thought for a moment. "I should very much like to serve the nuns in the refectory. It would at least give me the feeling that I belong to you for a brief spell." Her aunt laughed. "You have always hankered for the cloister. I shall never forget when you were a little girl, Madame de Marsan told me that when you visited the convent of the Holy Child Jesus, you wanted to wear one of the novices' habits, and, when you were told that there were none to fit you, you went purple with rage and stamped your feet and howled. A true sign of vocation!"

In the refectory, bare trestles against three sides of the white-washed walls. Above, painted in black, the somewhat terrifying Carmelite maxims, such as:

"Take up thy cross and follow Me."

In their brown habits, with their hands up their ample sleeves, Carmelites sit on hard benches on one side of the tables only. Like good religious, they are trying to keep their eyes down, but to-day it is very difficult. It is hard not to look up at the royal figure in the pale green satin bodice with its snowy muslin fichu and the ample billowing white skirts. And to make things harder, she was wearing a large and most intriguing hat, turned up at one side and surmounted with a spray of cocks' feathers and geraniums. Beneath those brown habits, women's hearts still beat, and one has yet to meet the nun who is impervious to the excitement of a fashionable hat. Oh dear! what a

clowder of faults against our Holy Rule will have to be confessed at
the next Chapter meeting! The princess has gone to the serving hatch
with her plank of wood. On it are about six earthenware platters filled
with cold beans. Such a feast! Plonk! the board has tipped. A platter
falls off! One of the novices titters. Elisabeth goes as red as a cockatoo.
Mère Thérèse de St. Augustin, controlling her voice as best she can,
says: "After such an act of clumsiness, my daughter, it is customary
for the culprit to kiss the ground." Elisabeth does this to the manner
born, though the hat is a bit of a hindrance in the process. What a lot
of laughter that caused afterwards at recreation!

When she got into her carriage to be driven back to Versailles,
Elisabeth had that uncanny feeling, which happens to people with
religious vocations, that she had left her heart behind. Only an outer
shell was going to Versailles. The knees which had knelt in prayer,
must now bend for great ceremonial curtsies. An immense nostalgia
filled her. It was a blessing that she had her beloved Louise de Causans
with her; she was so very devout, that she would go to all lengths to
get to Mass every day, in all weathers. As for Angélique de Bombelles,
well, one could not expect so much enthusiasm from such a happy
young wife, whose thoughts were always with her husband. To cheer
herself up, Elisabeth started to tease Angélique. "I am going to write
to your husband and tell him how you cried your eyes out at the
Clothing ceremony the other day. How I enjoyed giving all those
nuns the kiss of peace afterwards. It really is a foretaste of Paradise.
One doesn't know half of them, and yet we kiss each other so whole-
heartedly."

Angélique sighed: "I am so moved at these sort of functions, that
I get a migraine for the rest of the day, and everybody teases me about
my red eyes."

Only the coaches of princes were allowed into the Cour de Marbre
at Versailles. As Elisabeth stepped out, one of the Queen's young pages,
in red and silver livery, came to her, bowed low and said that her
Majesty would be grateful if she could come and talk to her. Followed
by her squire and her page, Elisabeth went up the staircase and walked
through the state apartments, with that peculiar gliding step which all
court ladies had learnt to adopt to avoid falling on the slippery parquet.

She went through the Queen's bedchamber, where two men had just turned the mattress. Two chambermaids were putting on clean sheets, while the gloves and spare handkerchief trimmed with Valenciennes lace just brought down from the attics were laid in a basket lined with green taffeta. Another maid was taking up the book[1] filled with tiny samples of the Queen's dresses which she chose for the day by putting a pin against the sample. Court ladies who were pregnant were excused from going to Mass; they were now sitting on large tapestry stools, looking out of the windows. Two footmen were wheeling the exquisitely beautiful dressing-table away from its place of honour in the middle of the room. Carved Cupids holding great copper lilies played in the garlands on the baldachino of the immense bed, behind its balustrade. The ladies rose and curtsied to Elisabeth as she passed through a little door behind the arras; this led to the private room called a *"méridienne"* in which her Majesty always had a rest after the mid-day meal. The sofa was in a niche of mirrors. The sculptures by Rousseau were enchanting: the flowers, buds and leaves of the rose-tree were the principal motifs of decoration. Falling roses framed all the panels. The gilding of the wood was so perfect that it looked like bronze. There were crowns of roses intertwined, hearts pierced with arrows, all these emblems of love and feminine seduction surmounted by the heraldic dolphin, surrounded with lilies.

Monsieur André Maurois says somewhere that a woman can only create the climate which is her special personal atmosphere or perfume, when she is in a setting contrived by herself, and surrounded by objects of her personal taste. A woman enhances her personality by expressing it in her surroundings. Marie-Antoinette's *petits cabinets* were entrancing, and a fitting background for her glowing beauty. She was at long last expecting her first child at the end of the year, and the happiness seemed to have transformed her. However, a keen observer might notice a somewhat harder expression than when she first came to Versailles as a heedless young Dauphine. But how could she help that, when the Prince de Ligne has said: "I have never known her have a perfectly happy day." The cure of the King's impotence had come too late: the emotional damage was already done.

[1] Exhibited at the National Book League.

Madame Campan has written of Marie-Antoinette: "One is captivated by her smile, and French gaiety sparkles in this entirely enchanting being. An indefinable august serenity, perhaps also the somewhat proud attitude of the head and shoulders, reminds one of a daughter of the Cæsars." The Queen had just returned from mid-day Mass, and had thrown off her panniers, her head-dress, and her black lace mantle.

"Ah, *ma petite sœur*, here you are at last. I thought you were never coming back from St. Denis! I get quite frightened sometimes that you are going to leave us."

Elisabeth said gaily: "Would that be such a great tragedy? You've got so many friends of your own age, and you've made yourself such an intimate little niche here, you can't be lonely in a room like this." And she glanced around at the delicate furniture—the harp, the harpsichord, the music scattered about, her work-boxes and taffeta sacks by her side, full of brightly coloured wools for her tapestries, the red marble chimney-piece and the great marquetry table covered with *chinoiseries* and family miniatures. Just then, a lady-in-waiting whose sole duty it was to fill the flower vases, brought in a great Chinese pot on a tray and several little crystal and Sèvres and Venetian vases filled with the old-fashioned pink moss roses which would have delighted Redouté. The Queen was never unoccupied. When she was alone, she plied her needle, and only left her tambour frame when she had to go out, taking it up again when she returned. On a tray were her golden thimble and her scissors, as well as her *écritoire* on which she wrote short missives to her intimates. On another tray, there were boxes of silver and gold, finely engraved, and perfume burners and crystal cornucopias for the roses she had picked at Petit Trianon. The lady-in-waiting curtsied and went out again.

Elisabeth continued. "And then, when your child is born, you will never be lonely again. You won't need me."

"On the contrary, *ma petite sœur*, I will need you more than ever. There are very few people around here whom I would trust with any young person. I've already been going through the list suggested for the child's future household, and so few of them are at all reliable. A good aunt in the background can be such a blessing."

"Did you want to see me about anything special?" The Queen hesitated and then said: "The King wants to see you. Oh no, you needn't look so upset. He's not going to scold you for going to St. Denis again. Anyway, go and find him. He's either in the library or the smithy."

Elisabeth walked along narrow corridors and up tortuous dark staircases overlooking gloomy courtyards. Her brother was not in the smithy. As a matter of fact, he had climbed up to the garrets, and, having opened a door communicating with the secondary kitchens for the *petits appartements*, he was talking with great kindness to the first person he met there, and this time it was a little scullion. "Ah, here you are," he said to his sister, "let's go to the library. Rousseau and Gabriel have been showing me their designs of trophies for the panels. It is going to be delightful. There will be rustic bagpipes and castanets and shepherd's hats and crooks and the most superb bouquets of field flowers tied loosely with ribbons. There'll be roses and dahlias and poppies, marguerites and sunflowers. As for Gouthière, he is going to surpass himself with the bronze appliqué work on the white marble chimney-piece." The King waxed eloquent. "All my hunts will be depicted on Sèvres plaques, and your Van Blarenberghe is going to do me some fine battle scenes. I have told him to take great care with the uniforms of the soldiers."[1]

It was pleasant to hear him being enthusiastic about his surroundings. Falling in love with the Queen had certainly refined his tastes. He loved her dearly, and had just proved it in such a charming way at Carnival time, by arranging for a fancy dress party when the Queen was in bed. This party must have been very funny, for some of the old courtiers came as Cupids with diaphanous wings. Monsieur de Sartine was disguised as Neptune, the Princesse de Chimay was a fairy, the Maréchal de Biron a Druid, all the pages were jockeys. The Queen hugely enjoyed trying to guess the identity of her friends. At one o'clock, the King said it was time to go to bed, and everybody was regaled with chocolate, both hot and iced.

[1] We are able to date these delightful pieces of woodcarving, for there are even four *montgolfières* among the sextants, the thermometer and the agricultural implements.

To-day, the King seemed ill at ease. His sister could not help noticing that he had put on odd shoes, one with a red heel, the other with a black. It was always those with many lackeys who were worst served. Brother and sister strolled over to the window overlooking the Cour de Marbre, and saw an officer carrying away an immense hamper, looking furtively to right and left. The King said, "What does that fellow think he's doing?" Elisabeth laughed merrily. "Haven't you heard? It's extraordinary how you don't know anything about your own household. He collects all the tit-bits left over from your meals and sells them at a market in the town at a great profit."

"The villain. . . . But what's the use of saying anything? I can't put my foot down. The bills are simply enormous. Why, I only drink lemonade twice a year, and yet they make that single item come to about a hundred pounds or so. As for the candles, I wish I could stop even the unused candles becoming the private perquisites of the staff. I'm feeding an army of parasites. However, I didn't invite you here to talk about the servant problem." He peered at her with his rather short-sighted eyes. "Elisabeth, you've been to St. Denis again. I can see it on your face. I just wanted to tell you that I don't mind how often you go, as long as you don't decide to remain there. You see . . . you see, my dear, I, ahem, I need you here. . . ."

CHAPTER VIII

Elisabeth surveys her new apartment

IN her great life of Madame Elisabeth, E-M. du L. (Sœur Aimée du Sacré Cœur) has said: "At Gethsemane, and during the passion of the French monarchy, there had to be a consoling angel: God who alone foresees all, assigned this rôle to this chosen soul. . . ."

The King and Queen had tried their best to give Elisabeth a taste for worldliness. They had successively appointed the Princesse de Guémenée and the Comtesse Diane de Polignac to her household, but this had only strengthened Elisabeth's reaction against the world. The Queen said: "Anyway, in two years from now, she will have her own household and move to the best suite on the first floor. She'll then probably become more attached to her surroundings."

On December the 19th, according to the barbarous custom of the French court, Marie-Antoinette had her first child in public. It was a daughter, Madame Royale. Elisabeth, being unmarried, did not assist at the confinement, but Angélique de Bombelles was there and came back quivering. The room had been absolutely packed, and some odious men had even climbed on to the chimney-piece to get a better view. The Queen was heroic. She clenched her teeth throughout and did not scream until the very end. The King had tied some screens together with thick rope, hoping to hide the bed. When the Queen was told it was a daughter, she thought to herself, "She will be my friend." In spite of all appearances to the contrary, she was shrewd enough to see through her entourage, and she knew that her loneliness would increase with every passing day.

The following year, 1779, Angélique de Bombelles went to rejoin her husband at Ratisbonne. Elisabeth caught measles in April and the Queen followed suit in the summer. They both recuperated together at Petit Trianon.

It is in this year 1779 that Comte Axel Fersen made his appearance at court. Comte de Tilly said he had a beautiful though cold-looking face, which is not displeasing to women. He loved all that the Queen loved—music, the arts, and a quiet life. There was nothing of the courtier about him. All his skill was to be simple. When he was presented to the Queen at Versailles, she exclaimed, "Ah, but Monsieur is an old acquaintance." She had, indeed, provoked him at a Carnival ball in disguise. She insisted that he should come and show himself to her in his new uniform of the King of Sweden's Light Dragoons. He appeared in a short white tunic, opening on to a blue doublet, skin-tight chamois breeches, silk stockings, blue garters, little Hungarian boots, a black shako with a blue and yellow aigrette, a gold belt and ceremonial court sword.

Though the Queen fell in love with him, she did not succumb to her passion. Monsieur de Nolhac has called it *"une grande passion naissante et combattue"*—a great passion conquered from the beginning. As for Fersen himself, he was a "very perfect gentle knight", who safeguarded the reputation of his friend. During that year, before he decided to leave for the American War of Independence, he came to Versailles two or three times a week. It is very improbable that Marie-Antoinette ever confided any of her emotions to her young sister-in-law. She was too inexperienced, and it would have been most unsuitable from every point of view. But Elisabeth, who was no fool, and who was used to the ways of the world, was not unaware of the gossip which this friendship excited at court. Her aunts at Bellevue even went so far as to think that the Queen was Fersen's mistress. If Elisabeth had believed this to be true, she would never have continued to be such a good friend to her sister-in-law. In March 1780, Fersen left for the American War of Independence. One day the Queen was singing to her friends in the drawing-room at Petit Trianon: "Ah que j'étais bien inspirée quand je le reçus à ma cour. . . ."—"Ah! how well inspired I was, when I received him at my court." Some people noticed that, as she turned to glance at Fersen, her eyes were filled with unshed tears. Afterwards, somebody twitted him on leaving his new conquest, but he replied with a prudence and dignity far above his years.

And so Marie-Antoinette was left alone again. She could not take refuge in the nursery of her first child. That would have upset the staff.

Indeed, she had been so delightedly amazed when the child recognized her for the first time and said "*Maman*", that it appears as if this were unusual. How any child of the royal house of France ever survived the etiquette of its nursery days is a wonder. The women quarrelled and intrigued amongst themselves, trying to filch as many perquisites as they could. When the children grew older, some of the women put them against their unhappy mother, with all the baseness of servant mentality. That they did not succeed is a great proof of Marie-Antoinette's charm and goodness as a mother. So, in that March of 1780, particularly as this was the Lenten season and all festivities at an end, Marie-Antoinette felt very despondent. She turned instinctively to Elisabeth and decided to go and view the new suite of rooms into which she and the Comtesse Diane de Polignac were moving in May, when she was sixteen. Followed by her page, the Comte de Tilly, who had been in disgrace again, she called him into an antechamber, as he needed a scolding, and anyway had asked for a private interview.

The Memoirs of the bad page, Monsieur de Tilly, record a lifelike conversation with the Queen which is absolutely unique. One can almost hear the sound of her voice. The Queen, for all her frivolity, thought it her duty to supervise her pages, just as she considered it an obligation to read the plays which her ladies-in-waiting, some of them young girls from St. Cyr, were going to see in Paris. The Queen was forever receiving complaints about Tilly—how he was always going to Paris, having illicit love affairs and getting into debt. She said to him once: "Be more simply dressed; in the space of a few days, you have worn already two embroidered suits. Your fortune will not be sufficient for you, your tastes exceed it. Simplicity does not make you conspicuous, but it brings you esteem." The day before, Tilly had asked her, in the Galerie des Glaces, for permission to place a request at her feet. She said, "Be with me before five o'clock." When she appeared she said: "*Bonjour*. Where have you dined?"

"At Madame de Beauvilliers', Madame."

"With mine?"

"No, Madame, with Madame Adélaïde's."

"Does she give dinners?"

"Yes, Madame, to me at any rate, whom she knew as a very young child, and with whom she feels at home."

"If Monsieur de Champcenetz had been at Versailles, you would have dined with him. Now, there's good company for you!"

"Madame, he has some intelligence and much gaiety."

"Oh! That's charming. That will get him a long way. Well, Monsieur, what do you want? Come in."

"I beg the Queen to listen to me with a little indulgence, because I will perhaps be a little longer than I should."

"But of course I will listen to you."

"Madame, there has arrived here a Monsieur . . . a kind of magistrate, to whom my parents wish well, and I also. He would like to obtain a place at Alençon. It is vacant. Here it is on a piece of paper. . . ."

"That depends on Monsieur de Miromesnil."

"My Monsieur is an excellent subject. A word from the Queen to Monsieur the Keeper of the Seals, and it is clear. . . ."

"*Eh bien*, it is clear . . . ?"

"Yes, Madame . . . that he could not refuse. . . ."

"Is that all?"

"Yes, Madame."

"I will write. Give me that piece of paper. Come back to-morrow at 3.30. The letter will be written. *Adieu*."

"I do not know how to express to the Queen all my gratitude. . . ."

"By behaving yourself!"

Later, the Queen met Elisabeth in the nobles' antechamber which was upholstered with crimson Genoese damask trimmed with gold galloons and fringes. The stools and tapestry-covered benches had only just been finished.

"Ah! here you are, *ma petite sœur*. The King and I have just been making up the list of your new household."

(One only has to read the "Almanach de Versailles" to count the numbers of these servitors, most of whom were mere parasites, with posts which were sinecures.)

Elisabeth said a little timidly: "If I may say so, I don't know that I am altogether pleased with the choice of Chamfort as my librarian. He is an unbeliever and very cynical, and then, my dear sister, he has no great love for soap and water. He gives me the impression of being one of those hangers-on at court, rather dangerous because he is very touchy; he may some day turn round and attack his benefactors. And then, most important of all, I'm quite certain that he will never choose the kind of books I should like to read."

The Queen laughed. "Alas, that is exactly what I have to suffer from with my own librarian, Campan. If complete strangers were to look at all the titles of the naughty novels on my new shelves, they would form a poor opinion of my tastes and morals. Campan chooses exactly what he wants to read himself. No, but seriously, about Chamfort, I think he is intelligent enough. Now let us go and look at your boudoir." This was at the very end of the suite, overlooking the woods of Satory and the road leading to St. Cyr. Unfortunately, when King Louis Philippe tried to save the palace of Versailles from destruction by dedicating it "to all the glories of France", he tore down the partitions between these rooms on the first floor, and it is now a most uninteresting museum. The only thing which has not changed is the view, but even so, one must remember that five years previously, in 1775, there had been a tremendous cutting down of old trees and replanting of new ones in the much neglected park. The new trees that were planted would not, of course, be as high as they are now, and Elisabeth could therefore see the Grand Canal more clearly, with its gondolas manned by Venetian gondoliers. In winter, if the Canal had frozen over, she would watch the courtiers skating, or duchesses being pushed in gorgeously carved and caparisoned sledges. And on hot summer nights, ladies attended by their chevaliers and pages would visit the neighbouring menagerie.

Just as her brother Louis XVI, in the north-east side of the palace, would sit cosily ensconced at his library window, peering through a spyglass at the varied crowds coming and going in the courtyards, so Elisabeth his sister, in the south-west wing, must often have enjoyed the view of that glorious expanse of water. Fennebresque describes the charming scene around the great gondola. "A court lady crossed the bridge, a page holding the train of her dress. Aft is a siren, astern a Cupid hurling his dart. On the banks are the wheeled chairs, covered with baldachinos, drawn by footmen."

During that time of the park's replanting, there was chaos. Hubert Robert portrays it so charmingly in his picture—the trees felled, the workmen sawing, a dog playing in the ravine where the roots had been, the King and Queen making an informal tour of inspection. *Le Roi Soleil* would have turned in his leaden coffin at St. Denis, had he seen his gardens and park at that time—he who had taken the trouble to write a detailed guide—"Manner of showing the gardens of Versailles". The superintendents, whose responsibility was to keep the park tidy, had collected their wages without doing the work. The marble pools were never cleaned: brimming over with dead leaves and rubbish, they stank in hot weather. Under the arched aisles of the trees, the long green alleys, with their ruts and stumps, were very dangerous for horsemen. Elisabeth actually had a fall from her horse before the officers in charge realised that something must be done. There was little privacy and quiet for her, even on that side of the palace. The usual troop of low lackeys and kitchen aids, and men emptying the *porte-chaises d'affaires* in the thickets, swarmed about the gardens. The children of the townsfolk played hopscotch around the newly planted trees, very soon making pathways, to the despair of the gardeners. The Versailles populace had free access to the gardens, just as they do to-day. One could hear pleasurable hunting sounds coming from the woods of Satory, the hounds giving tongue, the horns sounding the "view halloo" and the raucous yodelling cries of huntsmen. At nightfall, when the King rode back from hunting, and there was no moon, the park alleys were so pitch dark that he had to be preceded by torch bearers, or he would have lost his way.

Elisabeth's view faced south-west, so that she could admire some of those golden sunsets which are the glory of Versailles. She said, in one of her later letters: "There is no place in the world like Versailles for me." From her windows she could see the immense bronze urns with their impish children and frolicking cherubs. They had been placed there by her great-great-grandfather, who had told his architects and sculptors that he wanted to have children everywhere. For festive occasions, after the pools had been hastily cleared, the fountains plashed and glittered in the sunlight, drenching the Tritons, the dolphins and the sea-gods. In the happy days before herbaceous borders had ever been heard of, the flower beds were massed with blooms of one colour—the deep purple expanse of sweet-smelling heliotrope, the red and purple of fuchsias, crimson salvias by the thousand, potted out overnight, the misty pink of night-scented stocks, and of course, in spring, the hyacinths and jonquils, and sometimes the glorious anemones of which Louis XIV had been so fond, and over whose cultivation he had watched with such intense interest. Looking over the balustrades southwards, Elisabeth could see the immense Orangery, which, in those times, was a dream of beauty, for it was well filled and well tended. On state occasions in summer, lackeys would haul the great orange trees up into the Galerie des Glaces, where they were placed in the silver tubs which had survived the melting pot of Louis XIV's last wars.[1] Our ancestors were better able to tolerate heavy scents. The picking of the orange blossom was quite a ritual at court. It was given to the princesses, who had it distilled into orange-flower water for the poor. Elisabeth only had to walk down that glorious pink marble stairway to reach the Orangery. Alfred de Musset has written delightfully about those steps:

> But do you remember, my friend,
> Those pink marble steps,
> As you go to the lake
> Near the orangery,
> On the left, going away from the château?
> It was there, I warrant,
> That the matchless King came,
> In the evening, at sunset,
> In silence, to watch in the forest
> The day vanish and hide itself
> (If in his presence
> The sun dared go to bed).
> How pretty these three steps are!
> How fine and smooth is this marble!

[1] When the late King George VI and his Queen were entertained at a State banquet in 1938, the château officials tried to revive that old tradition, in the Galerie des Glaces, but the perfume of the orange blossom was so overpowering that some of the blossoms had to be replaced by artificial ones.

Do you see those azure veins,
Light, delicate and polished,
Running, under the faded roses
In the whiteness of a pure marble?
So, in the robust and hardy breast
Of the huntress Diana
A divine blood would course.

Oh my God! In such a little thing,
How much grace and beauty.[1]

So, on this March day in 1780, the Queen and Elisabeth gazed out of the boudoir window at the lake beyond. At length, Marie-Antoinette turned round and, casting an admiring glance at the crimson and white damask, with scroll-designs in flowers and ribbons, depicting hanging baskets with bouquets in the centre, she said: "As this boudoir is at the end of the suite, you will have a little privacy, and you won't hear all the coming and going of your household. You've got the Master of the Horse overhead, I hope he won't make a noise with his great boots. He gets to the riding school to coach the pages at five o'clock every morning, doesn't he, Monsieur de Tilly? However, privacy and quiet are considered luxuries for princesses. Now, let's go back and look at your bedroom."

The curtains and upholstery at Versailles were changed summer and winter. The summer bed was up. It was a four-poster whose domed roof was surmounted by a carved cornice of acanthus leaves, studded with pearls. It had four mattresses, a white taffeta eiderdown, and a footboard of crimson damask. As Elisabeth glanced at it, she could not help smiling at the contrast with the Carmelite palliasse on its wooden plank. Marie-Antoinette, who guessed her thoughts, and who had greatly hoped that having her own personal quarters would distract her sister-in-law's attention for a time, prattled on. "The winter bed is 'à la Duchesse'. You know, like a *lit d'ange*." This had a tall headboard, supporting a draped canopy. The back rest was cut out in profile and embroidered in gold. (There was once a bed like that on show in Marie-Antoinette's bedchamber at Petit Trianon, before it was replaced by a three-sided one placed against the wall.) In

[1] "Sur Trois Marches de Marbre Rose."

the winter, Elisabeth's hangings and curtains were of crimson silk velvet, and in summer of green Lyons damask, with a gold-embroidered palm design. There was a marquetry chest-of-drawers with a green marble top.

The suite consisted of eight main rooms: the first and second ante-chambers, the nobles' chamber, the bedroom, the "grand cabinet", the billiard room and the library, and lastly, at the very end, the boudoir, from which the royal ladies had just come. One can find an almost complete inventory of the furniture in the appendix of Beauchesne's life of Madame Elisabeth. In the first antechamber, the benches were covered with Savonnerie tapestries and the screens were crimson; in the second antechamber, the chests-of-drawers were veneered with rosewood and topped with marble. In the middle of this room was a table with a large silver inkstand on it. It was in here that at night time, behind the screens, they made up beds for the maids on duty. Everywhere were branched candlesticks surmounted with fleurs-de-lys and candelabra of gilded copper. They must have looked magnificent at night, with all their lighted candles reflected in the large mirrors. The nobles' chamber was furnished with Genoese damask. It had twelve stools of crimson silk velvet, and the corners of the room were filled by consoles of marquetry and gilded bronze. The chimney-piece was immense. The "grand cabinet" had a day bed with its mattress and pillows, and hangings of *Gros de Tours* in blue and white. The billiard room and library were hung with green and white Lyons damask depicting children, cascades and flowers. The question of Elisabeth's books is so fascinating, that it will have to be pursued later; for the time being, one may in passing mention Pliny's letters, Plutarch's Lives, Racine, books on Port Royal, for Elisabeth had a great admiration for "*ces messieurs de Port Royal*", medicinal treatises, like the one on diseases of the eye, procured probably so that she could help the poor whom she visited, Abbé Nollet on physics. . . . There were some novels, provided by the cynical and dissolute Chamfort, but she asked her ladies not to read them. Elisabeth really loved arranging her books. They were friends, not merely ornaments, though they were very decorative as well. Some of them can still be seen to-day in the library of the rue de Richelieu. Ernest Quentin-Bauchart, in "*Les femmes bibliophiles de France*", says: "They are very simply bound, and engraved with the Arms of France, with the lozenge-shaped shield surmounted by a ducal crown, some of them in morocco leather, almost all in fawn-coloured calf, marbled or speckled with granite black spots and sometimes with the *ex-libris* of the princess stuck on the inside, the word Montreuil inscribed in gold letters on a little band of green sheepskin at the base of the spine." He tells us that a prayer-book of hers was left to the library of St. Petersburg, by Donbrowsky, the famous collector. From the large list of smaller personal possessions, among her silver, one selects a silver *pot à pâte*, probably for make-up, cream or rouge, a silver glove box and a silver Holy Water stoup. Like all the royal princesses, she must have had an important jewel chest, for amongst other things, she possessed a large pair of sprigs, encrusted with brilliants, five bodice brooches, a watch and chain surrounded in diamonds, two rings, one with a large diamond in the middle and smaller ones at the sides, and one of the fashionable sentimental rings containing a locket of hair. In her accounts, one sees that she had spent some money on porcelain at the Sèvres manufacture. A short visit to the Wallace Collection or to the eighteenth-century rooms in the Victoria and Albert Museum would evoke for us the glowing colours of some of that porcelain—that pure golden yellow, that deep rich blue called *bleu de roi* and that paler blue called *œil de perdrix*. Some of the new furniture had blue Sèvres plaques on it, and of course, there were those charming groups of white Cupids by Falconet in *biscuit de Sèvres*. But this first suite of Elisabeth's, in spite of all its grandeur and beauty, seems to lack the personal touch which comes from individual choice. The King had probably given orders to the Superintendent of the *Garde Meuble* in the Place Louis XV, without consulting his sister's taste. It was not until the following year, when she had her own private country house at Montreuil, that one gets any impression of personality. To begin with, she had no privacy here at all. How could there be, with such an immense household always coming and going? The list of it in the "Almanach de Versailles" for 1784 is positively baffling. Her household and staff numbered sixty-six persons, at least. The names are fascinating. Her four "premières femmes de chambre" were all called Madeleine. She had twelve ladies-in-waiting. M. de Martineau was her

G

"Porte-Manteau". Bosserelle was her "Coiffeuse", and M. Léonard the younger, her "Coiffeur". M. de Boilly, "Maître de Harpe". She had two furnace attendants. Her laundress was La Dame Albert.

"You must really get one of your ladies to be responsible for the flowers," continued the Queen. "It's no use leaving it to the servants. You can always send a footman to Petit Trianon with a note to my gardeners." Just then, the Comtesse Diane de Polignac came in. She too had wanted to inspect her new quarters. She curtsied and then asked Elisabeth what were her plans for the day. "I am going to St. Cyr." The Comtesse gave a little contemptuous pout, and thought to herself, "Well, I shall not be needed on that pious journey." She planned to steal time off with her lover, the Marquis d'Autichamp, who had left Chantilly for a few days.

The Queen and her page went away, and Elisabeth went downstairs to her old ground-floor suite to do her accounts with her secretary. She always looked through the list of gratuities personally. There were tips to the chimney sweeps, to the fishwives of Paris and Versailles, to the employees of the Ministry of Works who lit the street lamps, to the lamplighters in her apartments, something for the gondoliers' yule log, or for the men who carried up the coal and the man who brought the newspaper. In February, there was the candle for Passiontide, and at Easter for the Easter sepulchre, and one for Notre Dame de Bonne Délivrance (that was a candle lit for her dear Angélique in Ratisbonne, expecting her first child in July). In May she had bought some oranges, in June some little orange-flower cakes and some orange-flower water. There were alms to the extern Sister at the Carmelites, a bill for asses' milk and something for Bourdet, the dentist, for Beaulieu for embroidery silks, for Letellier for writing paper (she was writing so many letters to Angélique), something for the woman who mended laces and a sum for de la Roue for parasols, for Bataille the perfumer, and Dauge the bathing woman. Two porcelain pot-pourris, for the *lieu à l'anglaise*, and lastly, she had bought a microscope glass mounted on copper.

She sighed, thinking to herself: "How small these alms, compared with all the luxury prepared for me upstairs. And to think that all I ask for is a small Carmelite cell."

CHAPTER IX

Elisabeth's friends

ELISABETH moved in on her sixteenth birthday. It was in that new apartment that, after some weeks of anxious waiting, she heard about the birth of Angélique's child at Ratisbonne. We must allow the Baronne de Mackau, the new grandmother, in her letter to the Marquis de Bombelles, to describe how the news was received (July 11th, 1780). ". . . Trembling, dishevelled, half undressed, I run to Madame Elisabeth's; as I was coming in, I want to make some excuses on my appearance: I was holding the letter in my hand; she stares at me, the embroidery at which she was working is flung into the middle of the room; she flies into my arms, I feel that my legs are giving way, and fearing, because of the strength of her hug, that I would drag her down as I fell, I reach an arm-chair, into which I throw myself and her. In this position, she falls at my feet, I throw myself at hers, and, in this attitude, our arms interlocked, we stay pressed close to one another without uttering a word. Her ladies, my sister, the charming la Rochelambert, whom I should have mentioned earlier, and who were present at that happy moment, all burst into tears and lifted us up. My little princess, who notices that I feel faint, is now only engaged in assisting me."

A circle formed around the Baronne de Mackau, all the ladies were laughing and crying at the same time. Suddenly Madame Elisabeth said: "Oh, but most important, is it a boy or a girl?" "It's a boy." More cries of joy, universal jubilation and mutual embraces. And that is how the news of Bombon's birth was made known to Elisabeth. We shall hear more later of this engaging little boy, who won all hearts wherever he went, including the Queen's, and who, when he was an old man, loved to come back to Versailles and recall the happy days he had spent there.

As Elisabeth was nearly always surrounded by her ladies-in-waiting, it would be good to take a fleeting glimpse at her entourage.

The Comte d'Adhémar, a member of her household, was so insinuating, always in such a good temper. Being of humble birth, he was a social climber who had made his way by little talents. He sang in a trembling voice, which always made the Queen laugh. He had married a rich widow from ambition. He ill-treated her and used to declare quite openly to everyone: "One must succeed through women. For my part I take it upon myself to get all I want out of her." Under his frivolous exterior, as he turned a madrigal or played on the spinet, he concealed boundless ambition and an iron will, and one regrets to say he became ambassador to England.

A certain Madame de Canillac had been placed in Elisabeth's household, through the combined efforts of her aunt and the Duc de Coigny. Before that, she had been *dame de compagnie* to the Duchesse d'Orléans. Unfortunately, Monsieur de Bourbon fell in love with her, his wife was furious and Madame de Canillac retired—all Paris was talking about it. When she reached Elisabeth's household, she was such a success with the men, that the Princesse de Guémenée used to encourage her to come to her place because she brought the men along with her. She was just a pretty woman, whom everyone flirted with. Unfortunately the Comte d'Artois pursued her, and this again infuriated the Duchesse de Bourbon, for she was jealous a second time. She made a scene at a masked Opera ball, in the hope of compromising and embarrassing the young woman. The Comte d'Artois was so furious that he was rude to her, and on Shrove Tuesday, 1778, he and the Duc de Bourbon fought a duel. All the women at court were on Madame de Canillac's side. Whilst this was going on, Elisabeth treated her as if nothing had happened. She may not, of course, have heard the gossip, for she says herself that she was always the last to hear any piece of news, but it is likely that the Queen told her everything, for she did all she could to prevent the duel.

Among her men friends, Elisabeth counted her younger brother the Comte d'Artois, whom she idolised, although she sometimes tried to lecture him a little on his wildness. Le Monnier, her botany master, and another botanist, called Dassy, for whom she says that she had "quite a little passion". Dassy had bought, in his name, a small house at Fontainebleau, where Elisabeth hoped to pursue her botanical studies. But she was never able to go there.

Last but not least, the Queen was her friend. The friendship had been strengthened in 1779, after a visit to Trianon. Madame de Bombelles wrote: "The Queen is delighted with her. She tells everybody that there is nobody as amiable as she, that she has not known her well until now, but that she has made her her friend and that it would be for all her life."

Elisabeth sometimes found the small-talk of her women very fatiguing. She complains that some of them chattered like one-eyed magpies and that the liveliness of two of them nearly killed her. She got bored with the smallness of their outlook and their lack of discretion in admitting others to intimacy: "Young women have no idea of the shades that one should use in one's friendships. It is sufficient that they please one another, to say that they are intimate friends." She herself believed in the proverb "Birds of a feather flock together", and that you could judge a woman by her friends. She could only give her friendship to persons she really respected, but once her allegiance was given, it was very constant. Even Diane de Polignac owned to that. Elisabeth realised that friendships need to be cultivated to be kept alive, and she was always giving charming little surprises and gifts to her friends. "Friendship, you see, my dear Bombelles, is a second life, which upholds us in this world."

CHAPTER X

Elisabeth stays at Petit Trianon, and meets the Queen's friends

WHEN a whole section of society is frustrated, it may develop sadistic tendencies. This accounts for some of the horror stories of the late eighteenth century. The Maréchale de Luxembourg, who hated her daughter-in-law, came into her room as she lay dying of consumption. "Oh, what an intolerable stench!" she cried. How could one expect real charity and disinterested friendship from a society which could produce women like that? It is not surprising that most of the members of the Queen's set were incapable of friendship. Many of them were in financial straits, and clung to court circles in the hopes of toadying for rich appointments. One evening, at the Princesse de Guémenée's, the Comte de Vaudreuil exclaimed: "A writer whom you know, Chamfort, makes out that young women have one misfortune: that of having no friends." The Comtesse Diane de Polignac replied testily: "How could your Chamfort believe in disinterested feeling? For him, women only give to friendship what they borrow from love."

In that year, 1780, the Queen's men friends were all past their first youth. Madame de Bombelles wrote to her husband: "In all, this famous clique is composed of very malicious people. . . . They think they are in a position to judge the rest of the world. . . . They are so frightened that someone should insinuate themselves into favour, that they hardly ever praise anyone, but tear them to pieces at their leisure."

Most of the men in the Queen's set were lechers, and most of them so vain, that they kept imagining that the Queen's free and easy manner betrayed a weakness for them. Indeed, two of them in their memoirs have not scrupled to throw out dark hints about her virtue. It is surprising that the Queen, who refused to receive officially at court any women living apart from their husbands, and who scratched out from the list of her balls anyone accused of improper behaviour, should yet in her own private circle have been surrounded by men and women who thought nothing of their marriage vows. Even the charming Prince de Ligne went on breaking the sixth commandment until extreme old age, when he raped his cook among the cabbages of his kitchen garden. The Queen was not very fastidious in her choice of friends. She took the first people who came her way and who happened to amuse her. She was so lonely. When her first little daughter died, and her over-zealous friends were trying to console her, she said: "Do you forget that she could have been a friend?" It was her loneliness which drew her to Elisabeth; she too was very lonely, for the Marquise de Bombelles has written: " . . . we have tried to amuse with our follies, Madame Elisabeth, who really needs to be dissipated sometimes, with the life she leads; it would be very sad for any other person less reasonable than herself." Almost the only disinterested secret adorer of Marie-Antoinette was a man who did not live at court. He had been a member of the Parliament of Bordeaux, Monsieur de Castelnau. Suddenly, when he was long past his first youth, he fell madly in love with her. All his happiness consisted in seeing her, and he spent his life in the Galerie des Glaces. Always alone, he calculated the moments when she would be passing. He was very assiduous in going to the royal Mass, where no doubt he had his private distractions, and, after it was over, he used to run to see the Queen returning to her apartments. If he heard her carriage, he would tear down to the bottom of the staircase. However icy cold it was—and the cold at Versailles could be terrible—he was always there, sad and taciturn, speaking to no-one. He followed the court to Paris in 1789 and was killed in the massacres of August the 10th, for of course he was not far away from the object of his devotion at the Tuileries.

The Queen's first great woman friend was the Princesse de Lamballe. She was very beautiful, with a serene expression, in spite of suffering tortures from a nervous malady which left her stiff and unconscious for hours on end and which the great Tronchin tried to cure. The wretched Duc d'Orléans had got hold of her husband early in life, and, by causing his early death, through encouraging his dissipations, had inherited his vast fortune. The Princesse de Lamballe's friendship for her royal mistress was completely disinterested. Her rank was of the highest, she was very wealthy and she refused to solicit favours for her friends. If she had one fault, it was too great a liking for the minutiae of etiquette. When the Queen made her the Superintendent of her household, some of the ladies were so furiously jealous, that they resigned. The Princesse de Lamballe was a sincerely devoted and faithful friend, and, after the period when she had been temporarily eclipsed by the Duchesse de Polignac, Marie-Antoinette, with that bitter wisdom bought by experience, at last learned to appreciate her.

Unfortunately Madame de Lamballe was at daggers drawn with this Gabrielle Duchesse de Polignac who had been pushed into favour by her sister-in-law, Diane de Polignac. She too was extremely graceful and beautiful, with expressive blue eyes, a high forehead, a nose slightly tip-tilted without being *retroussé*, a charming mouth, a celestial glance, and a smile full of grace. This creature, whose features breathed nothing but modesty and sweetness, was the mistress of the Comte de Vaudreuil. The page Tilly said: "Her walk was seductively free and easy, and this distinguished her in a special way from the other court ladies, who only had all the bustling ways of pride and vanity."

Nothing was to warn the Queen of how dangerous this woman was, for she had an angelic expression.

The two favourites spent all 1776 quarrelling. The power of the Polignac clan, under cover of fun, poked gentle ridicule at the Princesse de Lamballe. They laughed at her fanatic tenderness for the Queen, her attacks of nerves, the way she swooned if she saw a bunch of violets or shrimps or crabs. They even went so far as to say that the company of this sick woman would injure the Queen.

The Comte de Vaudreuil, *"le divin Vaudreuil"* as he was nicknamed, was very seductive in spite of having had smallpox. He had the boundless vanity of a nobody, for, though he always spoke as if he were a man of noble birth, he had no known ancestors. The Queen would certainly not have invited him to Petit Trianon, had it not been for Gabrielle de Polignac. She hated him for the hold he had over her friend. One good point: he appreciated Elisabeth.

The Comte de Guines, the perfect flutist, had an enormous paunch. He was so heavy that the parquet floors of Trianon cracked under his red heels as he walked. He wore very tight clothes in the vain hope of concealing his girth. Each morning, at his toilet, his valets asked him whether he was going to sit down that day, and fetched the appropriate trousers. He would climb on to two chairs and descend into his trousers held up by two servants.

The Baron de Besenval, an ageing, white-haired roué, was the Lieutenant-Colonel of the Swiss Guards and a friend of the Comte d'Artois. He had fought in the Seven Years' War, with the fire and gaiety which characterise the French soldier. At one point, in a battle, when his division was hacked to pieces, he rushed back to the field of battle to fight. Somebody called out to him, "What are you still doing here, Baron?" and he made this elegant reply: "It's like the Opera ball—one is bored, and one stays as long as one hears the violins." With such dash, it is not surprising that he was a great success with women, and his calculated brusqueries were forgiven. The ladies used to cry out in mock horror: "Baron, what bad form! You are frightful!" As the de Goncourts say, ". . . He had that great charm and that great art: *l'excellent ton dans le mauvais ton*—elegance in bad manners." He never married, but lived entirely for himself, like Vaudreuil. He had the fashionable passion for designing gardens, and was always advising the Queen about new improvements for Petit Trianon. In his own way, he did her much harm, for the motif of all his flatteries was "You are young, you are beautiful, why shouldn't you indulge in a few of the simple pleasures for which you crave? I really don't think you should reproach yourself for this little knick-knack, or ordering just a few more shrubs to put round the *Temple de l'Amour*. When I think of the hard life you lead, always a slave to etiquette, you must not be at the mercy of the old ladies." Not only was he cynical about the virtue of women, but quite flippant about how to get on at court, telling a duke who was returning to Versailles after six months' absence: "I will put you wise: have a puce coloured outfit, a puce coloured jacket, a puce coloured pair of breeches, and present yourself with confidence: that is all that is needed to-day to succeed." He never kept the Queen's secrets.

Comte d'Adhémar, described before as a member of Elisabeth's household, was also an *habitué* of the Queen's clique.

The Duc de Lauzan had excited the Queen's curiosity in the early days, in the Princesse de Guémenée's drawing-room. With all the vanity of a professional seducer, he had talked of his conquests and she had listened. She did not realize that he would soon be boasting to everybody at court that he would conquer her.

After this somewhat sombre picture, one must turn to a pleasanter man, Prince Charles de Ligne, nicknamed "Charlot", Austrian by birth, but French at heart. He was a great friend of the Chevalier de Boufflers, and consequently generous and madly gay. His manners were so perfect that, when he was turning out trespassers from his estate during a hunt, he would take off his hat and say: "Go to the Devil, please, Sirs, and leave my woods." He loved Petit Trianon. The Polignacs and the royal family adored "Charlot". They knew that when this charming madcap appeared at the door, boredom would vanish through the window. He had been in love with the Queen, secretly and respectfully, but all the rest of his life he was her sincere friend, so that he could truthfully say: "She behaves like a Queen without knowing it. One adores her without dreaming of falling in love with her." The Queen must have felt completely at ease with him, for he is the only person to give us an intimate and amusing side-light on her behaviour. "She is charming to catch out. If one interprets some of the things she says too freely or in a malicious kind of fashion, she gets cross and laughs and becomes even more delightful."

The Queen was often criticised for making friends with foreigners, but she said sadly: "They never ask me for anything."

The Princesse de Lamballe, the Duchesse Jules de Polignac, the Comte de Vaudreuil, the Comte de Guines, the Baron de Besenval, the Comte d'Adhémar, the Duc de Lauzan, the Prince de Ligne. But there are two men at the end of this formidable list who are not so depressing: the Hungarian Comte d'Esterhazy, a brilliant horseman, and a friend whom the Queen could trust, and the Duc de Coigny, upright, moral, endowed with a grand air and exquisite manners which made him sought after by all. He never asked for anything. Marie-Antoinette took to him because of his refusal to bow to the du

Barry, but even his greying hairs did not save the Queen from calumnies in connection with him.

The Queen is known to have stayed at Petit Trianon from the 10th to the 12th of October, 1780.[1] After the death of Louis XV, when the du Barry had been temporarily packed off to a convent, the King, imbued with grace by love, is supposed to have said to his wife: "The Petit Trianon has been the home of the King's favourites, therefore I want to present it to you." She was delighted to have somewhere to which only her intimate circle of friends had the right to come. The court ladies on duty, whose privilege was to attend the Queen all day, could only come there by invitation. And what a joy to escape that *lever* and that *coucher* in public; those awful family suppers, with her hideous sisters-in-law; those crowds who watched her eat and who gaped at her as she walked on hot summer nights, and listened to the band. Here at last, she could be herself, see Rose Bertin without upsetting the ladies of her household, wear simple white dresses and straw hats, enjoy the company of her little daughter, pick flowers, listen to the birds, choose and arrange the furnishings she liked, give parties, have amateur theatricals in a wood, dispense with etiquette. Indeed, she made it a rule that, when she came into the drawing-room, the women were to continue their embroidery and the men their billiards and cards. She wanted to perpetuate the illusion of a country-house party, such as was enjoyed by many other French châtelaines up and down the kingdom in those happy years before the end. She always asked Elisabeth to come with her, and put her in a suite on the second floor, where the rooms were low and square, with charming views of the gardens, and where it is now very easy to lose one's way.

It was autumn, 1780. Many of the guests much preferred stuffing away in a drawing-room by a big log fire, to taking a constitutional in a west wind. We will postpone the delights of a tour of the domain until it is completely finished, and the weather is warmer, and instead, take a glimpse at the Queen's entourage, and listen to their conversation. Elisabeth, who could not live without fresh air, and whose

[1] The Temple of Love was finished, but the Belvedere and Rocher had not yet been built, and as for the model village and farm, they were not begun until 1783, and not completely finished until 1788.

letters are full of the delights of a brisk walk, was exercising her own pug with Marcassin, the Queen's little dog. Her cheeks were a fine colour. The falling leaves were blowing about her feet. The Comtesse Diane de Polignac was watching her charge from the window of the drawing-room, where she was sitting with the clique, and indulging in a little low gossip. The Queen was upstairs in her bedroom, at her dressing-table, where Monsieur Léonard, her hairdresser, to his great despair, had been ordered to undo the high head-dress she had worn at Versailles for Mass that morning. Gabrielle de Polignac was moodily twizzling her muff and looking out of the window, wondering what her lover Vaudreuil was doing. The charming room, with its poppies and other little flowers carved around the woodwork, its bed smothered in white silk lace, its chairs upholstered in blue paduasoy and its curtains looped up by pearl-embroidered scarves, was full of the scent of orris root. Monsieur Léonard, with all the gestures of a comic-opera hairdresser, was pirouetting around on his toes, trying to please the Queen by arranging a very simple coiffure, and then spraying the finished result with scent. "Madame," he cried, "a touch, a suspicion of powder on the hair?"

"No, no, no, my good Léonard. It hardens the features, and makes blondes look insipid. I'm so delighted to launch a change of fashions this year." Then, turning to Gabrielle, "Which reminds me, *mon cœur*, since I've given up high-heeled shoes, can you tell me the name of a new shoemaker?"

"What about Charpentier?" Just then the Princesse de Lamballe came in from the dressing-room and interposed: "What! Charpentier! That impertinent little *parvenu*! You'll never be able to make him keep his place!"

"Oh!" exclaimed Gabrielle, "but he is *such* an artist!"

"That is as may be, but I must tell you how he received Monsieur de la Luzerne the other day, who went to order a pair of shoes for a friend of his who lives in the country. He was admiring his splendid cabinet full of portraits of court ladies, and who do you think was among them? Why, your own Princesse de Guémenée, who holds the highest position at court. And when Monsieur de la Luzerne showed Charpentier the model of shoes that he wanted, he exclaimed, 'Ah! I know that pretty foot, one would travel twenty leagues to see it. Do you know that, after *la petite Guémenée*, your friend has the prettiest foot in the world!'"

The Queen and Gabrielle burst out laughing.

"It is no laughing matter," exclaimed the Princesse de Lamballe dramatically. "One must keep that sort of person in his place."

To keep the peace, the Queen changed the subject of conversation. "I must show you Rose Bertin's new design for a fancy dress ball: large panniers, white background, padded with light-coloured Italian gauze, held up with blue satin draperies patterned with peacocks' feathers. On my head, large aigrettes of the same feathers. And of course, over the whole thing, a white taffeta domino with large sleeves."

The wind blew a lot of leaves up against the window. "What a pity," said the Queen, "that we won't be able to go out to-day." The little bedchamber looked very snug in the equinoctial weather, the blue silk chairs with their large eiderdown cushions almost inviting one to stay in and gossip.

In the meantime, the *coterie* in the drawing-room had divided into groups, some embroidering near the fire which was crackling in the hearth, others playing cards by the windows. The Comte d'Artois' mistress, fragile-looking Madame de Polastron who had a weak chest, held out her delicate white hands to the blaze and sighed contentedly: "I'm so glad that we are not making the usual autumn visit to Fontainebleau, it's so cold there. Even with a roaring fire day and night, and the warming pan put into the bed, it is impossible to get warm, and of course those rats scuttling overhead all night keep me awake. In the morning I look dreadful." Diane de Polignac laughed. "Why don't you imitate my royal charge out there and take more outdoor exercise?"

"Oh, I don't want to get plump. All this walking and riding is so bad for the figure!"

Diane did not contradict her. She was a mistress of the disloyal and unkind silence. Hearing the talk turn to riding, Comte Valentin Esterhazy moved towards the fireplace and stood behind Madame de Polastron's little sofa. (In those days it was undreamed of for a man to sit on the same sofa as a woman, or even to rest his hand on the back of her chair.) Diane looked up at him and said: "Did you know that Madame Elisabeth is going to ask you to be her squire? She has such a great admiration for your horsemanship."

Esterhazy was too ambitious to accept what he called "an unimportant post", but he was too good a courtier to let his face fall. He merely murmured, "I am greatly honoured. She is a splendid horsewoman herself."

"Well, she must have something to occupy her," said Diane spitefully. "She won't read novels, she doesn't particularly like dancing, and she simply refuses to act in any plays, because she might have to take part in a love scene."

Madame de Polastron, who, at the end of her life, was to repent so bitterly for the years which the locusts had eaten, gave another imperceptible sigh, and, for a moment, almost envied the detachment of the angelic young princess. Her rather languorous eyes wandered over the Cupids frolicking in the four cornices of the drawing-room, and at the crowns of roses in full bloom sculptured on the panels. "Ah," she thought, "*les roses et les amours*—happy the woman who can forsake them."

Diane went on being catty. "Oh, yes, Madame Elisabeth may be quite a good horsewoman, but even going to the races near the Bois de Boulogne bores her." At the word "races", the Comte d'Artois joined the group. "Oh, that's only a rumour. I think Babet secretly enjoys those races, just as much as all of us."

The Prince de Ligne laughed at the Comte d'Artois: "I shall never forget you, on those days, dressed as a jockey, running up and down the stairs to the Queen's stand, shouting your bets, bemoaning your losses, introducing the winning jockeys to the Queen, and then joining the group of hungry young men who fell upon the buffets. You were just as excited as when you egged Lord Fitzgerald to do that marvellous jump over another horseman. Do you remember? By the way, Baron," he said turning to Besenval, "you were going to tell us about that famous race to Chantilly and back. You're the only one here who can remember it well, I think."

"Don't remind me of my white hairs, my good friend," said Besenval with mock despair. "Yes, I'd have given anything to see that.

One August day, the Marquis de Saillans bet 20,000 pistoles that he'd race from the Porte St. Denis to the château of Chantilly, twice, from six in the morning till noon. Monsieur le Duc, for his part, took up wagers against different men at court. I think the total of the betting was 80,000 pistoles. It was nine leagues to Chantilly, therefore he'd undertaken to do thirty-six leagues in six hours. He was allowed to change horses as often as he wanted, and to choose his mounts from the King's stables and those of various friends. They say that, after trying more than two hundred, he picked out sixteen as the very best for speed in the whole kingdom. These horses were chosen for being able to gallop at full speed for long stretches at a time. A platform was set up under the Porte St. Denis, for the ladies, for Monsieur le Duc, and the Prince de Conti, not to speak of a large clock, which all watched with bated breath. There were about four thousand people, either in the Faubourg St. Denis itself, or on the road, on horses or in coaches. The Marquis de Saillans arrived at the Porte St. Denis at nine o'clock, having gained fifteen minutes on his time-table. He drank a glass of wine to the health of the ladies, threw the glass in the air and was off again to Chantilly like a flash of lightning. He returned to the Porte Sr. Denis at thirty-five minutes past eleven, having gained twenty-five minutes on the whole race. You can imagine the commotion and excitement."

"He must have been *exhausted*," panted the Comte de Guines, who had been unable to sit down all morning. This was one of his stand-upright days. He was even afraid to laugh, lest his breeches split from top to bottom.

Besenval glanced at him rather superciliously. "He was a hardy fellow. When it was over, they prepared a bed for him at a lemonade seller's of the Porte St. Denis, but he wanted to go off at once to the King's luncheon. They prevented him, of course. In the afternoon he went to the Opera and was cheered to the echo. He was a magnificent horseman, as strong as ten lions. He won the race more on his own skill and physique than on the qualities of his sixteen mounts. The men who followed him were completely out of breath and wet through too, for it rained continuously from eight till twelve."

"I'm surprised he didn't slip in the rain," said the Duc de Coigny. Besenval replied: "Monsieur le Duc had sanded all the roads. He never got off once. His fresh mount was brought up to his side and he passed from one stirrup to another. By the way, there is a rumour that the Duc de Chartres wants to put in his Cantator for the Derby. I'd love to see a Frenchman score over the English on a racecourse." Turning to the Comte d'Artois, he said, "I'm hoping great things from that Comus you bought four years ago."

The Comte d'Artois laughed. "I don't know what grand-papa would have said. He used to make fun of me when I used the English word 'sport'. He had to put a stop to the races between Englishmen and Frenchmen after the time when they accused Lord Forbes of poisoning a French horse. They say that Newmarket is now infested by Frenchman. Horace Walpole told me that the celebrated sportsman Hugo Meynell took it so much to heart in his day, that he said with grim humour, he wished the peace were all over and that the English were comfortably at war again with the French. Personally, I am delighted when Lord March and other of their leading racing men send their horses to run against ours. Orléans appears to have been made an honorary member of the Jockey Club. If grand-papa was horrified, how much more shocked great-great-grandfather would have been! What a contrast between his huge opulent cart-horses with their arched necks and our modern race-horses, thin-limbed and nervous, stretching their necks right out! Our thorough-breds would certainly not appeal to the men of the last century, who loved to clothe their horses in superb plumes and trappings, so as to peacock and prance about at tilting matches under the eyes of their lady-loves."

Esterhazy said: "But you, Charlot, don't you secretly blame the habits of the great English milords, their racing dinners, their races, their bets, their orgies and their stable-boy appearance?"

The Duc de Lauzan, who had been rather silent until then, said: "I have had all the trouble in the world to prevent the Queen from owning race-horses and from mounting like an Englishwoman."

The Prince de Ligne, who never could bear the slightest innuendo against her, exclaimed: "No horsewoman could be pluckier or more graceful than the Queen." Madame de Polastron tried to turn the conversation, for she knew from experience that any criticism of the

Queen infuriated the Prince de Ligne. "I heard Madame de Genlis, *la chère amie* of the Duc d'Orléans, say the other day that she hated racing, because it was profaning nature to drive away innocent shepherds and their flocks from the green fields."

Diane de Polignac exclaimed caustically: "What a silly woman that is!"

.   .   .   .   .   .

In the meantime, Elisabeth was chasing her dogs in the arbours of latticed and pleached limes around the *Pavillon Français*. These breezy autumn days exhilarated her. She was still so desperately shy, that she welcomed any excuse to escape from the Queen's guests in the drawing-room. Just then, she caught sight of the Princesse de Lamballe, her eyes red with weeping, walking agitatedly up and down the alleys of the *jardin français*. Elisabeth ran to her, gave her a friendly hug, and said: "You look rather depressed this morning, *ma cousine*."

For half an hour they walked up and down the pink-sanded alleys, while the poor Princesse de Lamballe opened her heart to her, and told her how sad she was to have fallen from the Queen's good graces: "I am prepared to die for my royal mistress and to do anything to serve her faithfully, which is more than I can say about many others, who only came to Trianon to ask for favours." With a prudence rare in one so young, Elisabeth never allowed herself to take sides, but tried to comfort and cheer her. Just then the chaplain rang the Angelus in the tiny chapel next to the château. Tethering the dogs outside, they slipped in to the royal gallery for a moment or two, much to the surprise of the chaplain, whose post here was almost a sinecure. Why, only that morning he had picked up what he thought was a stray missal, and on looking to see the name of its owner, was horrified to find inside "*Le Sopha*" by Crébillon fils. He was afraid to give it to a flunkey to return to its owner, in case of causing a scandal. The only person who really used this simple country chapel habitually was Madame Elisabeth. There was a rumour that she had wanted to be a Carmelite, and he knew that she often went to St. Cyr to spend the day in retreat. There she was now, looking so happy and peaceful, like a young angel who had strayed away from a group of bacchantes.

H

In the meantime, the Queen, who had joined her friends in the drawing-room at the precise moment when they were mocking Madame de Genlis and her pastoral tastes, was saying: "Though I certainly do not approve of Madame de Genlis, who I think is a sanctimonious hypocrite, I confess I have a sneaking liking for pastoral pleasures. When Petit Trianon is completely finished, I should like to keep lambs and shepherdesses! But I've already spent so much here, and it has caused such a lot of scandal, that I dare not risk it."

"What!" cried Besenval. "Is your Majesty always to have her wings clipped? Let Charlot de Ligne and myself draw you another plan for a rustic village with thatched roofs, built around a lake. It would cost *nothing*. And there your Majesty, for a brief spell, could forget the cares of Queenship and taste the pleasures of being a woman. Just think how delicious it would be on spring mornings to listen to the birds singing in the bushes, and to collect one's own eggs in a rush basket. I would send Swiss cows to you from my native land and you could have your own dairy with marble-topped tables and taste some of that delicious Swiss whipped cream which is unequalled anywhere else."

Said Lauzan in an aside, "Oh, there he is again, becoming all rustic! How I hate his bucolic effusions!"

The Prince de Ligne, who loved planning other people's gardens, took out a drawing board in a corner of the room where the Queen kept her paint boxes (she had been trying to paint a late autumn rose in the manner of her master Redouté). In the meantime, Lauzan was telling the Comte de Vaudreuil in a whisper the amusing story of his first seduction, and they were trying very hard not to laugh. "It was a little actress from the theatre of Versailles. I had gone in to her minute bedchamber, so small that it only held a bed and two chairs. My dear fellow, a veritable Cupid's paradise! But alas, our amorous dalliance was interrupted by——"

"A husband!"

"*Non, mon cher*, something much more terrifying . . . a positively *enormous* black spider, which fell on to the pillow! It frightened both of us so much that we simply fled!"

Esterhazy was reading "Aline, Reine de Golconde" by his friend the Chevalier de Boufflers, and thinking what a good play it would be to act in the new little blue theatre here. Elisabeth came in and found him thus. She took the opportunity to ask him whether he would accept the post of her squire, and he apologised profusely and said he must decline the honour. He went on apologising until she stopped him graciously: "Let's think no more about it."

After a pause, he said: "I'm so glad, Madame, that Madame de Bombelles learned to ride with you at Marly. I expect you miss her greatly."

"Oh, but she is coming back to Versailles next year, I hope. The climate of Ratisbonne does not suit her at all."

"Will her husband be coming too?"

"I think so, they are quite inseparable, you know. I am longing to see their darling little Bombon."

In another corner of the room, Diane de Polignac and Louise de Polastron were talking about Comte Axel Fersen. "What a charmer. Do you think it is true . . . ?"

"Who knows? Wouldn't you? With a husband like that. She sleeps alone here."

"How is that?"

"Didn't you know? The King only comes to Trianon by invitation."

CHAPTER XI

In which Bombon makes his appearance at Court and Elisabeth becomes Châtelaine of Montreuil

ELISABETH, feeling that her beloved Angélique secretly preferred being with her husband and child, to remaining on as her lady-in-waiting, did all to make things agreeable for her at court. The night that she returned from Portugal, a messenger met her coach to say that the Hôtel des Ambassadeurs was full and would she go to another lodging in the town. This was part of a charming surprise prepared for her: good rooms, a fine dinner: Elisabeth had even given her a gift of white and gold porcelain with her crest on it. The following morning, Angélique hurried to Elisabeth's suite at Versailles, with Bombon. It is easy to imagine the re-union of the two friends. Angélique wrote to her husband: "Bombon was not forgotten. He was as sweet as he possibly could be. He went to sleep this morning in her apartment as I was suckling him; she wanted to put him in one of the low rooms under the first floor, but Madame de Sérent, whom we consulted, advised us not to do so, on account of his sex, assuring us that people would not fail to use it as a pretext to say that I dressed and undressed the child in front of Madame. He was therefore put to sleep at Mamma's.

"The Queen, who lodges underneath Madame Elisabeth, came to the window directly she noticed me, she called me, asked me how I was and where my son was. . . . She added that she was charmed to have the pleasure of seeing me. I made her a beautiful curtsey and then I went. In the evening, coming out of Madame Elisabeth's apartment with Bombon, I again met the Queen with Madame and Madame la Comtesse d'Artois; she stopped to see him and told me that she thought him charming. The little one snatched her fan from her hands, which made her laugh a great deal. She told him he was a little rascal, played with him a little and then went away. Madame Elisabeth with whom I dined, has showered more kindness upon me.

"Yesterday I had a great treat, *mon petit chat*. Your portrait came at six o'clock in the evening. I jumped for joy in seeing the packing case: I thought they were never going to open it quickly enough. When I saw your face, I wept for joy: I caressed you; I carried my folly as far as to kiss you.

"As for Madame Elisabeth, there is no attention she does not shower upon her friend's son. *Mon Dieu*, how obliging she is! On my word of honour, I love her madly. If you had seen how pleased she was with my little successes the day before yesterday: how she came very quietly and sweetly to arrange my neckerchief so that it would sit more becomingly. Really I am quite overcome by the interest she takes in me, and I wish I had a thousand ways of showing her my gratitude. . . ."

". . . I am prodigiously bored, I don't hide it from you, and if the Lord and you had not given me Bombon, I assure you that I would not remain here, for we would always have enough to live on, you and I. But this child, he must not be unhappy. . . ."

Her letters are full of the raptures of motherhood.

"It is no longer a dream, it is no longer an illusion! A tooth as white as milk; it was at two o'clock yesterday that we discovered it."

". . . Bombon is going to be weaned. To-morrow the 22nd of July is the great day. He slept perfectly the other night, and last night too, but the one before that, which was the second after our separation, that poor little thing was very unhappy. He was determined that I should feed him: he wept; he called out: '*Maman, maman*', looked for me everywhere and after heaving great sighs, began to weep again. He talks of me all day long and makes a sign with his finger that they must go to the garden door, because I am there. I wept when they told me these details. I adore that child. . . ."

"Bombon is as usual very well. He is falling in love with all the little girls he meets."

"When he is hungry, he goes to the cupboard in the ante-room, takes the hand of Lentz, puts it on the key to make her understand that he wants it opened. He helps himself to some biscuit, some raisins or a pear, in short, everything that he needs: he closes the cupboard himself very carefully and goes off with his provisions. More often than not, he brings them to my knees; he starts eating, standing up in front of me, and gives me something to eat. But what is so charming about this child is, that if he is not hungry, even if he is offered the thing he likes most, he will not eat it. It is impossible for anyone to be sweeter, and to have more intelligence than this jewel. But expect to find him ugly when you see him again, because even I find him so. . . ."

November 9th. "All the time he sees coaches and people passing by, and that amuses him . . . Bombon loves music more than ever; when I want to amuse him, I take him on my knee and I play him a little air on the spinet. And when I want to rest, he takes my hand and places it on the spinet. The first nights that he had the smallpox, he had a terribly high fever and was very fractious. I played the spinet to him and that calmed him down. This child will surely become musical. Can you believe it? He plays the drum beautifully in time!"

December the 3rd, during a visit to Chantilly. "He wants to be out of doors all day and nothing amuses him so much as being in the fresh air. If you could see his joy when I come back to my apartment; and he cries '*Maman, maman*', stretches out his little arms for me, devours me with caresses and does not want to leave me any more. I have never seen such a caressing child, and one so attached to his nurse: and so, when I am obliged to leave him, I have to resort to all kinds of ruses to slip away."

It is impossible to resist quoting a letter in which the adorable Bombon is shown displaying his talents as a dancer.

"Versailles, January 16, 1782. Madame Elisabeth came to see me after dinner. She had Bombon brought in, and he was charming. She had not yet seen him walk absolutely alone, and to make him shine in all his glory, I started playing a little air on the spinet; he took his little tight-fitting frock in both hands and began to dance and turn all round the room, which greatly amused Madame Elisabeth. As I made him dance, I thought of you and I kept saying to myself, 'If he were here, he would be mad about that child.' . . ."

On October the 22nd, 1781, Elisabeth was alone in her boudoir. She had been waiting there all morning; it was now after one o'clock in the afternoon. Angélique with the rest of the court had gone to assist at the Queen's second confinement. If only it were a boy! The clock chimed the half hour. A scurry of footsteps coming through the library . . . the door was flung open . . . Angélique and she flew into each other's arms. "It's a Dauphin! they're both well. He's so strong! Everybody is in floods of tears! You should have seen Madame de Guémenée, radiant with joy, carrying him across the apartments. Everybody wanted to touch her chair. Why! What's the matter, Elisabeth? Don't tell me you're going to faint!"

And Angélique wrote later to her husband that she found it almost impossible to persuade her friend that a Dauphin had at last been born to France. "No, you mustn't cry. You've got to be in the chapel by three o'clock to hold him for his christening. Oh, you should see his Majesty! All smiles! And people everywhere, complete strangers, are falling into each other's arms and kissing one another."

When Marie-Antoinette was expecting this child, she said to her husband: "Sire, I have a complaint to make. One of your subjects has just kicked me in the stomach." The Comte d'Artois whispered in an aside, "Yes, and he's giving me a kick in the tail." The brothers and sisters-in-law were the only people who did not share in the rejoicing. As for Mesdames Tantes at Bellevue, they began spreading the rumour that he was a bastard. This did not, however, prevent the spinsters from coming over in their carriage at full speed, in order to watch from the windows a procession of the craft guilds from Paris, in honour of the baby.

Madame Adélaïde began: "Ah, here is Madame Poitrine, the wet-nurse. Good morning, my good woman. Who is your husband?"

"If you please, Ma'am, a gardener at Sceaux."

"You've to curtsey when you address me."

"*Saccrré tonnerre,*" said the wet-nurse, who had the tone of a Grenadier Guard and swore with the greatest of ease. The rich laces and fine linen in which they had rigged her looked most incongruous. She had flatly refused to have her hair powdered or to put on a high bonnet. She kept the royal family in fits of laughter, but needless to say, greatly shocked Mesdames Tantes.

While brilliant festivities were taking place in all the towns and villages of France, these Paris guilds had spent considerable sums in going to Versailles in a body, bearing the different tools of their trades. They were all in fresh, elegant new clothes, and each group had its own musicians. When they reached the *Cour de Marbre*, they arranged themselves with charming effect. Quizzing glasses were raised at all the balconies. Exclamations of delighted sensibility from the courtiers: "Oh, but look at these adorable little chimney sweeps! Do you see that one carrying a beautifully decorated chimney, and on the top of it is perched a tiny sweep?" The men who carried sedan chairs had produced a gilded chair in which were installed a fine wet-nurse and a little Dauphin. Butchers, pastrycooks, masons, locksmiths—all came by in turn. The shoemakers were putting the finishing touches to a little pair of shoes for the Dauphin. The tailors brought a minute regimental uniform. The King was in ecstasies. Never had he looked so happy. Suddenly Madame Adélaïde gave a scream. "But here are the grave-diggers. What a terrible omen! Somebody run down quickly and tell them to hide."

.   .   .   .   .   .

The day that the Princesse de Guémenée had sailed through the royal apartments so proudly holding the Dauphin, had been her swan-song at Versailles. Quite soon after that, she was forced to resign her appointment and sell her fine house at Montreuil, for her husband went bankrupt. It was a terrible and notorious bankruptcy, which not only ruined some of their friends, but also many little tradespeople who had trusted in them. The Guémenées had lived in high style, and perhaps had placed too great a confidence in their agent. It was considered most un-aristocratic for a prince or a duke to sift through his account books very carefully and ask awkward questions. One was expected to behave in a princely manner and spend money like water. And of course, in those days, when the many servants were nothing more nor less than parasites, a great deal of petty pilfering and thieving went on.

The Guémenées disappeared from Versailles and were hardly ever heard of again. Practically nobody called on them.

One day, the King and Queen were alone, talking about Elisabeth who seemed far from happy.

The King said: "Do you think she is still pining to become a Carmelite?"

"Yes, I think so. I wonder what we can do to distract her. She seems happy enough when she comes to Trianon for the day." There was a silence. "Ah, I know. Supposing she had a place of her own like Trianon. What about Madame de Guémenée's house at Montreuil? It's up for sale, and we'd be doing her a service if we were to buy it. . . ."

Elisabeth was to write to one of her friends: "I am at Trianon, where I lead a very solitary life, but which pleases me greatly, and all the more because the site is charming. It rouses my envy; I should like to be able to carry the garden to my place and especially the water, which is not beautiful but very abundant."

The poet Delille wrote of Montreuil:

"Les graces en riant dessinèrent Montreuil." ("The Graces smiled when they drew Montreuil.")

It reminds one of Chateaubriand's country estate, La Vallée-aux-Loups, though the atmosphere in the two places is very different. The one was the domain of a saintly young girl who went there with her friends to do good to all the villagers, and there are, to this very day, great-grandchildren of these people at Montreuil, who speak of her with bated breath. The other place was the lair of a vain and egocentric lecher, who did not scruple to insult his wife by spending a long time there alone with Madame Récamier.

The day after secretly buying the estate, Marie-Antoinette suggested to Elisabeth that they should drive in the direction of Montreuil. "Wouldn't you enjoy visiting Madame de Guémenée's house where you played when you were a child?"

"That would give me great pleasure. Alas, it will no doubt be my last visit."

They rode down the Avenue de Paris, then turned to the left, up a narrow lane called Ruelle du Bon Conseil (now Rue Dussieu), and went through the grilles of the entrance. The concierge's wife dropped a curtsey. The footman lowered the footboard. They stepped out on to the pillared portico. A caretaker opened the door. When they had reached the entrance hall, with its floor paved in white and deep blue marble, and its fine staircase, the Queen turned to Elisabeth with a charming smile. "My sister, you are here in your own home. This will be your Trianon. The King, who has taken pleasure in offering it to you, has left me that of telling you the news."

And, as always when something too delightful happened, the young girl felt faint. After a while, she said: "Do you mean to say, *ma sœur*, that it will be my very own, to arrange as I like, and that I can entertain my friends here? And I'll be able to plant shrubs and trees, and to call on the villagers?"

"Yes, all that," laughed the Queen affectionately. "And I hope you will invite me and the children, and Madame Poitrine. But you understand, the King doesn't want you to sleep here until you are twenty-five, because it would need a lot more sentries and guards and a larger staff. You can come here early in the morning, and leave in the evening."

The rest of the time was spent in exploring. The house, built in 1776, was a white, semi-circular, two-storied building, with the stables on one side and the kitchen offices on the other, quite far away from the dining-room. On the ground floor, a circular chapel occupied the centre. The principal rooms were the boudoir, with wainscoting and a cupboard decorated with arabesques, the library with bookcases paned in clear glass, the buffet warming room paved in white marble, the dining-room, the billiard room, the music room, the drawing-room and some antechambers. Some of the old floors in small parquet squares are still there. Upstairs, twenty-one panelled rooms. On the other side, french windows looked on to a park. One could walk straight out of the drawing-room into the garden. On the right-hand side was the alley of lime-trees on the top of the terrace whose wall separated the estate from the Avenue de Paris. On the left, hidden by trees and quite a distance away, an orangery, a dairy, cow-sheds, farm buildings and the gardener's cottage. There were also kitchen gardens and hot-houses. The Prince Charles de Ligne, who was an amateur of gardens, describes it: "The garden of Madame la Princesse de Guémenée proves that, with skill, one can supplement what was lacking. The grounds are not very extensive, but everything has been so cleverly arranged, the clusters of shrubs so well placed, the objects of decoration so skilfully hidden from one another, that one is astonished to see how even the neighbours' territory has been used to advantage. The river and the beautiful meadow on the other side of the road to Versailles are very pleasant to discover from the mountain." There is an old engraving of this *petit monticule* or miniature mountain from which one could see Paris in the distance. The summit was reached by a spiral staircase hidden in a clump of little trees.

To-day, the Orangery has been turned into a private residence and is occupied by a great admirer of Madame Elisabeth. The *monticule* has disappeared, the dairy is still there, though the porcelain flooring is getting more and more worn. The park is not as extensive as it was. In 1781, Montreuil was a poor lost little hamlet with a population of nursery gardeners, château servants and paupers. Now there are fairly good roads and streets; in those days, the lanes were so muddy, and the roads so full of ruts, that Elisabeth had to walk to the parish church instead of going in her carriage. The church of St. Symphorien is exactly the same, built on classical lines, and the bell calling the villagers to Mass was Elisabeth's own gift. Instead of streets, there were meadows, fields and hedges, and a sprinkling of tiny thatched cottages.

When Elisabeth's plants were sold during the Revolution, an inventory was made, and it is from this that we learn the names of the pot plants and shrubs in her nurseries: salvia, ixia, gladiolus, lavender, japonica, mimosa, chrysanthemum, orange trees, pomegranate trees, myrtles, olives, oleanders, cypresses, different kinds of geraniums —some in earthenware flower pots. In the nursery, three hundred Scotch pines, forty chestnuts, one hundred and fifty "arbres de Saint Lucie", one hundred and fifty maples with ash leaves, thuyas, two hundred and fifty cherry trees, sixty ebony trees, forty syringas, eighty lilacs, fifty pots of roses. There were rare trees called juncorilobars and sequoias, there were cedars, pines, oaks, and beeches, cherries, dogwood trees, lilacs, ashes, and Canadian maples. There was plenty of water about, some coming from the reservoirs of the Butte Montbauran,

and according to the 1802 inventory, there were no less than five wells
on the estate.

"How Le Monnier and Dassy will enjoy themselves in this garden!"
exclaimed Elisabeth as she wandered about happily.

It was typical of her to think of sharing her joy with her old
friends. She gave a tiny house near by to Madame de Mackau. Angélique tells us that her mother's house had a door which communicated
with Madame Elisabeth's garden. Le Monnier lived near in a pavilion
which had belonged to Madame de Marsan. Here he had arranged a
botanist's paradise. All the strange seeds which had been brought to
him from America or the Cape were planted in the glass frames of his
garden. His library of botanical books, his albums of flowers and
herbs, his samples of ochre, iron, antimony and his amethysts from
Auvergne were arranged in show-cases. Dassy used to come from
Fontainebleau to talk with his two friends. He was one of the many
solitary long-distance walkers of the age of Rousseau.

The Ministry of Works, officially in charge of the furnishings,
provided all the grand stuff from the *Garde Meuble* in 1789, so one con-
jectures that Elisabeth, until that date, made do with pieces of furniture
of her own choice. In 1935, the owner had furnished the house most
delightfully in the Louis XVI style. By pure chance, she had bought
some chairs which had belonged to Elisabeth at Montreuil. The
original label in eighteenth-century handwriting was nailed underneath a chair. Although she didn't sleep there at night, Elisabeth had a
bedchamber, and in it was a *bergère*, or large, deep armchair by Boulard,
covered in striped tapestry, also a chair signed by Jacob, a pair of
candlesticks with their sconces in gilded bronze ornamented with
madonna lilies chiselled by Gouthière. As she was an exquisite needlewoman, Elisabeth covered many of the chairs with her own em-
broideries. We have a record that she bought a Christmas present for
Angélique of three Sèvres figures, one of Hebe and the other two of
Vestals: one may conclude therefore that she also bought Sèvres
porcelain for Montreuil, for every year at Christmas time the Sèvres
manufacture would hold a sale for the courtiers at Versailles, and the
King used to help to open the packing cases, sometimes smashing things
as he did so.

Elisabeth wanted the furniture to be simple and severe. She often modified the plans of the *Garde Meuble* officials, when she thought they were being extravagant. The National Archives preserved a note of hers saying: "One must for example have mirrors of 24 to 30 *sols*, instead of those costing from 6 to 8 *livres*." One can imagine that she soon put her foot down about the plans for the boudoir furniture, which, according to the records, was more suitable to a *petite maitresse* than to a princess. She says in one of her letters: "I have learnt that at the château they are making fun a little of the simplicity of my entourage." That is exactly what one would expect of the Polignac clan, which, according to Madame de Bombelles, was so malicious. But in Montreuil itself Elisabeth was independent and she was held in high honour. Monsieur de Lescure tells us that "The poor kissed the hem of her dress when she passed as if she were a saint." Her reputation for sanctity filtered through even to that insubordinate little institution, the school for pages: Félix d'Hézecques was thrilled that such an accomplished horsewoman and such a good dancer should also be a pattern of Christian living. Helping the poor was almost a family tradition: it was in her blood. An iron balcony had been put up soon after her parents' marriage, by their ground floor drawing-room, to protect them from the horde of beggars who came there daily, certain of never being sent away.

Let us spend a day with the princess and her ladies in the month of May 1782. On January 21st (ominous date), the Queen had gone in state to Notre Dame to give thanks for the birth of the Dauphin, and then supped with the Comte d'Artois at the Temple. In early March, Tante Sophie, who had been so frightened of thunderstorms, had died; the sight of her death-bed upset Elisabeth so much that she wept a great deal, and Angélique had to comfort her. In May, there was an interim of calm before the visit of Prince Paul of Russia and his wife, who were travelling under the names of the Comte and Comtesse du Nord. On great feast days and state occasions, Elisabeth would hear High Mass at Versailles at mid-day, before driving or riding to Montreuil. As the tribune reserved for the royal family was icy cold in the winter, it was walled in with a great gilded screen with windows, which turned it into a beautiful drawing-room. The balustrade was covered with a

crimson velvet carpet fringed with gold. At the door, the lackeys
gave their mistresses missals in large sacks of gold-fringed red velvet.
Each lady, as she came into the chapel, would throw her heavy train
over the side of her pannier. The King's chapel music was noted for its
beauty: everybody greatly admired the little airs which the celebrated
Bezonni played on the oboe. When Mass was over, the courtiers used
to rush up, so as to be on the path of the King and Queen, as they came
back through the state apartments. This was when Marie-Antoinette
would give her celebrated smiles and bows. She looked every inch
a Queen, taller than any of the ladies, whose nodding white ostrich
feathers gave the impression of a snowy forest. Immediately after Mass,
on festal days, Elisabeth would get into her sedan chair, go to her suite
overlooking the Orangery, and change into simple country clothes or
into her riding habit. But on ordinary days, when she would hear a
low Mass early, perhaps at the altar of the Sacred Heart, she would not
need to wear court clothes, and would go straight from the chapel
to her coach, waiting outside. Another coach would bring her ladies
who were on duty for the week. In ten minutes' time they would
reach Montreuil. Her page, Adalbert de Chamisot, followed her into
the house and then straight through to the garden on the other side.
"Ah! how glad I am to be here," she would exclaim. Montreuil owed
a great deal of its charm to the majestic shade of its fine trees, and to the
depth and beauty of its glades, which resembled Petit Trianon. Her
maid took her little black lace cape and her hat before they all had
breakfast together on the lawn.

In 1817, the painter Richard, a pupil of David, painted Elisabeth
on her farm giving milk to the villagers. She is hatless, carrying a light
parasol. Her white dress is airy and diaphanous and makes her look
like an eighteenth-century Vestal. As 1817 was only twenty-three years
after her death, oral traditions about her appearance still existed, and
these the painter must have followed. These breakfast parties in the
sunlight must have been very merry. Madame de Bombelles wrote:
"Our life at Montreuil was uniform, just like that spent by any united
family in a château a hundred leagues from Paris. Hours devoted to
work, to walks, to reading, either alone or in common. Everything
was methodically regulated. The luncheon hour reunited the princess

and her ladies around the same table. She had fixed her habits in this way.

"Towards evening, before the hour for returning to court, we all gathered in the drawing-room, and, as is the custom in some families, we had evening prayers all together. Then we set out again towards that palace which was at the same time so far and so near, one's heart refreshed by the impression of a day filled with work and friendship, and sanctified by prayer and charity." The Comte Ferrand, quoting Feuillet de Conches, says that this was not a prison of *ennui* or sadness, but that the princess lived with her ladies as if they were sisters, loving gaiety, taking part in it and often inciting it by one of those sudden sallies which were characteristic of her. In her society, the amorous intrigues of Versailles and Paris were never mentioned, and some of the ladies only heard about notorious scandals many years later, when they had emigrated. The French have a proverb "A sad saint is a sorry kind of saint." Gaiety is the hall-mark of French sanctity. They say that Sainte Thérèse de Lisieux, destined to die so young of consumption, was the life and soul of Carmelite recreations, by her anecdotes and her mimicry. And of course, Joan of Arc's gaiety has become proverbial. The quality of Elisabeth's good spirits has something individual about it. The de Goncourt brothers say there was something boyish and very "Ancien Régime" about her. Although she was never uncharitable, she had a high sense of the ridiculous and once wrote to a friend asking her to tell her about a family wedding and whether so and so had put on a lot of airs. She was a Carmelite at heart. Probably St. Teresa of Avila would have nicknamed her "my little varmint". One can imagine how Elisabeth would have rocked with laughter on the day when a lizard crept up St. Teresa's habit sleeve ("how terrible if it had been anywhere else but my sleeve!" she cried), and her brother seized the lizard by its tail, threw it into the air, and it fell into somebody's open mouth! The smallest things made her merry, as when she and the Queen both turned the mattress for little Adèle de Boigne's doll's bed "with gleeful jubilations", as if they had done nothing but make beds all their lives. When she was a guest of the Bombelles for luncheon—"we leave you to imagine how gay was this intimate *déjeuner*: we can hear Madame Elisabeth teasing her friends and the children. . . ." St.

Thomas Aquinas has classified amiability under the heading of a pleasant countenance, endearing language, unswerving gentleness of behaviour. He might have added the finishing touch of bubbling gaiety. The Psalmist speaks of the overflowing joy of the man who looks at his Lord. In the midst of the horrors of the Revolution, after the failure of attempted flight, Elisabeth could still write to the Marquise de Raigecourt: ". . . I have even kept some gaiety. Yesterday, I laughed a lot, recalling some of the ridiculous anecdotes of our journey." She also wrote to the Abbé de Lubersac: "God has given me the grace to keep some gaiety." The magnitude of her own griefs at the end of her life never led her to minimise the little troubles of her friends. With teasing affection, giving them such loving nicknames, she would enquire about their headaches or their children's teething worries, as if the monarchy and French society were not crumbling about her feet.

The morning at Montreuil was spent in a multitude of tasks. Hubert at the porter's lodge had orders never to turn away any poor persons. Elisabeth and Le Monnier used to concoct herb ointments and lotions for sores, and she would distribute vegetables from her garden and milk from her dairy, Even before the Swiss cows came in 1788, the quality of that milk was so good that the only children who survived the severe winter of 1783 were those who had drunk it. Then, of course, she would interview her staff, the Sieur Brown, the gardener, her maid who did her accounts with her every month, perhaps her hairdressers or her fine starcher—"*empeseuse et faiseuse de colorettes*", Demoiselle Marie Catherine. When she had overspent her pocket money for one month, she would arrange to spend less in proportion the following month. Furniture makers would come along with tempting *objets d'art*, and she once refused to buy a beautiful chimney-piece because she said that the money could have set up three poor households. There were sometimes harder temptations to resist: nursery gardeners would bring expensive exotic shrubs for her park, and she often had to refuse those. When she particularly wished to help some poor family, she would sell her own jewels, trinkets or watches. She certainly never spent very much on dress, though she once lavished quite a fortune on giving Angélique a glorious ball-gown. On Fridays and Saturdays, which in those days were fast and abstinence days, she gave orders that anything left over from her table should be given, morning and evening, to *les filles de la Charité*. Madame de Causans had certainly taught her thrift, for when she commissioned the Marquis de Bombelles to buy her some special lined writing-paper and some low-crowned straw hats from England, she begged him to be careful of her finances.

A great deal of her time was spent in visiting the sick and poor. She would often arrive just as the priest was bringing Viaticum to the cottage. Once the parish priest said: "Madame sets a very great example here," and she replied: "Monsieur, I receive a greater one from this, and I shall never forget it." Another day it was "poor Mother Rendoulet" who was dying peacefully, and the good princess stayed with her for an hour to aid her in her death agony. Occasionally she would go to St. Symphorien for Vespers. "I look like a real country woman," she wrote. ". . . I am at Montreuil since mid-day. I have been to Vespers at the parish church; they are as long as they were last year and your dear vicar sings the *O filii* in the same agreeable manner. Des Es(sarts) nearly burst out laughing, and I too." The *O filii* was a favourite liturgical chant of her father's; he had always loved to sing at his parish church, as if he were an ordinary village squire instead of a prince. By then, Elisabeth was saying the whole Office each day, though one must remember that in devout circles, even in the late eighteenth century, this was quite usual.

As some of her ladies were married, the children would come to Montreuil occasionally, and the new-born infants would have to be fed. Elisabeth mentions amusingly how two of the babies howled their heads off at their christening, and how their mammas had fussed her for a whole week about their christening robes. Since Rousseau, children had become fashionable, and Moreau's delightful engravings of the pleasures of family life were all the rage. Elisabeth's large household needed a lot of looking after. There might be a disagreeable duty to perform with Chamfort the librarian for example, if he brought dangerous books. Madame Vigée le Brun detested him: "His conversation was very witty, but caustic, full of rancour and without any charm for me, who disliked intensely his cynicism and his dirty appearance." No doubt the reliable older women of her entourage would

I

warn her against any unsuitable books he might put into her library—
volumes like "*Les Liaisons Dangereuses*", or that "*Nouvelle Héloïse*",
of which Madame de Sabran had been so frightened as a girl, that she
thought she would lose her honour if she so much as opened its pages.
No two people could have been more temperamentally unsuited than
Elisabeth and her librarian. Emmanuel Berl says of him: "He subsisted
on a pension. It is he who asked that pensions be suppressed. . . . High
society entertained him—Chamfort was devoured with hatred for it
and he sought its destruction, not without bitterness. . . . He says that
when he was returning from Versailles, he loved to see dogs gnawing
bones: an authentic passion, after the spectacle of so many friendships
without friendship, of loves without love. . . ." Berl rather admires
him, because he showed: ". . . that same disgust of what is slimy, of
what is sugared, of what is glib, of the *petite compassion*, of false sympathy, of all faked feelings. . . ." The fact remains that he was a snake-
in-the-bosom and that he became one of Mirabeau's chief supporters.
At the end, he committed suicide in prison.

Elisabeth could not do much about him, for, as well as being
patronised by the Comte de Vaudreuil, he was the protégé of the
Comtesse Diane.

It is extraordinary how these men of insignificant background,
who owed their livelihood to the great, grew to hate their patrons in
the end. The same was true of Beaumarchais, who had begun as a
kitchen boy. How truly it has been said that the razor of his "Barbier
de Séville" became the blade of guillotine!

One day, Elisabeth had a trying interview with the Prince de
Condé, about a pension for the widow of her butler. She wrote:
". . . Well, I'm sorry to say perhaps the King has not many people in
his employment who would prefer to break their heads in his service
than to smash his porcelain. This is, however, what has happened to
my poor Buisson, who was carrying the dessert of my dinner. His
foot slipped on the staircase and all the porcelain on his tray would
have been broken if that excellent fellow had not held it up horizontally, by hitting his head against the wall. The shock which he received
from this was so violent that he fainted directly his tray was placed
intact on the ground." Six weeks later, when he appeared to have

recovered, he died suddenly, leaving a wife and six children. Buisson's wife would not have received a widow's pension, for her husband's name was not on the list, unless Elisabeth had told the Prince de Condé that the family was dying of hunger and cold. In the end, she helped to support them.

On another morning, she had to reprimand her coachman very severely. The Duke of Bedford tells us about this. "The princess loved to drive very fast and her coachman had knocked someone down on the road. Because they were frightened of being punished, her servants did not speak to her about it. She was only told a few days later. Instantly she had the poor man sought out and gave him all the help that she could."

At the mid-day meal, everybody felt completely at home. So much so, that Elisabeth complained that her ladies "chattered like one-eyed magpies". Two of them in particular had exhausted her. In the afternoons, she would indulge her personal tastes: working her printing-press, particularly in Lent, drawing and painting. Sometimes, followed by her page Adalbert de Chamisot, she would go to look at some new plants with Le Monnier. Directly he saw the white-clad figure of his princess, he would leave his work and they would all spend a happy afternoon botanising together. So serious were those studies, that, when the page was exiled during the Revolution, he was able to earn his living by giving botany lessons.

Diane de Polignac, who was always kept politely but firmly at a distance by Elisabeth, tried to squeeze in somehow, and in her wake, unsuitable young persons like Madame de Canillac and Madame de Polastron would call. They, of course, remembered Montreuil in the days when it had been Madame de Guémenée's gambling hell, and they recalled the cheating exposed when some stranger from Paris was caught giving counters instead of coins. It was here that Madame de Canillac, surrounded by all her admirers, had queened it during the days when she was flirting with the Comte d'Artois. Now Madame de Polastron was his mistress. The tone of the conversation sank when women like these two appeared, and the châtelaine's back was turned.

"Do you think it's really true about the Comte de Fersen?"

"Who can tell, one hears so many things. He's extremely romantic, but then he's as close as a clam. I've never seen a colder face."

"I wonder if he'll be at the parties at Trianon, for the Comte and Comtesse du Nord? The Queen is absolutely transformed when she is near him. She is not in love with the King, though he certainly adores her."

"Have you seen her performance at the little theatre?"

"Oh yes, indeed, I acted in 'Le sabot perdu' only last week: the Queen was enchanting as Babet, though, I must confess, the Comte d'Artois as Colin sang a little out of tune."

Just then, Elisabeth appeared, carrying a large bouquet of spring flowers. "What is the plot of 'Le sabot perdu'?" Elisabeth asked the Comtesse Diane, more to hide her vexation at seeing her, than out of curiosity.

"I will tell you: to meet her lover Colin, Babet puts on her mother's clogs. The lovers are surprised by the village school-master, Babet flees, leaving behind one of the clogs. Great complications, the mother's reputation is at stake, but all ends happily with marriage bells. I love these simple village scenes. I think that a performance should be given for the Russian visit. Which reminds me, Madame, have you tried on your ball-gowns?"

CHAPTER XII

The Russian Visit and the Chantilly house-party

THE Queen, knowing that the Empress of Russia disliked her, was so nervous before receiving the Comte and Comtesse du Nord, that she asked for a glass of water. This fascinating visit is described at great length by the enthusiastic Baronne d'Oberkirch, who was a personal friend of the Comtesse. It is almost exhausting to read, particularly as the Baronne made the daily journey back to Paris in the small hours of the morning, after balls, a trip which took about an hour and a half. And then, she had to rise again very soon because her head-dresses were so complicated. She had glass flower containers made to the shape of her head, and she said that these real flowers coming out of the hair powdered snow-white looked delightful. The Comtesse du Nord herself had a jewelled bird in her hair, which sprang forward and was so dazzling that one could not look at it. Poised on a rose, he balanced on a spring, flapping his wings. She also had such a fine set of chalcedonies, that all the court ladies formed an admiring circle around her. The Comte, in spite of his ugly face, had charming manners, and great tact. It is eerie to think that this monarch was eventually assassinated by his courtiers, and that Gustavus III of Sweden, who came two years later, was to suffer a like fate. But there were no omens or portents about this visit.

To get a glimpse of the courtiers of Versailles at this time, one should study Carmontelle's gallery of portraits at the Musée de Chantilly. Oh those charming little figurines in profile, strutting about in backgrounds of princely parks and trellises, arbours, quincunxes, springing fountains and Temples of Love! Against that operatic décor, such elegant women, both old and young, smiling urbanely at the azure and gold of wonderful sunsets, or lost in the froth of their panniers, as they sit in carved armchairs against the woodwork and damasks of their drawing-rooms. There are bouquets of flowers at their bodices, and tiny posies poised on their closely cropped curls.

During the royal visit, Angélique de Bombelles wore the wonderful multi-coloured ball-gown, embroidered in gold and silver, which Elisabeth had given her the previous year, with a note attached: "To my tender friend. Receive kindly, my dear little guardian angel, this token of my tender friendship."

What a charming hostess Marie-Antoinette must have been! She soon treated the tall, portly grand duchess as a friend, asked her about her children and the education she gave them, and tried to find out what she could do to please her. The royal guests were under Elisabeth's suite, in a small apartment on the ground floor overlooking the Orangery. The Queen, who had supervised everything, saw to it that a harpsichord and great bunches of flowers were put in the rooms of the grand duchess. The grand duke was given maps of Versailles and its neighbourhood, with a choice of engravings to look through. When the Queen took her guest to the *manufacture de Sèvres*, she showed her a magnificent toilet set of lapis lazuli porcelain mounted on gold. Three Graces held a mirror around which Cupids frolicked. The grand duchess exclaimed: "This is no doubt for the Queen!" As she looked at it more closely, however, she saw that her own crest had been painted on it: this was a present for her.

On the first evening at Versailles, when she was watching the play, the Queen said: "It seems to me, Madame, that you and I have the same defect. Your sight is not very good. I help myself out with a lorgnette hidden in my fan. Would you like to see whether this little aid would suit you?" She presented her with a fan richly encrusted with diamonds. The grand duchess tried it and exclaimed that now she could see perfectly. The Queen then said: "I am delighted, and I beg you to keep it." Her guest replied: "I accept with pleasure, as it will serve me to see your Majesty more clearly."

The most delicious festivities took place in the gardens of Petit Trianon. This jewel of French architecture had been designed by Gabriel for Madame de Pompadour, but she never lived to enjoy it. It is a miniature palace, composed of a ground floor and two other floors, between columns and Corinthian pilasters, beautifully fluted.

An Italian terrace looks over the French garden, with its conventional green lawn and its flower beds where new pots of flowers were planted overnight. From the windows can be seen a pavilion containing a boudoir, kitchen, warming-up room and closet built around a central circular room. It is in this Pavillon Français that Louis XV used to drink iced champagne in hot weather. This traditional French garden consoled the gardener Richard a little, for he was broken-hearted at being deprived of his hot-houses; Richard had so greatly enjoyed seeing Louis XV botanising with the Duc D'Ayen. But at right angles to it, the Queen had had her way: there was the new English garden, designed by Mique, which she could gaze at from her bedroom window; here were the weeping willows swaying over the sinuous, sleepy stream, winding in a green meadow, and meandering around the island of the Temple of Love where Bouchardon's Cupid was carving his bow. On a hillock on the left was the Belvedere, where the Queen used to breakfast in summer. The artist had fore-shadowed the taste for Pompeian decoration. The de Goncourt brothers have described this Belvedere: "A delicate fugitive, enchanted paint-brush has splashed these porcelain walls with caprices and bursts of light. The painter has taken up again the poem of the palace wainscoting. He has brought it to life with sunshine and peopled it with animals: and again one sees quivers, arrows, garlands, white roses, loosely tied bouquets and cascades of flowers . . . open cages, hanging by ribbons, crossed by little monkeys and squirrels who scratch a crystal vase in which some fish are playing. . . . Here, the most ordinary objects of domestic life—a glass, a plate of biscuits, a fan, a woman's scarf, are so exquisitely painted that they acquire the value of precious *objets d'art.*"

Quite near is the grotto, overlooking the lake, and the wooded hillock with intertwining paths where the courtiers could have their secret flirtations. Everywhere, Chinese apple trees, quinces, almonds, hawthorns, pears, chestnuts, ashes, the crimson embroidery of Judas trees and the green velvet of that immense cedar of Lebanon which the Queen loved to gaze at. She wrote an order for a meal to be given to the Sieur de Jussieu, when she went to watch him watering this great cedar. Everywhere in the grass, scattered at random, tulips, pansies and hyacinths. Many poems have been written about Petit Trianon. In 1780, Bertin sang:

> "Charming Trianon, how many diverse transports
> You inspire in love-lorn souls!
> When I came to your green shades, I thought
> I had seen the dwelling of happy phantoms.
> See this brook which flows so idly,
> Murmuring its little sound.
> It is hushed, murmurs again, makes a loop and twines,
> Comes, goes, disappears, further off it shines and flees,
> Losing itself in the meadow
> Among the clover and the leaves. . . ."

The Chevalier Bertin became ecstatic when he described the shrubs and trees.

> "What art has assembled all these divers guests
> And nurslings transplanted from the other end of the Universe?
> The brown persicaria,
> The Virginian tulip tree displaying its richest tints to the airs,
> The catalpa of India, proud of its shade,
> The precious maple and the sombre larch
> Which nurtures tender griefs?
> Each path bordered with a hundred flowering shrubs
> Leads indirectly to new groves.
> The resinous bark and the Judas tree,
> Even the cedar grow there among the young elms,
> The fragile bean-trefoil drinks from a pure spring,
> And the foreign oak on verdant beds,
> Spreads its pliant branches like a parasol.
> But through these hallowed groves,
> What an elegant colonnade
> In white marble, aspires towards the skies!
> It is the Temple of Love, it is the sacred precinct
> Which the Queen of these haunts reserves for her son.
> Two weeping willows guard the entrance
> From any bold mortal.
> The statue on the altar is of a child.

It is he himself, he is trampling a buckler,
And the helmet of Alcides and his broken sword.
His knotty club, he is carving
Into a polished bow,
And with a cunning smile, already he defies us."

For this royal occasion, the gardeners had placed tubs of orange trees in the alleys and groves, and the perfume mingled with that of the roses, honeysuckle flowers and jasmine.

The festivities began with a performance in the Queen's little blue theatre. The principal guests were presented with copies of the play bound in morocco and gold, and engraved with the arms of the Queen and the grand duke. Between the acts, there was plenty of small talk, and the Baronne d'Oberkirch was as enthusiastic as ever. With Angélique de Bombelles she went into ecstasies about all the different shades of yellow, gold and green-gold in the mouldings, and the naked children playing with the long garlands of flowers and fruit. As Monsieur de Nolhac has said, this little theatre is "as appetising as an eighteenth-century ball gown". If Monsieur Taine had been there, he would have found much material to inspire him to write his famous passage about a vanishing society: "There is not a toilette here, not a pose of the head, not a tone of the voice, which is not . . . the distilled essence of all the most exquisite products of social art. It takes, we are told, a thousand roses to produce an ounce of that unique attar made for the Kings of Persia. This drawing-room is like that, a minute flask of golden crystal. . . . To fill it, a great aristocracy was transplanted into a hot-house, and thereby made sterile of fruit, though rich in flowers, in order that in the royal crucible, all its purified essences should be concentrated into a few drops of scent. Its cost is most extravagant, but only in that way are delicate perfumes made."

"Do any other members of the royal family act with her Majesty?" asked the Baronne d'Oberkirch innocently.

Madame de Mackau unfurled her fan and whispered confidentially: "Ah, *ma chère Baronne*, once her Majesty very graciously asked one of her sisters-in-law to act in a little play with her, but she replied that the daughters of the House of Savoy were not buffoons. Her Majesty was so hurt, that she burst into tears. The Comte d'Artois lost his temper when he heard that and gave the Comtesse a good snubbing."

"I find the Comte d'Artois so very charming," said the Baronne.

"So do I, *chère Baronne*. He is so devil-may-care. I cannot resist telling you something amusing about him. Some time ago, we were all very much intrigued by his comings and goings. Every morning he went to Petit Trianon, and for several hours on end, gave himself up to a mysterious occupation. And what do you think it was? He was taking lessons in tight-rope dancing from Sieur Placide! He gave an exhibition of his newly acquired talent to her Majesty. Oh, I well remember those early days! The Queen used to have great fun with Madame Elisabeth, going for donkey rides. When she fell off, she used to cry out: 'Don't pick me up, we must go and consult Madame L'Etiquette'—that was the Duchesse de Noailles—'on how to pick up a Queen of France when she has fallen from her donkey.' I remember the day Monsieur Mique brought her the new plan of the gardens: she spread it out on the lawn and said she must have flowers everywhere. But . . . sh . . . sh . . . , the curtain is going up."

. . . . .

At the supper which took place at Petit Trianon after the play, Madame d'Oberkirch was placed next to Elisabeth and they had an important conversation which she recorded in her Journal: "Afterwards, there was a supper of three tables with 100 places at each. I had the honour of being placed near Madame Elisabeth and to look at this saintly princess at my leisure. She was in the full glow of youth and beauty, and refused all marriage proposals in order to stay with her family. 'I can only marry a king's son,' she said, 'and a king's son must reign in his father's states; I would no longer be a Frenchwoman, I don't want to cease being one. Better to stay here at the foot of my brother's throne, than to ascend another.'"

On the ground floor supped '*les Seigneurs Russiens*', the French and Italian actors, the musicians. Elsewhere were tables for Madame de Polignac, the Queen's ladies, the suite of the grand duchess, the guards, the *officiers de bouche*, the footmen, the stable assistants, the men who carried sedan chairs, even the laundresses and kitchen hands. Indeed there were more than twelve hundred people at supper that night.

Afterwards, there was the influx of all the courtiers who had not been invited to the supper. They wandered about the gardens to listen to the music of the French and Swiss guards. The artists in charge of those nocturnal festivities were past masters in scenic effects, as one can see in the enchanting engravings of the time, particularly in Hubert Robert's sketch and the painting by Lavreince. "The art with which they had . . . lit up the English garden, produced a charming effect: earthen dishes hidden by green-painted wooden planks, illuminated all the clumps of shrubs or flowers, and brought out the different colours in the most varied and agreeable manner. Several hundred bundles of sticks had been set alight in a ditch, behind the Temple of Love, giving a great glow which made it the most brilliant spot of the garden." Madame de Sabran, in speaking of similar evenings at Montreuil and Bellevue, says that the discreet lighting of the clumps gave to objects "such light shadows that the water, trees and the people, everything appeared ethereal". Elisabeth, in her glorious court panniers and high plumed head-dress, wandered about, entertaining the Russian guests, who, of course, all spoke French. Madame d'Oberkirch made her laugh by telling her that one night, she had been to supper after the Opera with the Princesse de Chimay, and had had a terrible fright. "The princess's tiny monkey broke its chain whilst we were away at the theatre. He went to find his old friend, a little dog, and between them, they broke into the princess's dressing-room. Her toilet table had long been the object of his ambition. Pouf! He overturned the boxes of powder-puffs, the hairpins, combs and brushes, sprayed perfume on to himself and the dog, rolled himself in powder, applied rouge and patches, just as he had seen his mistress do, except that he added a patch on his nose. He made himself a head-dress out of one of her lace ruffs, and, thus bedecked, he walked into the room where we were all having supper, jumped on to the table and ran towards the Princesse de Chimay. All the ladies fled, shrieking, thinking it was the Devil in person. Even his mistress did not recognise him. Dear little Almanzor was enchanted with himself. I confess I was not at all amused at the time. I think he should have been smacked, but instead he was given gingerbread and filberts."

Elisabeth laughed heartily: "I think my Aunt Victoire would have died of fright: she has a particular horror of monkeys. That is why I never keep one."

On these great occasions, the pages were always extremely useful. They rushed about fetching cloaks for the ladies or bringing refreshments. At the end, they helped the footmen to call the carriages. In the small hours of the morning, the poor mites were sometimes so tired, that it was quite usual to see a page fast asleep in a corner, with his pockets stuffed with oranges. What a charming subject for an engraving by Cochin! Whilst Elisabeth's page went to fetch her cloak, the Baronne exclaimed ecstatically: "I think your pages here are little cherubs." "Ah, Madame," said Elisabeth, "if you only knew! They're utterly undisciplined. They complain about everything—even the food. They have far too much free time. Sometimes I see them running in bands through the streets of Versailles, breaking windows and teasing the women. Once, they even went to a grocer's shop armed with sticks and pillaged everything. They're a perfect nuisance in the royal gardens, they ruin the flower beds, paddle in the lakes, turn on the taps, hide the keys of the turncock, smash the trellises. I hear they sell their beautiful embroidered habits in Versailles second-hand clothes shops for a few *écus*. They poach the King's game, thrash the grooms, threaten passers-by with pistols if they don't like their faces, in fact, the inhabitants of the town are simply terrified of them. The owners of billiard rooms allow them to come and play free of charge, and the innkeepers rent private rooms for them, just because they dare not say no."

A Russian lady who was listening, exclaimed in horror: "Why, if a page did that sort of thing in the entourage of our Empress, he would be given the knout."

Elisabeth smiled urbanely. "Madame, one of the first things my brother did on ascending the throne, was to abolish torture. However, I sometimes feel like giving them a good smacking, particularly when they're cheeky to my brother and the Queen. The other day, would you believe it, they went up to the gallery of the théâtre Montansier and splashed a bowl of burning punch on to the people in the stalls."

She did not add that one of these horrible youths had publicly and cynically used the Queen's theatre box as a *lieu à l'Anglaise*. What a pity they could not all be sent back to their parents! And what a good thing that her own page, little Adalbert de Chamisot, was so well behaved!

Louise de Causans, whose mother had allowed her to come to the party, said: "But Madame, do you recall the year when the pages let out the boars, and they were chased by all the hordes of dogs in Versailles? I shall always remember the great packs of hounds, overturning the vegetable and fruit barrows and knocking down passers-by. There were still some boars roaming about Montreuil, seven months later."

Just then the Prince Charles de Ligne joined the group. "Well, *chère Baronne*," he said, "if you are, like myself, an amateur of gardens, you must go and call on Madame Elisabeth at Montreuil."

"Yes, please come and see me when you have a free moment," said Elisabeth hospitably. "Though, of course, my humble abode is nothing compared with Petit Trianon."

The Prince de Ligne said:[1] "I have just been dreaming of an ideal little rustic village for her Majesty. The cottages of my shepherds will be clean, uniform, covered with thatch. Each night, the sleek Swiss cows will present to my herdsmen their udders as bountiful as those of Cybele. The shepherds' wives and mistresses will sing, they will play on their simple instruments—the bagpipes, horns, pipes and flutes. The shepherds and shepherdesses will wear a costume worthy of the dignity and simplicity of nature."

The Baron de Besenval, tall and rather sinister, exclaimed: "Yes, I am always telling her Majesty that she should have cows from my native land."

Elisabeth enquired: "Is the quality of their milk so superior to that of French cows? You see, I have a dairy, and there is a daily distribution of milk to the Montreuil villagers. I get the impression that the milk isn't rich enough. The population of my hamlet is a poor one—paviors, navvies, tinkers, carters, old clothes dealers, sellers of songs, beggars, and a quantity of paupers without hovels. I would so like to provide their babies with rich, pure milk."

[1] From "Prospect of Bel Œil".

Besenval felt slightly irritated by Madame Elisabeth's tastes. It was really ridiculous and naïve to talk of good works and the poor on an evening such as this. Soon, he changed the conversation: "I think you will find a model dairy, Baronne, when you go to Chantilly."

The Comte d'Artois exclaimed: "I can assure you, *chère Baronne*, that our poor entertainments here will pale into insignificance when you get to Chantilly. Already all Paris is saying that the King entertains the Comte and Comtesse du Nord as friends, the Duc d'Orléans as a bourgeois, but the Condés as princes."

"I will not be coming," said Elisabeth, "but I know you will enjoy meeting my cousin, Louise de Condé. We vowed eternal friendship when we were young and I wish I could see more of her. Please give her all kinds of messages from me."

.   .   .   .   .

The Comtesse du Nord told her friend the Baronne d'Oberkirch that there were two people with whom she could become friendly in France. The first, the Queen, and the second Louise de Condé. This future Benedictine nun, intimate friend of Elisabeth and one who resembled her greatly, distinguished herself during this royal visit by appearing in a gilded gondola "as a voluptuous water nymph, with mocking lips and angelic eyes".

The entertainment at this house-party was so fabulous that it deserves more than passing mention. The King and Queen of France did not go, for the simple reason that the widower Prince de Condé lived in open sin with the beautiful Princesse de Monaco. She was not received at court by Marie-Antoinette and had therefore joined the ranks of her enemies. The whole situation was very embarrassing indeed. True, the Princesse de Monaco had a terrible husband, but she broke all the unwritten laws of society by flaunting her adultery quite shamelessly. Needless to say, she did not get on with Louise de Condé, or with her brother, the Prince de Bourbon, who treated her with cold looks and haughty silences.

It had taken three hundred years of continuous effort by successive generations of Montmorencys and Condés to bring the park and château to the point of perfection which it had reached in that year 1782. The vast deep forest, replete with game, had now been pierced with carefully tended alleys, radiating like stars from central points. The marshlands near the château had been drained and the waters used to fill lovely pools. The Chantilly lakes were much more alive than at Versailles, sometimes more so than was pleasant, for the prince had concealed some of those horrid eighteenth-century contraptions on the paths, whereby jets of water would suddenly spring up under the panniers of the ladies. (A trick of this kind had killed a young girl from shock in the Folie Monceau.) There were carp in the moats around the castle, and some of them were so tame that you could pat their snouts like dogs. The cascades were beautifully designed—vivid, roaring, limpid, musical. It would take too long to describe the green *boudoirs* in the parks, the statues and bowers, the English garden, the gondolas, the orange trees on an enchanted isle, the deceptively rustic hamlet in which one of the poorest-looking cottages was beautiful inside, with flowers painted on the ceilings, enormous mirrors, and furniture upholstered with pink taffeta and silver. In the dairy, ornamented with country scenes and paved in multi-coloured marble, rams' heads poured jets of water into marble shells. In the menagerie, there were swans, peacocks, exotic ducks, an orang-outang and even a tiger. Vialon had stuck on to a great alabaster column, eight sundials, giving the time in the principal cities of the globe. Then there was the indoor tennis court, very well lit, with lamps that you could switch at will. There was the Orangery, the theatre, the Island of Love, with its pavilion of Venus with pictures by Boucher, not to mention the kitchen gardens, the melon house, the figgery, the hot-houses.

The staff was legion, just as in other princely households. There was even a special guardian for the gold and silver plate and for the Sèvres and Saxe porcelain which decorated the tables. The unruly pages had their own riding masters, their tutors in mathematics, fencing, handwriting and dancing, and the tutors, in their turn, were served by special valets. Everybody wore the Condé livery, *"couleur ventre de biche"* (rosy-white like a hind's belly), with crimson breeches. The prince paid all fees connected with illness, gave pensions to his own servants and kept up the hospital at his own expense. The stables, which still exist to-day, were stupendous, with their two hundred and forty horses and two packs of hounds. The carriage houses were simply packed with every kind of vehicle, and there were special rooms for the spurs and the women's blue velvet saddles, the golden bridles and so on. These coaches, with their Genoese, Venetian and Dutch velvets, their paintings and scutcheons, were works of art in themselves. There were also seven sledges, twenty sedan chairs and five gondolas. It would be impossible to give an idea of the treasures inside the château. Several things, though, stand out in one's memory—the deer in the dining-room spouting water into a granite container in which the wine glasses were rinsed, the central heating under the white marble of the dining-room floor, the botanical room to which the sovereigns of Europe sent rare exotic plants, the charming boudoir, still intact to-day, on whose walls Huet painted his bright, delicious little monkeys in fine raiment.

The guests, strangely enough, were lodged in the attics, and they could walk right round the castle on the tiles. The Prince de Croÿ said: "It seemed astonishing to me to be able to get into my room from the windows. From the roof one enjoyed a splendid view of the forests, the hillocks, the villages nestling in the greenery."

And yet, when we read the letters of Madame de Sévigné, we recall it was here that the steward Vatel committed suicide because the fish had not come in time for Louis XIV's visit. La Bruyère, who belonged to the household, had written this reflection: "The great ones of the earth pride themselves on opening an alley in a forest . . . of gilding ceilings, of producing ten inches of water, of furnishing an orangery, but their activity does not extent as far as to make a heart content, to fill a soul with joy, to foresee extreme needs or to remedy them."

The Princesse Louise de Condé might have echoed this view, for, in spite of all this opulence, she was very unhappy. The Baronne d'Oberkirch soon fell under her charm during this visit. She speaks of her "innate distinction", her "queenly beauty" and the great tenderness of her heart. ". . . it is a brow which should wear either a crown or a nun's veil." She speaks also of her angelic piety, the serenity of her soul and the calm of her glance, which indicated a creature privileged by God; lastly she extolled her gifts as musician and painter.

Just as the Baronne had led Elisabeth to divulge her reason for not marrying, so at Chantilly the conversation turned to matrimonial affairs. The Baronne wrote: "She is quite determined not to marry. Madame la Duchesse de Bourbon assures one that she loves somebody and that the somebody is not of royal birth, and that she will go to the convent, pure and holy as she is, rather than give her hand without her heart." She noticed, even then, the invincible melancholy on her face. Louise, however, tried to keep gay for her father's sake.

Angélique de Bombelles, who had been to stay at Chantilly in December 1781, had said about Louise de Condé: ". . . Mademoiselle always shows me the greatest friendships; I love her madly. There is in her manners, a great analogy with those of Madame Elisabeth."

It is no wonder, then, that at this great reception on June 10th the Baronne exclaimed: "Chantilly is the most beautiful place in the world. The lakes, the woods, the gardens are delightful. The water nymphs and the fountains have quite the air of the court. . . . The princes of the House of Condé have always been more popular with the nobility than their elders the princes of Orléans."

At meals, the table was covered with an inexhaustible supply of gold and silver plate. After each course, the servants, without confusion or noise, threw it all out of the window. It fell into the waters of the moat and was taken out in large nets.

At the play, the back of the stage opened, disclosing woods, fields, fountains and lawns in a magnificent *trompe œil* effect, and the great Vestris himself, attired as Zephyr, was seen dancing on the grass. Supper was served in the hamlet with little comic-opera huts in the middle of an English garden. The guests passed through an Isle of Love, such as Watteau would have loved. Cupid holding a burning heart stood on a pedestal, and the prince's secretary (who was to turn Judas with the Revolution) had written the poem carved on the pedestal:

> Offering but a heart to beauty
> As naked as truth.
> Unarmed like innocence,
> Wingless like constancy,
> Such was Love in the golden age.
> We find him not but still we seek him.

K

At length, the Baronne returned to Versailles, rather spoilt by the pleasures of Chantilly. However, she admired the chandeliers and branched candlesticks, sparkling with lights, the orchestra on the tiers, the miraculous dresses of the women, the Queen, beautiful as the day, enlivening all with her glowing presence. On the last evening at Versailles, there was a fancy dress ball in the Galerie des Glaces. Those mirrors, which, since the days of Louis XIV, had seen so many intrigues, now reflected Marie-Antoinette's ladies in white satin dominoes. One can picture Elisabeth enjoying herself hugely. It would be a mistake to think that she felt out of things. Angélique records, almost with a sigh of exhaustion, how she could hunt eleven hours a day and then watch dancing till the small hours of the morning without showing fatigue. After this ball, there was a supper party at the Princesse de Lamballe's, at which the Queen danced in a quadrille. "Madame d'Oberkirch," said the Queen that evening, "speak a little German to me, I want to know if I remember it." And when the charming Baronne from Alsace obeyed, the Queen went off into a day-dream for several moments. "Yes," she said at last, "I am charmed to hear *ce vieux Tudesque*; German is a beautiful language; but French! On my children's lips, it seems to me the sweetest language of the universe."

After one of those balls, the Baronne, returning to Paris from Versailles in broad day-light, saw "the peasants repairing to their daily labours, and noticed the contrast between their calm, contented faces, and the weary expression of our features—rouge had fallen from our cheeks, powder was shaken from our hair".

A few days later, this historic visit came to an end. And so, after all the fatigue, all the expense, all the enormous efforts made on their behalf, the Comtesse du Nord wrote to the Empress Catherine II, her mother-in-law, that the King was a bore, and Marie-Antoinette empty-headed and frivolous!

"Put not thy trust in princes! . . ."

.   .   .   .

When Frederick the Great wanted to have a good laugh, he used to say to Voltaire, "Come on then, describe the King of France's *lever*."

His *coucher* was even more diverting.

At last, the guests have gone! Louis XVI, like the cat, always became singularly impish towards bed-time. Jocularly throwing his Cordon Bleu at someone's nose, he would allow two of his valets to undo his breeches, and then stumble around to each of his nobles in turn, shuffling along, because his feet got caught in his breeches. At length he consented to sink into a chair, and lift his feet for two pages to take off his shoes. Etiquette decreed that those shoes should fall with a certain clacking sound. The two little pages on duty for the week were so tired that they could hardly keep their eyes open. When the gentlemen tried to slip the night-shift over the King's head, he pirouetted and gavotted about, making little passes, and was extremely hard to catch. Then there was all the tomfoolery connected with teasing a certain fabulous court personage, bristling with jewels, who stank like a boar. (He looked after the menagerie.) The thing was to get hold of his plumed hat and throw it up into the canopy of the King's bed, where he could not reach it. On hot nights, showers were played on a cloth tent near the window, to cool the air, and the King loved to push some unwary gentleman under the spray and go into fits of laughter when he was drenched to the skin. The exhausted staff dutifully roared with laughter too. At length the King was safely tucked up in bed. "Ouf," he said to himself on the night when the Comte and Comtesse du Nord had gone back to Russia. "Ouf! In bed at a reasonable hour at last! And to-morrow I'll make a new lock in my smithy."

CHAPTER XIII

A bad winter, and balloons

ON June 12th, 1783, the King forbade the performance of "Le Mariage de Figaro". Beaumarchais was furious. He exclaimed: "Well, gentlemen, it seems my play cannot be performed here, but I take my oath that it will eventually be acted—perhaps in the very choir of Notre Dame." The King had seen, as Sainte-Beuve was to say later, that "Figaro is a sort of professor who gives systematic instructions—I will not say to the middle classes, but to upstarts and pretenders of every class—in insolence."

Had it been Napoleon, who knew how to rule his court, and who certainly had the art of keeping turbulent Frenchmen in order, he would have seen to it that his orders were properly carried out. Disobedience was in the air, an almost fashionable complaint, just as obedience had been the thing in the times of Louis XIV. Nothing amused the nobles like a satire on nobility. Three months later, on September 26th, 1783, the Comte de Vaudreuil had this play performed in the private theatre of his château of Gennevilliers by the Comédie Française before an audience of three hundred people. For that, he should have been locked up in the prison of St. Lazare, or the Bastille. (It will be remembered that in "An Adventure" by Miss Moberley and Miss Jourdain, when they saw what they believed to be the ghost of Vaudreuil at Petit Trianon, they were impressed by his evil countenance.) There is no doubt that he did incalculable harm to his royal master.

Alas and alack! The first public performance of "Le Mariage de Figaro" took place in Paris in 1784, in the theatre of the Comédie Française, which is now the Odéon. One can be pretty sure that Mesdames de Canillac and de Polastron both went, and probably returned to Montreuil to recount their adventures to the peaceful little dovecote of Elisabeth's ladies.

"Such a wild struggle for tickets! All our duchesses and marchionesses had taken their places in the early morning in the actresses' boxes, even breakfasting and dining there. The guards were swept aside, the doors burst open, the barriers torn down, people were smothered."

Elisabeth said with her usual dry humour: "Indeed, you seem to have had a charming excursion."

The naughty young protégée of Elisabeth's nicknamed Démon asked: "Is the play as dangerous as they make out?"

"I don't know about dangerous, but I found it diverting. That little Beaumarchais—what impertinence!" Then turning to Elisabeth, "Madame, I don't know how your venerable aunts Mesdames Victoire and Adélaïde endured him. I'm told he started as a kitchen boy."

Démon interrupted, "But do tell us some of the bits of the play for which they say he ought to be imprisoned."

Madame de Canillac opened her reticule and brought out a copy. "Now, just listen to this:

FIGARO: I'm born to be a courtier.
SUZANNE: I'm told it is a difficult profession.
FIGARO: Receive, take, ask. There is the secret in three words."

There was a titter of shocked amusement. Elisabeth said to Adalbert de Chamisot, "Stay outside the door, and prevent any footmen from coming in."

Madame de Polastron took up the play again: "Just listen to this one.

THE COUNT: The servants in this house take longer to dress than
                      their masters.
FIGARO: It's because they have no valets to help them."

The ladies laughed, and she continued: "And then, isn't it wicked when Suzanne says: 'Do women of my station have the vapours? It is a malady of fashionable people and prevails only in boudoirs.'"

Madame de Canillac went on to describe the delirium of the audience when the barber turned towards all the peers, the knights of St. Louis and the Knights of the Holy Ghost and exclaimed: "Because you are a great Lord, you fancy yourself a great genius! Nobility, wealth, rank, office—all that makes you very proud! What have you done for all these blessings? You have taken the trouble to be born and nothing else."

Elisabeth said, "I am told there was a very dangerous passage about gaming." "Oh yes," said Madame de Polastron, "here it is. 'There was nothing left for me to do except steal. I made myself banker at a faro table. Since then, good people, I sup out, and people who are called *"comme il faut"* open their houses to me very politely, reserving to themselves three quarters of the profits.'" Madame de Canillac had turned rather pale. She felt quite certain that the quotation referred to the Princesse de Guémenée's gambling hell in this very château of Montreuil. Just then, Monsieur de Chamisot opened the door and admitted the Comte d'Artois, who was looking in high spirits. Madame de Polastron gave him a melting look. He kissed his sister's hand, and she said to him mockingly: "There is no need to tell me where you have been."

"My dear, there has been a terrible scene with the Marquis de . . . He swears that Beaumarchais pokes fun at him in his play, and that he'll have him thrashed by his lackeys."

"What passage does he refer to?" cried the ladies in turn.

"This one: 'I was poor and I was despised. I showed some wit and I was pitied. A pretty wife and a fortune, every heart will turn to you.' But seriously, Babet, when Beaumarchais was making clocks and finding musical instruments for Aunt Adélaïde, I never guessed that we were nursing such a viper in our bosoms. Perhaps I ought to warn Vaudreuil against patronising your librarian Chamfort. I always think it so unwise to patronise the lower classes. You never know when they're going to turn against you."

And indeed, Chamfort, in spite of all the great favours he had received, became a rabid revolutionary.

The weather of that summer of 1783 had been odd, as if in sympathy with the growing turbulence of the times. Strange phenomena in the skies filled superstitious souls with foreboding. The sun, of a pale russet-colour, gave a sad and sombre light. In spite of the thick fog which surrounded it, the heat was stifling. Angélique, who was expecting another child in the autumn, was exhausted. The moon was the colour of blood. As there were earthquakes in Calabria, everybody began prophesying about the Last Judgement. There was an atmosphere of tension everywhere. At her balls in the past, when the Queen had seen the young men lounging in groups, talking politics and neglecting their partners, she used to go up to them and disperse them with a little tap of her fan. But now, they flatly disobeyed the orders of their gracious hostess, and the balls were a dismal failure. The people who had not been invited to Petit Trianon, took their revenge by not coming to Versailles to pay their court. Extraordinary rumours began to spread about the enormous sums spent on the Queen's Hameau or comic-opera hamlet. A severe winter followed this strange summer. The manuscript of St. Cyr tells us: "The snow and ice lasted very long and produced a thin coating of ice which made the roads very dangerous. The poor began to increase in numbers because of the difficulty of finding work; several families died of hunger, cold and poverty . . . the King showed himself to be a real father of his people. . . . He gave abundant alms; and the rich, drawn by the example of the master, showed themselves benevolent. . . ." Elisabeth deprived herself of everything, so that the villagers in her hamlet should suffer as little as possible. She and Le Monnier were kept very busy at her dispensary, tending sick people.

In the immense palace of Versailles, with its army of underlings, no space could be found for drying firewood. So the fires smoked, particularly after a wet autumn, and everybody shivered. Sometimes the chimneys smoked and soot fell down in pailfuls. Monsieur Lenôtre, in a chapter of his *"Versailles au temps des Rois"*, tells us about the Marquise de Rambouillet who used to sew herself into a bear-skin, and of another lady who, at the risk of being grilled alive, used to hide herself in a barrel placed on a warming-pan full of live charcoal, of the Maréchale de Luxembourg who spent the winter in her sedan chair, lapped round with numberless hot-water bottles. In the vast rooms, gales blew and blizzards froze sauces and wines. The white and gold drawing-rooms became invisible in the thick, soot-laden, breath-impested smog!

"Brrr," said Elisabeth, blowing on her frozen hands as she stood by her window at Versailles. She had scratched a little portion of pane and was trying to peer through at the gardens. Across the dark, threatening sky, a crow flew towards the bare, shivering elms. "Monsieur de Chamisot," she said, turning to her page, "I don't seem to have heard your Prince de Lambesc overhead recently. I begin to miss the clacking of his riding boots on the parquet. Is he away?"

"No, Madame. His horse kicked him in the stomach. He's only just recovering, and he is champing because his apothecary won't let him ride for another month. I think he is going to die of melancholy, for I saw him reading a book about the solitaries of Pont Royal the other evening: so unlike him!"

Elisabeth laughed. "Go up to him at once. Present him with my compliments and beg him to come down and talk to me."

In a quarter of an hour, the prince appeared, looking quite unlike his old self. His ambition was to die in the saddle. "Come and sit by the fire. I'll ring for the footman to stoke it up a little. I'm so sorry to hear of your ill-luck."

"*Tonnerre! Tonnerre!*" exploded the prince in the voice he used at five in the mornings when teaching horsemanship to young pages. "It's all that confounded apothecary—saving your presence, Madame. He said if I were to get on a horse before Christmas, I'd be a raving lunatic, and he'd have me locked up at Charenton. And here am I biting my fists with rage, to think of all I'm missing. I've hunted six days a week since I was out of swaddling bands."

The princess's blue eyes twinkled with amusement. "Come, come, prince, you couldn't be hunting in this weather, anyway. But tell me how your accident happened."

"Well, Ma'am, you know that walloping great stallion called Brutus, the one I lost my heart to. By St. Martin's bones, what thundering great hocks he's got! Well, I was stupid enough to be near by at his supper time. The stable lad was just bringing in his mash. Brutus rolled his eye at it, and, through sheer *joie de vivre*, Ma'am, sheer *joie de vivre*—and nothing else—there's not a spot of mischief in the fellah—he kicked out with his back legs and got me full in the belly. The next thing I knew I found myself in bed. Hope I didn't disturb you with my groans. Coughed up a lot of blood, you know. And to think I'd only had the fellah's portrait painted the week before. I noticed he cocked his eye at the easel. Perhaps he didn't like the picture."

Elisabeth held her sides with laughing. When she had recovered her breath, she said: "Oh, but you are so amusing."

"I like to hear a good honest laugh."

"When I was a child, the Vicomtesse d'Aumale always told me to laugh as much as I could, as it was good for the lungs. But I must confess these last few days I haven't felt like laughing at all."

"Have you been ill too, Madame?"

"Never better, thank you. I've got a constitution of iron, and I shall probably live to be a hundred, unless I'm assassinated. No, I'm miserable because of the sufferings of the poor in this terrible weather. The King has given great alms, and everybody has followed his example. Huge fires have been lit in all the courtyards. But it isn't enough. You should just see my hamlet of Montreuil. Oh, prince, I had you called down because I wanted somebody who could spare a little time to help me with my poor people."

Now the Prince de Lambesc had a great admiration for the princess. "One of the finest horsewomen in France: shall never forget the way she picked herself up after a fall and mounted again." She was a kindred spirit all right, and knew that one of the great pleasures of life was to have a good mount under you, who'd do anything you asked of it, and carry you over hill, over dale at break-neck speed. Oh, the good days he had spent with her boar-hunting in the forest of Fontainebleau! And when the quarry sounded and torches blazed in the immense courtyard, the great beast was disembowelled and the hounds were at last unleashed to gobble up his guts. Yes, manifestly she'd enjoyed all that, in spite of her reputation for piety. So he said gleefully: "Madame, I am at your service. I'm not allowed to go near those stables, in case the temptation is too great for me. I'm nearly ill with *ennui* upstairs. I'll do anything you like."

Elisabeth unfolded her plan which had secured the King's approval and which needed a great deal of help from the now unoccupied stable hands. "I want to organise a chain gang. I want to fill a lot of your carts with wood, and dry that wood at Montreuil, in the ovens and elsewhere. Then I'll assign several houses to each of your lads, and I want them to distribute the wood. Old people living alone in crumbling hovels will be brought out on stretchers, and I'm putting them up in camp beds in my Orangery."

"You won't have any oranges next year," he laughed.

"Oh, what do a few oranges matter when you think of human lives? Well, to continue. I'll send my squire on ahead with orders to the cooks to make quantities of good meat broth. I've got the wine. We'll make *chabrol*, as they do in the Limousin. Other boys will go to the bakers' to fetch bread, and, as I haven't got any old clothes left, nor have my friends, I'll send some of my chamber-maids to the old-clothes shops in Versailles, with particular orders to buy bed coverings. Let's have a glass of muscat ourselves before we start. The wind cuts like a knife. I'll go and dress myself as if I were starting on a campaign. This place is an ice-box. Look, you can't see to the other end of the room, there's such a fog with this smoking chimney. If we can feel wretched here, you can imagine what it must be like for my people in their hovels at Montreuil."

. . . .

The charities of the royal family were soon forgotten. There were even grumblings and murmurings in Paris because during those hard times the Queen's newly rigged yacht lay at anchor near the Pont Royal. The contrast was too great, and her enemies blew on the embers of calumny.

So much has been written on this exquisite civilisation before its decline. This time in mid-winter would be the moment to point out what Monsieur Lenotre calls "l'envers du décor"—the reverse of the medal at Versailles.

Elisabeth often had a bath, and so did other members of the royal family. But others did not. One can imagine what the white and gold painted walls in the state apartments looked like, smeared with hundreds of grimy hands. Other indispensable closets were very rare, and so, walking through the courtyards you were obliged to put up great leather umbrellas to protect yourself from what was thrown out of the windows. In fact, one day, Elisabeth's mother, the Dauphine, was left stranded in her sedan chair because her almoners and suite had been drenched by ordures hurled by servants from a second-floor window, and they'd rushed away to change their clothes. La Morandière, writing in 1764, said that the filthy odours of the park, the gardens and the château made one heave. "The communicating passages, the court-yards, the wings of the building, the corridors are filled with filth. At the bottom of the Ministers' wing, a pork butcher bleeds and grills his pigs every morning; the avenue of St. Cloud is covered with stagnant waters and dead cats."

Against the door of the King's bedchamber, the fat Swiss Guard had put up his screen, and lived there, morning, noon and night, even preparing his meals therein. Even so, the King's bedchamber was not properly guarded, for one morning somebody had stolen Louis XV's *pot de chambre*! In spite of his four thousand servants, Louis XV was so cold in bed, he used to rise before dawn, take refuge in some smaller apartment and light his own fire.

The highly paid official who went by the enigmatic title of "Porte Chaise d'Affaires" used to entertain his friends with very fine table napkins whose primary destination was happily unknown to them. These squares of fine linen were the perquisites of his office.

Prostitutes, some of them dead drunk, used to try and hide under the stairs to sleep there for the night. One little girl of fourteen, Suzanne Lenoir, had been soliciting in the corridors for three weeks.

When we look at engravings of Versailles, we see the horsemen, the fairy-tale coaches, the sedan chairs, the fine vistas and views, the soldiers, the pages; our eyes are blinded by powdered gold dust. The truth is so different. In the years before the Revolution, the Boulevard de la Reine and the Boulevard du Roi were lakes of mud, and people used to throw their rubbish in the great holes in the road where chickens flapped. No police, hardly any lanterns, and at twilight, sinister-looking figures loitered about in the shadows. Monsieur Lenôtre says: "If you get near the château, everywhere there are shanties . . . real lairs, where are sheltered, out of charity, the little officials who are too old to work and have been dismissed: porters, guardians of groves, grooms; you see store-yards, manure heaps, huts to house the horses overflowing from the royal stables. On the Place d'Armes, against the slope of the Ministers' wings, one-storied hovels serve at night as refuge for vagabonds. The Comte d'Angiviller, Director General of the buildings, writes: 'Soon there will not be a single wall which is not lined with a row of booths or shops.' In the Rue de Bel-Air—in contrast with this coquettish name—lodging house-keepers housed pedlars, masons, knife grinders, parasol merchants of Auvergne, hawkers. . . .''

Everyone in the town let out rooms or lodgings to somebody. The chamber-maids of the chamber-maids of great ladies had to stuff themselves somehow or other into rat-holes, where the rain filtered through the garret windows which were never mended, in attics without air or light, where one froze in winter and suffocated in summer. And of course the pubs were full of a noisy crowd of cheats, tricksters and quarrelsome pickpockets who were quite beyond the control of the police.

In November, something very exciting happened. The physicist Charles went up in a balloon. (True, Pilâtre de Rozier had preceded him by forty days. Twenty minutes after leaving La Muette, he came down in the Faubourg of the Gobelins without catastrophe.) But Charles was a scientist, not a madman. In five weeks he evolved, all of a piece, the science of air navigation. He discovered that he could blow up his "globe" not with hot air, but with hydrogen gas. He invented the escape valve for the gas, the nacelle for the passengers, the net which enveloped the balloon and supported the nacelle, and the coating of india-rubber which made the material waterproof. He had the brilliant idea of bringing some ballast, to regulate the ascent and moderate the descent, and took a barometer to verify the height reached by the aerostat. The excitement penetrated to Montreuil.

"Please, Madame, if you please, Madame."

"Yes, Monsieur de Chamisot?" said Elisabeth, glancing at her page on November 30th of that year. "What do you want?" (She knew without being told.)

"If Madame would graciously allow me to go to Paris with Monsieur de Tilly to-morrow . . . I want to see the balloon going up from the Tuileries gardens."

"Yes, you may go. As long as you don't get into mischief with Monsieur de Tilly afterwards. And," she added graciously, "come and tell me all about it."

On the evening of December 1st, he came back brimming over with enthusiasm. Indeed, there had been 400,000 Parisians squashed into the Tuileries gardens, and on the quays, squares and bridges. At a quarter to two, a cannon was fired. "And Madame, gently, gently, we saw a huge sphere painted with yellow and red stripes floating up into the air, and Monsieur Charles and his mechanic Robert waving streamers and greeting us all. The wind was in the north-east, the sky cloudless. It seems that the airmen, as they went by Argenteuil to l'Isle-Adam, talked to the peasants on the way. These peasants were absolutely stupefied and uttered great cries of admiration and fear; they tried to keep up with the balloon and kept calling out to the two passengers: 'Good friends, aren't you frightened? Aren't you ill? We pray God that He will keep you.' And Charles and Robert answered: 'God Save the King.'"

Elisabeth laughed her hearty laugh. "I must tell the King when I see him. But pray continue; your story is thrilling."

"Well, Madame, when they got to l'Isle-Adam, they asked for the Prince de Conti at his château. A man with a very strong carrying voice replied that Monseigneur was in Paris and would be so vexed at having missed them. After two hours of this delicious excursion, the airmen came down near Nesles. Just as the balloon was skimming the earth, hundreds of village people chased after it, just like children trying to catch a butterfly in a field. A troop of horsemen appeared from Paris. The Duc de Chartres was amongst them. He's absolutely enchanted and wants to try the experiment himself. But it was an Englishman, Ferrer, who had the joy of clasping the happy airman in his arms. He was trembling with joy and stammering 'Monsieur Charles! Me first!' It seems Charles was so overcome at being the first human creature to rise in infinite space among the eternal solitudes, that he swore never again to expose himself to such emotions."

Elisabeth went on sewing a night shift for a woman expecting her first child. Adalbert de Chamisot's cheeks were like poppies and his eyes like stars. "Oh, and Madame, please Madame, may I go and call on Monsieur Charles to-morrow? He lives in the Place des Victoires. Many masters are sending their servants with messages of congratulations. And the market women are going to crown him with laurels."

"Yes. Just for once I'll be lenient." And then Adalbert quite forgot himself—he pirouetted several times on one toe, in the way his dancing master had shown him Monsieur Vestris would do, and kept crying out "Madame! Madame!"

The next day, a procession of peasants and musicians accompanied the carriage of the deflated balloon. All the Parisian ladies began dreaming about the hero of the air, although he was far from being handsome, with that jutting-out nose which is so typical of airmen. And one young girl certainly lost her heart to him when she attended his lectures on the experiment, for she sent him a rose which she begged him to wear, and some touching letters.

Balloons formed the principal topic of conversation of the following year, and contributed to the entertainment of visiting sovereigns. Gustavus III of Sweden, travelling back from Italy incognito, reached Paris on June the 7th, and the same evening appeared at Versailles without announcing his visit beforehand. The King, who had been hunting at Rambouillet, hurried back, and, as he was not expected, probably failed to find his valets. He dressed quickly and appeared before his royal guest with one red-heeled and one black-heeled shoe— a gold buckle and a silver buckle. The Swedes were called the French of the North. The Queen's heart secretly beat a little faster, for Axel Fersen was coming too. "Your Majesty," she said to the King of Sweden, "if you are here towards the end of the month, you will see something *very* exciting."

On June 23rd, a fire balloon was sent up at Versailles from the Ministers' courtyard, in the presence of the King of Sweden. It was decorated with the initials of Louis XVI and Gustavus III and called the "Marie-Antoinette". This balloon, twenty-four feet high and fifty feet in diameter, piloted by Pilâtre de Rozier, rose without the slightest difficulty, to the great admiration of the spectators. The Duchesse de Polignac, who was now governess to the royal children, could be seen giving the Dauphin some useful information from the balcony and pointing to the skies. This balloon hovered over St. Denis, to the horror of the Carmelite nuns trembling in their garden. Madame Louise was quite perturbed. In the following September she wrote to her great friend the Cardinal de Bernis in Rome : "I bless God that it did not fall in our enclosure. If that sort of thing goes on, no-one will be safe in his own home: the company will fall from the clouds like hailstones. To what lengths will this folly of balloons go, since even a Carmelite is talking about it! Though, it is true, I am more concerned for what will become of the poor men nesting inside, than for the results that might occur, and I pray a good deal for them."

The ladies of the royal house of St. Cyr were no less agitated about these apparitions from the skies, than the Carmelites. The Manuscript tells us some amusing things. At his second experiment, Montgolfier launched his balloon from the Château of Versailles, in the presence of the King, all the royal family and a prodigious concourse of spectators. When it fell in the wood of Vaucresson, they found the balloon separated from the basket, into which some animals had been placed. The sheep was eating in his cage, the duck appeared not to have suffered from his journey, but the cock's head had been crushed in the fall. . . . The balloon had hovered for a long time over a ploughman in his field, and he was terribly frightened. Thinking it was the Devil or some evil sprite, he went promptly to fetch his neighbours, who were as much lacking in valour as himself, and did not know what to do. After many discussions on this phenomenon, they all decided to beg the parish priest to come and say the prayers for exorcism of devils.

Balloons become all the rage: they were painted on snuff-boxes, and fans, carved on woodwork. Hairdressers and dressmakers created fabulous "coiffures à la Montgolfière", with the same zest with which they had once concocted "poufs à l'inoculation", complete with serpents.

The dissolute Duc de Chartres arranged to go up in a balloon at Saint-Cloud. When he had ascended a mere hundred feet, he lost his head and insisted on coming down immediately. The conductors dared not refuse. He was hissed by the spectators, and his family was greatly grieved. It was a source of affliction to the Duc de Penthièvre, who spoke of it only to his confessor, and exhorted his grandsons to remember the dignity of their name and race and not to forget the deeds of their ancestors!

His wife, the Duchesse de Chartres, consoled herself by going for a country visit with the Duc de Penthièvre and the Princesse de Lamballe to a château near the Trappist Abbaye de Sept-Fons. She and the Princesse de Lamballe returned to court in ecstasies about a fascinating new novice at the Abbaye who had left a brilliant military career to bury himself alive there in eternal silence, because the woman he loved had died.

Madame de Lamballe chattered away about him to Marie-Antoinette and Elisabeth as they were walking around the lake of the Hameau, where the new cottages were being built. "We were *charmed* with this new novice in his long white habit, delighted by the qualities of his mind and the nobility of his thoughts. We became quite friendly with this lover who was faithful after death. I was glad that our rank allowed us to go into the enclosure. The Superior received us very hospitably; he said that when we came into the monastery, a ray of spring penetrated the eternal winter of his house." ("Humph," thought Elisabeth, to herself. "Can't have a vocation to think like that. Every good monk should love his cell.")

Marie-Antoinette's nebulous attention, which floated airily like the fashionable balloons, was tethered at last. She said enthusiastically: "Ah, *mon cher cœur*, if only I could meet your monk!"

François Bernard Auguste de Sallmard de Montfort did not visit Versailles till four years later, when he was forty-one. The Queen received him as a friend in her private suite. He had then been elected Superior of Sept-Fons and came to court to further the interests of his abbey. On his appointment, he wrote to his benefactor, the Duc de Penthièvre: "Your kindliness, Monseigneur, has brought me out of the shadow of the tomb, to give me back to the light of life. God, no doubt, has allowed this resurrection, and may His will be done!"

If at Versailles he became again a man of the world, at Sept-Fons he remained the strict Prior who would not allow any relaxing of the Rule. His monks still ate meagrely, out of pewter plates in the frozen refectory, vegetables cooked in water. They slept in their habits on hard boards. They never spoke. They rose at two o'clock in the morning to say Office and remained up.

However, in the few surviving letters which the Prior wrote to the Duchesse de Chartres, we see him again falling a victim to tender sentiment. Perhaps he felt sorry for this unhappy wife of the dissolute

Chartres. Elisabeth's feelings on meeting such a religious may safely be imagined. Her widening experience of life, her understanding of the vagaries of human beings, lent point to the advice she gave later to one of the de Causans girls about religious vocation.

In that June of 1784, Louise de Causans was married to the Marquis de Raigecourt, and thenceforward nicknamed Rage. In the same way that Angélique de Bombelles was called Bombe and the Marquise des Monstiers-Mérinville was Démon. This marriage was really a *tour de force* on the part of Elisabeth, who had intrigued so that she would never be parted from her beloved friend. First of all she begged the severe mother to let Louise be her lady-in-waiting. Madame de Causans had needed a good deal of wheedling and placating. Elisabeth hugged her several times, crying out: "Don't refuse me. Please let her stay on. I know your manner of thinking. Don't worry. I will see to everything." (And then, the bombshell!) "I'm going to get her married."

"But, my dear princess, she has no dowry."

"That's all right, that's exactly what I'm going to see the Queen about. Good-bye, good-bye. Come along, Monsieur de Chamisot. To the Queen's apartments as fast as we can go." Once there, Elisabeth made a frontal attack. "I have a favour to ask you, *ma sœur*. But a favour which does not brook the possibility of a refusal."

The Queen replied, "Is this favour then granted in advance?"

"No, but promise me that it will be."

"I won't do anything of the kind."

And they went on teasing and twitting one another for some time.

At last: "I want to give Causans fifty *écus* for her dowry: get the King to advance me for five years the thirty thousand livres which he gives me each New Year's Day."

The Queen promised, the King gave his consent, and the marriage took place.

And for several years, on New Year's Day, when people at court noticed that Elisabeth received no present from the King, she would always say: "I haven't any yet, but I have my Raigecourt.

·   ·   ·   ·   ·

L

One July night of that year, anyone wandering in the park might have seen a beautiful young woman, singularly like the Queen, slip out from behind a hornbeam hedge and give a rose to the Cardinal de Rohan: unknown to all but the criminals involved, the first act of the Necklace Affair was being enacted.

. . . . .

In 1785, on March 27th, a second prince was born to Marie-Antoinette, and called Louis Charles, with the title of Duc de Normandie. Knowing the filthy songs which were being sung all over Paris about her and her child, Marie-Antoinette trembled at the thought of driving to Notre Dame for her public thanksgiving. She announced that she was going to take the Dauphin with her in her carriage, hoping that the sight of this charming and lovable child would disarm the hatred of the populace.

"Oh, no, no!" cried the Comtesse de Provence, "I wouldn't hear of such a thing. It is quite against etiquette. I alone have the right to sit next to you in the carriage."

Marie-Antoinette bit her lip. How she longed to say: "I am the Queen here and I will do as I like in my own carriage." But it was no good. The dice were too heavily loaded against her. They all hated her —Mesdames Tantes, her two hideous sisters-in-law from Savoie, Madame de Marsan, Madame de Noailles. And all that crowd of women whom she would not receive at court: Madame de Balbi (the mistress of Provence), Madame de Genlis, the Princesse de Monaco. . . . In the nursery quarters, they were even trying to put the Dauphin against her. Whenever he was forbidden to do anything, they said that it was by her express orders. Her dear friend Gabrielle de Polignac was under the thumb of her lover Vaudreuil. How rapacious they all were! They only came to Trianon for what they could get out of her. Marie-Antoinette clenched her tambour-frame in a great effort at self-control. Just then, Elisabeth looked up at her across the supper table, with love and affection shining in her blue eyes. She did not speak, but Marie-Antoinette understood that she had a real friend very near. When they had been girls, they had romped and played hide-

and-seek together, in spite of Madame de Marsan's efforts to part them. Yes, from the first, she had loved the little wild creature who had been kept in the background. She had sensed that she would always be loyal to her. What a pity that she could not confide in her about Axel Fersen. But even without saying a word, she felt that Elisabeth understood everything. She was a peerless sister-in-law.

The procession to Notre Dame was a terrible ordeal. The Queen, exhausted with the heat, thought she must shorten the ceremonial at the Church of Sainte Geneviève, and the little people who loved the patroness of Paris even more than the Blessed Virgin Mary herself, all murmured against "the Queen's impiety". Not a single cheer in the streets. Dead silence. Madame de Provence at her side could not conceal a little victorious smile. On returning to the Tuileries, Marie-Antoinette was so upset, that she avoided her courtiers who were waiting for her. She went up by a small staircase, peremptorily dismissed Madame de Provence, and locked herself up in her room with Elisabeth. She burst into tears. "Ah, *ma sœur*, what have I done to the good people? They loved me once. I was born under a malignant star. If only Mamma were alive! She always used to say it was an ill omen to be born on the day of the Lisbon earthquake. I seem to bring bad luck wherever I go. Look at the stampede in the Place Louis XV during my wedding festivities! Why, there was even a thunderstorm on my wedding day!"

Elisabeth poured out some Hoffmann drops—the fashionable remedy for nerves. "What you need, my little sister, is a week or two at Petit Trianon, and we'll go and watch the progress of the Hameau. Now don't cry, or you will make your eyes red. I'll ring for Madame Campan. She'll get your hair arranged and you must lie down. Yes, we'll go and call on your old pensioned-off servants at Trianon or on some of your orphans."

CHAPTER XIV

The Model village at Petit Trianon, and the Necklace Affair

THE Hameau of Petit Trianon was a great consolation to Marie-Antoinette, particularly as she could take her children there. They played with their lambs and goats, fed the chickens, watched the baby chicks bursting their shells, and cultivated little cottage gardens of their own. Rustic hamlets were in the fashion. The Prince de Condé had a model village at Chantilly, though one will remember that his cottages were rather a sham, as the interiors were gilded drawing-rooms with blue brocade chairs. The Queen gave tea-parties for her children's friends, and she and the King used to serve them. Little Elzéar de Sabran boasted to the end of his days that the Queen had kissed him. Marie-Antoinette always adored children. In summer, she had an elegant tent put up in front of the château of Petit Trianon, and on Sunday afternoons the gates were opened and people from the neighbourhood were allowed in, if they were decently dressed, and they all danced quadrilles. The Queen would go around to the various groups and have the children presented to her. Even Madame Adélaïde could not have objected, for she herself played the violin for her own villagers when they danced at Bellevue. As Taine has said, "Everywhere, as society is approaching its end, there falls a common gentleness, an affectionate softness, like a mild breath of autumn, to temper whatever is hard or dry and to envelop in a perfume of dying roses, the refinement of its last moments." Yes, Le Nain, who painted the sad-faced peasants of the seventeenth century, would never have recognised their alleged descendants, dressed à la Greuze. Nor would brocaded Marie Leczinska have recognised a Queen of France dressed in this floating, fine lawn gown, with lace fichu and head-dress. How greatly she would have disapproved of those simple straw hats which were all the rage.

A lot of nonsense has been talked about the Hameau. People have

164

said that the Queen built twelve houses in which she put twelve poor families, even installing an old hermit in the presbytery to lead them in a virtuous life. This was quite untrue. There were only three families in the model village—the farmer, the guard, and the gardener. The place named *le presbytère* was nothing more or less than a chicken house. We may also discount the legend propagated by a German traveller, that the Queen used to disguise herself as a farmer's wife, the Cardinal de Rohan as the parish priest, the Comte de Provence as the schoolmaster. All this is just as ridiculous as the legends about the Queen's extravagance which circulated in Paris at the time, so that at the eve of the Revolution the country bumpkin deputies, pouring into Trianon from the provinces, were disappointed at the simplicity of it all and kept asking for the drawing-room with diamond-lined walls. "And where were the twisted columns studded with rubies and sapphires?"

We owe a great deal to the American millionaire who restored the cottages, for quite lately they were falling into ruin. The wooden houses form a semi-circle around the lake. They have exterior spiral staircases, and on each step, just as in her day, there are plants in blue Sèvres flower pots with her initials interlaced. There is the water mill, the boudoir, the Queen's house, the guard's lodging, the gardener's, a barn, a chicken house and "la tour de Marlborough", so called because of the tune *Marlboro s'en va-t-en guerre*, which Madame Poitrine, the wet-nurse, used to sing to the Dauphin. Near it is the dairy and the fishing tower. The farm proper was by the wood called "*le bois des onze arpents*". Each house still has its own little enclosure with its tiny garden filled with fruit trees—nuts, cherries, plums, pears, peaches, apricots. As the Queen insisted that all the gardens should be full of flowers as soon as it was spring, Mique had to order a hot-house, so that plants could be cultivated during the winter and be ready in time. The lake was stocked with carp and pike. How different all this was from the early days of 1781, when the Petit Trianon account books in the National Archives have the following delightful entry: "To Bellet, six livres for two days hiring of his donkeys, which same donkeys have stayed during the visit to Trianon and served every day for Madame Elisabeth and for the other ladies."

It is most interesting to find the names of the little colony. There is the English gardener Eggleton who was paid forty guineas a year, but he'd been sick for such a long time and had cost the Queen so much during his illnesses, that he had to be sent back to England with a gratuity. In the farm lodged Valy Bussard, the cow-herd, who earned 125 livres a month, and there was the mole-catcher Lecourt, the rat-catcher Samuel Hirsch (no modern "vermin exterminator" there!), the ferreter Chartier and the reaper Riaux.

The Queen would take her children into what was called the "*Laiterie de propreté*" to which were brought the finished products of the dairy. In there, her guests would taste her delicious cream in Sèvres bowls. And then she would collect eggs, obligingly placed under the bushes by the staff, drag away the King from the grove where he was reading, to eat wild strawberries with her in the meadow, or watch the cows being milked. There is an old engraving which shows Louis XVI at the top of the tower pointing out the view to the Dauphin. There are many fascinating engravings still extant. How pleasant it would be to discover one of the royal family fishing together, or Marie-Antoinette doing embroidery or network or even spinning a distaff. It would be so delightful to see her in her white cambric dress, playing with her children. She loved going for walks; as early as 1782 she was taking long walks alone in the country. One day, the painter Boze was in an inn at Rocquencourt near by. He noticed the Queen who was drinking a cup of milk. She lowered her veil and put her finger on her lips to forbid him to recognise her.

Trianon was a refuge for her in the most unhappy months of her whole life, during the Necklace Affair and the subsequent trial which unleashed all the slumbering hatred of her enemies and was really the first act of the Revolution.

For the benefit of those who are not familiar with this odious page in French history, or who have not yet read the great book "L'affaire du Collier" by Funck-Brentano, this is the story in a nutshell. The Cardinal de Rohan, hated by the Empress Marie Theresa for being "a huge volume of evil language", was a man who "preferred the boudoir to the sacristy". He has been described as "an ecclesiastical Don Juan glittering in golden chasubles". His pastoral ring was priceless and his lace rochets filled fashionable beauties with envy. In Vienna, where he kept a stable of 50 horses, 10 scarlet-clad musicians and a staff of 200, he wondered why he was so ill served. He was continually going to the theatre and always wearing the different hunting uniforms of the nobles he visited. One Corpus Christi day, he and all the men of his embassy, in green uniforms slashed with gold, broke through a religious procession which blocked the way to a princely hunting party. Marie-Antoinette took an instant dislike to him. She never invited him to Petit Trianon, although he once bribed the porter to let him in during a night party in the gardens. He looks extremely harmless in the picture which hung in the Hôpital des Quinze-Vingt, with his little white powdered wig, his graceful feminine features, his pretty, almost cherubic mouth, and his arched eyebrows. And yet it was the eighteenth-century cherubs who were its evil fates. Greatly interested in sorcery, he got mixed up with Cagliostro. It was at this charlatan's house that he met an unscrupulous adventuress, beautiful, intelligent and very bold, the Comtesse Jeanne de Lamotte-Valois, descended from a natural son of Henri II and Diane de Poitiers. (The forgotten sins of kings, rearing up from the dung-heap of oblivion, to scourge their far distant descendants. . . .) Penniless and ambitious, this Lamotte woman resorted to all manner of subterfuge to be received at court, even trying the usual trick of fainting in the Galerie des Glaces to attract the Queen's attention, but without effect. She must have been like Madame Roland, who went to stay with a servant at Versailles when she was a child, and who became so filled with envy of the nobility that she thought she would burst with hatred. Suddenly, the Lamotte was inspired with a brilliant idea. She'd exploit the passions of the Cardinal de Rohan. When she met him again and heard him complaining that he was in the Queen's bad books, she hinted that she was very much "in" with her Majesty, and saw her often. The Cardinal asked her if there could be any means of effecting a reconciliation. After a time, she assured him she had been able to do this. She even hired a prostitute called Oliva, whom she picked up in the Palais Royal gardens, and who greatly resembled the Queen, to impersonate her one dark night of July 28th, 1784, in the grove of Venus at Versailles. Dressed in a white gown and with her head wrapped in a floating veil, this Oliva suddenly appeared from behind a hedge, presenting the trembling Cardinal with a rose, but was prevented from saying very much to him, because the watchful Comtesse de Lamotte rushed out, whispering: "Quickly, quickly, someone is coming." Quite soon afterwards, Madame de Lamotte told the Cardinal she'd heard the Queen say that she wanted a magnificent diamond necklace, assembled by the jeweller Boëhmer, and that she had chosen him to negotiate the purchase in secret. His public forgiveness, indeed, perhaps a great deal more, would be the reward of this service. He was shown forged letters signed "Marie-Antoinette de France". He ordered the necklace in the Queen's name, brought it to Versailles and gave it to Madame de Lamotte. It has always been said that the adventuress kept the necklace, split it up, paid her debts and began to live in the lap of luxury. But recently there has been a theory that the Cardinal must have got his share of the winnings, because from then until the end of his life he was no longer financially embarrassed. Anyway, they say that a part of the necklace has been sold to an Indian prince and that it always brings ill-luck to the woman who wears it. The months went by. After a while, the Cardinal grew uneasy when he saw that the Queen never wore the necklace, and that she continued to treat him as coldly as ever. The jeweller, on his part, anxious to receive the first instalment of payment on the date promised, asked Marie-Antoinette to pay him. At first she thought he had gone mad, and then slowly the hideous truth began to dawn on her. She thought the Cardinal had used her name to steal the necklace and she rushed to the King demanding justice and prompt punishment. The Cardinal was arrested in his pontifical robes, on his way through the Galerie des Glaces to say Mass on the Feast of the Assumption, August the 15th, 1785. As he was connected with many of the great houses of France—Condé, Guémenée, Rohan-Soubise—one can imagine the commotion. Madame de Marsan, a Rohan-Soubise, and who already disliked the Queen sufficiently, was in a fine state of fury. It is a great pity that the King ever allowed this public trial to take place, for it overjoyed the Queen's enemies. Some even went so far as to think that she was the thief and the forger. Many whispered: "Oh, well, if the Cardinal had made a mistake, didn't he judge the Queen capable of selling herself for a jewel?" All the accumulated hatreds of years seethed up, rearing their heads like hissing snakes. During the Cardinal's imprisonment at the Bastille, the disloyal courtiers wore red and yellow ribbons which symbolised "the Cardinal on the straw". All the women of the Rohan family besieged the judges on their way to the Palais de Justice with flatteries, offers of bribes, and threats. When the Cardinal left the Bastille at six in the morning, to go to the Palais de Justice, he found all his family at the door, waiting for the judges. When they appeared, Madame de Marsan, in deep mourning, said to them, pointing to the other Rohans: "Sirs, you are going to judge us all." The Rohans were indeed petrified, because the rumour had spread through Paris that the Cardinal would be condemned. During his cross-examination, Madame de Marsan went to pray for him at Notre Dame.

According to the de Goncourts, this is what Elisabeth's governess had thought of Marie-Anoinette. "In the eyes of Madame de Marsan, this light, poised carriage of the Dauphine was the bearing of a courtesan: these ethereal lawns she wore were dubbed theatrical costumes to stir the senses. If the Dauphine lifted her eyes, Madame de Marsan saw in this the practised glance of a coquette. If she wore her hair free and floating, 'the hair of a bacchante!' she murmured: did the Dauphine speak with her natural vivacity, it seemed she spoke much without saying anything. In a conversation, if her face took on a sympathetic and intelligent look, it showed her intolerable pretence at understanding all; did she laugh with childlike gaiety, it was simulated cheerfulness and forced laughter. This old woman suspected and calumniated everything."

How independent and how loyal were Elisabeth's affections to have resisted this perpetual "drip-drip" since early childhood! One can imagine the Queen's intense anxiety before the final verdict on May the 31st, 1786. She was walking in the gardens of Petit Trianon with Elisabeth, heedless of the birds singing in the lilac bushes. "I've just been hearing about Lamotte woman's early life. She was a ragged urchin girl selling flowers in the Champs-Elysées. Because she looked pretty, a kind rich woman took her into her household and tried to bring her up properly. But she soon had to get rid of her, because she was so corrupt. Oh, the sublime audacity of it all! Do you know, when she was arrested at her birth-place at Bar-sur-Aube, she was just returning from a reception at the Abbaye de Clairvaux in honour of the feast of St. Bernard. The Prior, who lives like a prince, treated her with the greatest honour because of her association with the Cardinal: he had even invited her to the banquet. She had filled her house with pictures, fine silver and other *objets d'art*."

"Try not to think of it," said Elisabeth soothingly, "though I must say I am seething myself. I was furious in Lent about notices pasted up on the chapel doors, likening the imprisoned Cardinal to St. Paul. I don't relish the innuendo that my brother is Nero."

"I am afraid this is going to take the wind out of Madame de Marsan's sails. She won't dare appear at court."

Elisabeth sighed. "I hate to ask you this, you mustn't think I am being disloyal to you. You *must* know how I feel in all this, but Madame de Marsan brought me up. Would you mind if I went to call on her, very unobtrusively, for she is extremely upset?"

"No, I understand, *mon cœur*. Diane de Polignac always says that constancy was your chief virtue."

The Cardinal was acquitted by 26 votes to 23. Oliva was acquitted, Lamotte was ordered to be publicly whipped, branded with a hot iron and imprisoned at the Salpêtrière. The Cardinal was exiled to his abbey of La Chaise Dieu. One is rather shocked that the Princesse de Lamballe called at the Salpêtrière and asked to see the prisoner, but she was prevented from doing so by a humane Mother Superior, who said the prisoner was not on show. All Paris was bubbling with the scandal: Madame de Sabran wrote a very blood-curdling description of the branding in one of her letters to the Chevalier de Boufflers. Eventually Madame de Lamotte escaped and fled to London, where she published her odious memoirs, propagating the legend of the Queen's vices. It is from this book that the public prosecutor Fouquier-Tinville sought inspiration when he wanted to vilify the Queen during her trial before her execution.

The Comte de la Marck, who was a witness of all this, has written: "It is in the slanders and the lies spread between 1785 and 1786 against the Queen *by the court* that one must seek the pretext of the Revolutionary tribunal's accusations against Marie-Antoinette in 1793.

Obscene pamphlets, engraved, alas, with the arms of ancient houses, circulated in boudoirs. Some of them were put into elegant and powdered rhymes, and the great ladies would sing these obscenities to fashionable airs at intimate supper parties." As Monsieur de Nolhac has said, "But the windows are open. The passers-by in the street, listen, repeat, and from the drawing-room the songs descend to the tavern. This people to whom one teaches contempt for Queens and for mothers, will not forget any of the lessons it has received, and it is the refrains of the people of the court which will accompany them to the guillotine.

"From the Necklace Affair, France hastens towards the Revolution."

How strange that four days after the arrest of the Cardinal at Versailles, Marie-Antoinette acted the part of Rosine in the "Barbier de Séville" at Petit Trianon, in the presence of Beaumarchais. One will recall that he describes his heroine in these terms: "Imagine the pretty little pet, gentle, tender, easy, fresh, tempting, with her pretty foot, her slim waist, her trim figure, her plump arms, her pink lips and her hands! her cheeks! her teeth! her eyes!" And this was the Queen of France. Figaro was played by the Comte d'Artois, Almaviva by the Comte de Vaudreuil. How odd to hear Figaro exclaim: "Who knows if the world is going to last three weeks?" or again: "I hasten to laugh at everything, lest I should have to weep at everything." And here is his definition of the crescendo of calumny: "First a faint rumour, skimming the ground like a swallow before the storm, murmurs *pianissimo* and flits and drops the poisonous dart. A mouth picks it up, and piano, piano, drops it adroitly in someone's ear. The harm is done; it grows, spreads, makes its way, *rinforzando*, from mouth to mouth on its devilish path; then suddenly, no one knows how, you see calumny rise, hissing and growing before your eyes. It spreads, takes flight, whirls about, covers everything, rends, tears, thunders, and becomes, with the aid of heaven, a general cry, a public *crescendo*, an universal cause of hate and denunciation. The devil could withstand it."

. . . Four days after the Cardinal's arrest. . . .

CHAPTER XV

Louise de Condé, and last days at Versailles

IN June 1786, Princesse Louise de Condé, Elisabeth's great friend, fell in love, and so ruined the rest of her life. She did not confide any of this to her friend until the following year. Madame de la Ferté-Imbault, who had given Elisabeth lessons in philosophy, knew a great deal about the tribulations of the Condé family. It is not unlikely, when Elisabeth was tempted to judge the Princesse de Monaco severely for living in open sin with the Prince de Condé, that Madame de la Ferté-Imbault told her the truth about the whole affair. Indeed her story causes pity to overcome moral indignation, for the Princesse de Monaco had been hounded into marrying her mother's lover, and then was so ill-treated by this avaricious and violent lecher, that she left him and fell straight into the waiting arms of the Prince de Condé.

So this was the mistress of Louise de Condé's father. The tragedy of Louise's own life was that she fell in love with a man whom she could have married, and she was prevented from so doing by her father who was living in open adultery. When Elisabeth discussed this with Madame de la Ferté-Imbault, she must have been indignant at the unjust fate suffered by her friend. After it was all over, it is easy to picture Louise calling at Montreuil in early June of 1787. "Let us go to the rustic hut, I've told the footman to keep other callers away, and so we won't be disturbed." How changed was "Hébé-Bourbon"! Impossible to imagine her as a voluptuous water nymph entertaining the Comte and Comtesse du Nord. They said that after this unhappy love affair she never smiled again.

Louise began: "Elisabeth, have you heard anything of this from anybody?"

"Several people started telling me about something that had happened to you last year at Bourbon l'Archambault, but, as you know,

I never allow gossip in my entourage, so I changed the subject. The reputations of my friends are always quite safe here."

"I wish the same could be said in Paris, where no-one ever believes that a woman can have innocent motives. I think if some of the chatter had not reached my father's ears, he would not have been so set against it. Well, I see I must begin at the beginning and tell you. I went to Bourbon l'Archambault to take the waters, for I had been most unwell after breaking my leg. I arrived about the end of June, hoping to stay six weeks. I lodged in a small comfortable house, surrounded by a garden and a high hornbeam hedge. My father came ten days later, because he too did not feel very well. I followed the usual treatment—baths, massage, the waters. This was interspersed with short walks, rides or amateur theatricals. Poor father was so bored. . . . But I wasn't. I had met a Marquis de la Gervaisais, a small country squire from Brittany, who had been given leave by his regiment because he had hurt his ankle. At heart he wasn't a soldier, but a philosopher and a thinker. I was a little older than he was."

"What was his Christian name?" asked Elisabeth.

"Louis-Marc. He wasn't at all a man of the world, he was timid, even a little morose, and he certainly knew nothing about women. He'd just had an unhappy love affair which had put him against our sex. You would have loved him! He had such generous thoughts and noble ambitions. He was such an enthusiast, he loved mankind and felt sorry for its sufferings."

"Yes," said Elisabeth. "A great contrast to the men you usually meet. I can imagine that the irony of all your sceptical and blasé friends at Chantilly is not to your liking. Did he feel conscious of the difference in your position and ages?"

"Oh no. We felt completely equal. He used to say, the soul has no age, just as it has no sex. I didn't realise I was falling in love. To begin with, it was just a very deep, pure friendship. We seemed to understand one another after the first three days. Oh, how happy I was! He used to come and have breakfast with me in my room every day, and we went for quiet walks in the countryside, I leaning on his arm. Every morning, the time between six and half past eight seemed an eternity, and I spent that eternity in studying the clouds, for I was so frightened it might rain. We went for pilgrimages to the ruins of our ancestral seat, the old château de Bourbon, with its picturesque towers. We used to visit the poor, and I remember how his eyes filled with tears at the simplicity of one poor woman. Often, we never spoke at all. I was there with him, at his side, and I was content. I felt that he only needed to look at me to read what was taking place in my soul. And then, one day, we confessed our mutual tenderness to one another. Oh, Elisabeth, after that we indulged in day-dreams: we planned to have a little house in a vineyard, far away from prattling tongues, where we would live until we were old, never quarrelling. Alas! the time for parting came too quickly. I was in tears when I said good-bye to him. I felt I was choking. My last words were 'Love me well'. The dawn was breaking as I got into the travelling carriage to leave Bourbon l'Archambault. I gave one backward glance at the house where we had been so happy. For the rest of the journey, I had to pretend to bury my head in a book, so that they would not try and talk to me. During the night, I had to turn my face away, as I did not want the moonlight to reveal my tears. When I got back to Chantilly, I was obliged to smother everything, for the Comtesse d'Artois had announced her visit, and there were sixty guests to entertain."

"Ah! That is when you begin to wish you were not a princess," exclaimed Elisabeth. "I feel it myself when my friends are ill, and I have to leave with the court for Fontainebleau or Marly. We are never free. We are always the slaves of etiquette. But, were you able to write to one another?"

"Oh, often. It was my only delight. Every night I used to pour out my heart to him. And then father guessed. At first he was very kind and he wept when I did. I showed him one of Louis-Marc's letters and he realised that he loved me well. He even discussed with me how we could meet in Paris without attracting attention. Louis-Marc was planning to leave his regiment and join the Gardes Française in Paris. All was fixed for November. But alas! gossip had already begun. The people who had taken the waters at Bourbon were coming back to Paris and telling all kinds of stories about me. No one believed that our friendship had been completely innocent. I don't think there are ten people in Paris who put any faith in the chastity of women. The rumours spread to Chantilly. My faithful old maid, Lisette, asked me one day: 'Madame, is it true that at Bourbon there was a young man who came every day to have *déjeuner* with you?' Then a terrible thing happened. Father was informed of the suspicions against my honour. He overheard a very disagreeable conversation about me in his own drawing-room. He couldn't endure anything to tarnish the glory of the name of Condé."

"Humph!" thought Elisabeth to herself. "And what has he been doing to the illustrious name all these years?"

Louise continued: "His pride was wounded, he began to exert his paternal authority and he dictated a letter which I had to send, in which I put an end to the whole affair."

Elisabeth asked: "So you've been sacrificed to family pride?"

"Oh, I'm proud also. I confess that when I used to post my letters to him myself, so that my footmen should not read the name and address, I hated the whole clandestine business. But, oh! I've had to pay for my sacrifice. I've had a winter and spring of fevers and long swoons. However, I kept reminding myself that when one is very much in love, wisdom consists in flight. When I wrote my last letter to him in May, I was so afraid he would hate me afterwards. I begged him to put a little cross on the envelope, if his reply was not too upsetting. I was in my house of the Rue Monsieur at the time."

There was a long silence between the two friends. Then Elisabeth said gently, "Perhaps your election as Abbess of Remiremont will distract your mind from your troubles."

"Oh, that place, where you dance at carnival time! So you call that religious life? Imagine me making my solemn entry into Remiremont next August in a court gown, a sapphire ring on my hand and holding a golden crozier. And think of all the luxury of my Abbey drawing-rooms. . . . No, I would prefer the little house in the vineyard. But no, I must not allow myself to remember all that. Elisabeth, I should like to become a Poor Clare or a Benedictine, or even something more severe. A Trappistine."

"Or a Carmelite," said Elisabeth. "I am sure you'd love Carmel."

"Don't you ever wish you could become a Carmelite?"

"Oh! I have always wished it. But I feel they need me here. My poor Queen is terribly anxious about the baby—Madame Sophie. She's so ill. The Queen went through too much trouble with that Necklace Affair just before the child was born. I must stay here. However, I try to keep a rule of life at court. It's even harder here than it would be in the cloister."

"Elisabeth, aren't you ever very lonely?"

"Yes, I suppose I am. My intimate friends get married and then they become absorbed in their husbands and children. The Queen thinks it terrible to be a spinster. I suppose she's influenced by the fear that I might become embittered, like my poor aunts. But I don't feel bitter at all. I must stay by the Queen and my brother. I can't explain it to you, but I know they will need me very soon."

On June the 19th, eleven-months-old Madame Sophie died. Her tiny body was exposed at Petit Trianon, and she looked so adorably beautiful that no one believed she was dead. Madame Elisabeth wrote to Angélique de Bombelles: "If you only knew how pretty she was as she lay dying, it is incredible! Up to the day before, she was white and rosy, not emaciated, in a word, charming. If you had seen her, you would have become attached to her." The Queen wrote a letter to her beloved sister-in-law Elisabeth asking her to come and stay for a short time at Petit Trianon, to weep with her for the death of her poor little girl.

Elisabeth went on living her retired life. She had a new protégée. One of her friends, whom she always nicknamed Démon—Charlotte-Julie Hyacinthe de Labriffe d'Amilly—had married in January 1785 the Marquis des Monstiers-Mérinville and instantly began to have trouble with her mother-in-law. She was very pretty, witty, lively, but capricious and headstrong. Elisabeth did all she could to smoothe her way for her, and even spoil her a little. Some of the letters she has written to her are full of tenderness and worldly wisdom. One day, the severe mother-in-law refused to take Démon with her to the Opera. She was so furious that she started vituperating. When Elisabeth was informed of this, she summoned her and said: "My dear Démon, do you know that you are committing a very big sin here? I am going to the Opera to-night; I offer to take you there; for after all, if you do ill in going to the theatre, you are even more at fault when you rail against your mother-in-law." One day, Elisabeth said to her Démon: "You'll break your mother-in-law's heart." To which came the apt reply: "I can't: she hasn't got one."

On August the 1st of that year, St. Cyr celebrated its centenary. The crowds were so large that the eight Swiss Guards could not protect the doors. One night, Elisabeth came to the house she loved so much and saw fireworks and illuminations in her honour—six dozen Roman candles spelling out "Vive Elisabeth!" She listened to that fine air, which an Englishman, once overhearing, brought back to England, where it became our National Anthem. The Manuscrit of the house says that the festivities went on till midnight, and everybody wandered about the grounds, admiring the illuminations. They tell us how Madame Elisabeth, who was then twenty-two, "gave proof of her zeal for the upholding of propriety among our pupils. Seeing four *Demoiselles* straying a little from the mistresses, she took them up sharply, showing them what prudence demands in such circumstances." Indeed, she wrote in a letter to her dear Marie de Causans about her sister: "You are quite right not to leave her for a moment; nothing is more dangerous than the society of boarders; and as there are all types, it is safest to avoid them." Such a combination of chaste behaviour and worldly wisdom is rare. It was impossible to live long at Versailles without learning the depths to which women could sink. Elisabeth had a great sense of responsibility towards the ladies and young girls of her household, and was quite determined that under her care, they should come to no harm.

But they were far from being bored, as this last little anecdote about Montreuil will show. At the beginning of 1789, Elisabeth decided that the cows of her dairy should now be imported from Switzerland, as she wanted better quality milk for her poor people.

"Madame," said Madame de Diesbach, the wife of a Swiss officer, "Madame de Raigecourt tells me you want an honest Swiss cowherd from Fribourg. I think I know just the young man you need, who would not try and make a profit on the side—absolutely faithful and trustworthy."

"Yes, Madame, when it comes to the milk of my dairy, I am a

M

miser. I want the poor to be first served, and I will only accept some milk for my own household if there is a little over."

"Well, I think that Jacques is just the young man you need."

Jacques came, accompanied by his parents, and spent much of his time exclaiming to Madame de Diesbach: "Ah Madame, what a good princess! No, in the whole of Switzerland there is nothing so perfect."

Elisabeth was so struck with the uprightness and frankness of this young man, that she got Madame de Diesbach to enquire if he were quite happy at Montreuil, and not too home-sick. He confessed that he had left his cousin Marie Magnin in Switzerland, just as they were about to get married. She was breaking her heart at his absence, for she was afraid that he would forget her.

"Well," said Elisabeth in her gay voice, "let her be sent for, let them get married at St. Symphorien, and she will be the milkmaid."

Madame de Travanet, Angélique's sister-in-law, composed the air of "Pauvres Jacques" in honour of the occasion.

The dairy still exists to-day, though it is used as a laundry. It is easy to picture the Swiss cows with their coats spotted with black and russet, ambling in at milking time to the sound of Swiss cow-bells. The great nail-studded door through which the farm carts used to come, still exists, with its knocker, its iron bar, its antique hinges and enormous lock. One can also see the paving stones of the courtyard. The farm was an old house with dormer windows and two pavilions on either side. The stables opened out on to the courtyard, and there are still the iron rings to which the cows used to be tethered. The granary for hay over the stables still has its original roof. There is an uneven old staircase with an ancient iron handrail, and there is the same old sandstone drinking trough. On the right, as one goes in, is the original dairy, opening on to this yard. The walls are lined with eighteenth-century Delft ware—green and lapis lazuli stars on a white background. The original tiles are on the floor, but getting rather worn. It is delightful to think that the place where the poor used to come and fetch their milk had been practically undisturbed.

There is a record of Elisabeth's good deeds before the Revolution broke out. At the beginning of 1786, as a result of very dry weather, a great agricultural disaster threatened the countryside. The larvæ of cock-chafers were swarming in the ground and the sap of trees was being drained by millions of little worms called "*turcs*". The Montreuil gardeners hastened to tell their mistress, and she quickly informed all her neighbours. She then took energetic steps to deal with the scourge and much harm was averted.

She could never hear of people in need without doing something to help them. She heard of a man who had reached the age of 116 years; he was looked after by his only daughter who, of course, was also extremely old. She begged the King to send him some alms.

At the end of the second volume of the Beauchesne's life of Madame Elisabeth there is a pathetic account of how she gave employment on her estate to a poor man who used to clean the marbles at Versailles. She arranged that he was to be clothed and fed and given thirty *sols* a day. Unfortunately, the underling who was supposed to pay him, only gave him twenty-four *sols* and even less, and when the Revolution broke out, he was obliged to apply to the town hall for assistance. This only shows that often, the great enemy of the poor was the intermediate man and not the noble employer.

The King had promised that she should sleep at Montreuil when she was twenty-five. Alas! the day after her twenty-fifth birthday, in 1789, the Estates General went in solemn procession to the Cathedral of Saint Louis. The road from Paris was crowded with disquieting-looking people from all over the provinces, and it was considered unsafe for her to sleep away from the palace. During that procession, the Queen was insulted by women in the crowds, and she was so overcome that she nearly fainted and had to be supported by Elisabeth. Many noticed the changed expression of the Queen's face. Although she still held her head very proudly, she looked eaten away with care. And well she might be, for her eldest son, the Dauphin, was seriously ill, and on June the 4th he died.

No time for mourning.

On June the 20th the Tennis Court Oath, and all it implied. . . .

.   .   .   .   .   .

It was a terrible summer. No need to describe the capture of the Bastille by the Paris mob. Louis XVI is said to have exclaimed, "This

is a revolt"; and someone replied, "Sire, it is a revolution." And still
he went on hunting, and the days when he was not hunting, he wrote
in his famous journal the terrible little word "Nothing". How his
gallant sister's blood must have boiled. She knew that civil war was
looming ahead. She said that if the King didn't cut off two or three
heads now, there would be an immense carnage later. Gradually one
sees the whole situation getting more and more out of control. The
King, a good man, who did not want to shed French blood, was
pathologically unable to protect himself or his family. He was a man
of no personality, who could never inspire awe, although he often
aroused affection.

And then, what is mysteriously known as the "great terror",
swept over the land of France. Rumours of vague disaster, whole
countrysides trembling with terror of impending doom. Peasants
began burning down châteaux. If this had happened in England, the
English squires would quickly have organised a Home Guard and stood
no nonsense from the riff-raff. They would have arranged a day and
night watch from the roof or battlements, imprisoned any shifty
servants, and, if the armed bands had appeared at night, they would
have shot the lot at sight. But the nobles who burst into tears at the
pastorals of Florian, who wept copiously at the sentimental engravings
of squires inviting peasants to dine at their own tables, still believed
in the innate goodness of man, and were taken utterly by surprise.
Elisabeth, as the beloved châtelaine of Montreuil, was not insulted, but
Madame Vigée Le Brun tells us that, about that time, she noticed that
the peasants never took their hats off to their squires, and indeed sometimes they shook their fists at them. The general exodus of the nobility
began after the capture of the Bastille. The Polignacs, knowing how
unpopular they were, tearfully allowed themselves to be persuaded by
Marie-Antoinette to go into exile. The Rohans and the Duc de Coigny
also left. The Comte d'Artois followed suit: he was never to see his
sister again. She must have had some premonition of the finality of this
separation, for she was so upset when she said good-bye to him that
she fainted. Everybody begged her to go with her brother, but she
absolutely refused to leave the King and Queen. Madame de Raigecourt had just lost her first child, and indeed was to lose her second.

Elisabeth insisted on her going to the province of Berry with her husband. Angélique de Bombelles had just had a fourth child and was not really fit to travel, but Elisabeth said that she must go to her brother at Stuttgart before rejoining her husband in Venice. Angélique and Elisabeth were never to see one another again, although Angélique was always beseeching for permission to return to her princess. The heart-rending farewell took place very late at night. As usual the perfect friend, Elisabeth helped the young woman to prepare for her travels, made plans in the interests of her family and took every precaution that her journey should be a safe one. She showed her at which halting places she was to write to her. "We are parting for a time, but we will always be united in prayer and thought." It is in her long letters to her friends that we learn how Elisabeth spent the years of the Revolution. With great pluck she was always trying to reassure her friends about herself, and create an atmosphere of calm normality. "Montreuil and its mistress could not be in better trim (*se portent comme des cœurs*). This one writes to you from the closet at the end of the apartment. The books are placed in their cupboard: in truth it is a little jewel."

One evening, towards the end of September, the wife of a workman living in the Rue Porcherie-St Antoine, whom Elisabeth had helped during her husband's grave illness, came to talk to her privately. "Ah, *ma bonne princesse*, I feel I owe it to you to tell you of the danger which is threatening you. My husband has been influenced by one of his brothers, working in Paris, in fact he had queered his ideas. He's told him that the Parisians suspect the King of wanting to flee to Metz, but that they would know how to prevent him, and would soon come to take him away from his palace and bring him to Paris where they will keep an eye on him."

Elisabeth told all this to the Queen, who replied: "My sister, the King and I think there is a lot of exaggeration in all these rumours."

Ah, if only . . .

PART II

"The Refiner and Purifier of Silver"

CHAPTER XVI

Farewell, Versailles . . .

ON October the 2nd, Elisabeth's first woman of the bedchamber told her mistress about the guards' banquet, the night before. "Oh Madame, you should have heard the cheers, you should have seen the devotion on their faces. Monsieur le Dauphin was carried round from table to table, shoulder high, and he won all hearts by his charm. Why, the cheers could be heard in Paris."

And Elisabeth replied: "Let us hope that the people of Paris will not reply by insults."

．　　　．　　　．　　　．　　　．

October the 5th was a damp autumn day, with a promise of drizzle in the air. The King had gone hunting, the Queen went to sit in the grotto of Petit Trianon, alone with her sad thoughts. Elisabeth rode to Montreuil. She was just sitting down to luncheon, when someone came to tell her that all the women and brigands of Paris, fully armed, were marching on Versailles. (She wrote to Madame de Bombelles: "You can imagine that the princess was as quickly at Versailles, as I take time to tell you so. I learnt, however, before going, that there were 2,000 women armed with cords, with hunting knives etc. arriving at Versailles. They got there at 5 o'clock.")

When she reached the Place d'Armes, the soldiers of the Flanders regiment were quietly watching a puppet show.

The King was informed at Meudon, and, very anxious about his family, he galloped back through the Avenue de Paris. The women were so taken aback at his breakneck speed that they let him pass.

It began to rain. The family gathered in one room. Monsieur de Narbonne-Fritzlar said to the King: "The bridges of Sèvres and Saint-Cloud must be guarded; either the troop will renounce its project or it will pass by Meudon. Then, set on the height, I will pepper the troop with shot, and then pursue it with my cavalry, so that no one will return to Paris." The King refused, hoping to appeal to the better feelings of the mob.

By five o'clock, the mob had arrived. The "women" came first— men in disguise, placed there by the Duc d'Orléans, who counted on the King's soft-heartedness not to mow them down. Elisabeth, glancing out of the window of the King's council chamber, saw more and more shapes looming in the far distance, so that the Avenue was black with menacing figures, bristling with pikes, sticks and bayonets. Soon, shots were heard, and clamourings: "The guts of the Austrian woman, let's get her guts and take 'em to Paris." They invaded the two wings of the palace. The courtyards were soon filled with bare-armed females and butchers in woollen caps, howling and shaking their fists towards the balconies overlooking the Cour de Marbre. The King, refusing to listen to a plan of escape to Rambouillet, seemed dazed and stupefied, as if all control of the situation were slipping from his fingers. Weber, the foster-brother of the Queen, tells us that Elisabeth asked him to find out whether the great glow of light coming from the direction of the National Assembly, was not her country house, burnt by the Paris fish-wives.

It was a wet and windy night. The doors of the château were all guarded. Suddenly, towards two o'clock in the morning, the storm became a violent hurricane. The wind shook the château as if it would uproot it. At three o'clock, Elisabeth went to her suite in the south wing and fell into bed. She slept until half past seven, when she was woken by her maid saying breathlessly: "Madame, the King is sending a detachment of grenadiers to fetch you. The Queen's bodyguard has been attacked, some of the men were killed defending the Queen: she had to flee for her life down the secret passage to the King's suite."

The princess was so greatly upset to think of the dangers threatening her sister-in-law, that she ran through the blood-spattered rooms, without even noticing the corpses of the guards. When she reached the Queen, she was shaking in every limb.

Armed bands were still loose in the palace; some were breaking furniture and throwing it out of the windows. Women were shrieking: "The Queen's head for Paris. Her guts for ribbons."

Elisabeth soon mastered herself. She returned to her suite, leaving orders that the doors were to be left open, so that the wounded could be brought in and tended. She started bathing their wounds and bandaging them. Some of them escaped across fields and woods to Louveciennes, where, strangely enough, they were cared for by Madame du Barry (still beautiful, engaged in a love affair with a married man, the Duc de Cossé-Brissac, and totally unaware that she and her dead royal lover were among the main webs in this huge arras of doom). Afterwards, Elisabeth went back to the *petits appartements* and stood with the family at a window. The Dauphin, playing with his sister's hair, kept saying: "*Maman*, I'm hungry."

Suddenly, a horrible sight: the heads of the Queen's murdered guards shot up on the ends of pikes. Cries of "To Paris. To Paris." Madame Campan collected the Queen's jewels, Elisabeth went back to her rooms and packed her jewels and a few necessary clothes. It was nearly half past one, the hour at which they were due to start. The whole place was in disorder, and the maids seemed to have lost their heads. Elisabeth turned everyone out of her bedroom and locked the door for a moment. She went to the window and gazed out—for the last time. The rain had cleared, and it was a glorious autumn day. The wind had stripped the elm avenues, and dead leaves lay in sodden heaps on the paths. She glanced to the left, towards the Satory woods, where she had hunted so often. Then down at the pink marble steps of the *Cent Marches*, leading to the Orangery. A sudden pang went through her. Was this farewell? A knock at the door: "Madame, it is nearly half past one—his Majesty is waiting for you."

Monsieur Lenotre gives a fascinating account of the preparations at the Tuileries at that date. On October the 6th, Mique, the architect and inspector of the château, appeared all of a sudden, looking demented. We must imagine the whole place as it was then. The Place du Carrousel, which is now so spacious and well balanced, and from which we can see Cleopatra's Needle in the perspective of the Arc de Triomphe, was, in those days, a hotch-potch of private houses, barracks, huts, stables, (all so ill planned and huddled together that the

Queen lost her way in there on the night of the attempted escape to Varennes). The grille which we see nowadays dividing the Tuileries gardens from the Rue de Rivoli was then a high wall. The pavement of the Rue de Rivoli was a large grassy alley for horses. Where we now see the arcades of the shops, there were the boundary walls of the gardens of the Rue St. Honoré. That street—St. Honoré—contained three vast convents, and many orchards. The Palace of the Tuileries was divided into three pavilions, with high roofs. Pavillons de l'Horloge, de Flore, de Marsan. The Pavillon de Flore, destined for Madame Elisabeth, overlooked the wall of the terrace near the Seine. The château, which had not been occupied by a reigning monarch since the minority of Louis XV, had become a kind of "grace-and-favour" lodging where the inhabitants did pretty well what they liked. This historic place was invaded by an undisciplined, turbulent crowd. Lenotre tells us that the King's pensioners were nobles, artists and actors. They set about getting their own way, with a blend of patience and ruse; they made staircases, they turned drawing-rooms into kitchens, they pierced walls to get some daylight, they cut tall rooms horizontally into two storeys, they threw up partitions. Even so, they never had enough corridors, and often had to cross each other's kitchens. The place swarmed with heterogeneous and squabbling humans. It was icy cold in winter and very hot in summer. The chapel was so dilapidated that the priest said Mass in fear and trembling.

Mique gave a quick look round, collected his underlings and then dispatched them from one set of rooms to another, to tell the tenants they must be out by nightfall. There were cries, screams, imprecations, prayers, recriminations, hysterics, calls for indemnities for their expenses, but Mique was adamant. An army of porters fell on the place like a cloud of locusts, moving the furniture out. At the same time, a second cloud of carpenters came in to tear down the partitions, painters rushed in with their paint-brushes, and interior decorators tried in vain to hang curtains. The bedlam was indescribable. At seven o'clock at night, the functionaries of the King's household went round all the doors chalking up various hieroglyphics. If any of the infuriated inhabitants remained they would have seen extraordinary titles like these: the Waiters of Madame's ladies. Queen's kitchen, serving as Madame's warming-up room. The King's ice-house. The Creamery. The Fruit depôt, the German bakery (for the Queen's Viennese bread). And the physicians: the 1st and 2nd surgeon, the 1st and 2nd apothecary. The members of the royal households were scattered in lodgings all around. Some rooms were let in the Rue du Chantre for the Queen's maids, and the secretaries of the kitchen aids. These parasites, stifling the royal power, afforded such a contrast to the new ideas, and seemed hopelessly out of date, even mediaeval. Parisians who had not seen the functioning of the court for nearly a century, tittered at this avalanche of thousands of functionaries, with their antiquated and amusing titles.

In the meantime, the King got into his carriage with the Queen and Madame Royale. The Duchesse de Tourzel, the royal governess, sat in front, holding the Dauphin on her knees, with Madame de Provence by her side. Monsieur de Provence and Elisabeth were by the doors. "Look after my Versailles," the King had begged the Marquis de la Tour du Pin.

As the coach lumbered out into the Avenue de Paris, something terrible happened. The inhabitants of Versailles, who owed everything to the presence of the monarch and his court, and who were to be ruined by the Revolution, all swarmed into the roadway, cheered and clapped their hands with glee and jeered at the royal family. To her dying day, Elisabeth never got over this. She often bewailed this act of treachery in letters to her friends. "But the people of Versailles, Monsieur, have you ever seen such frightful ingratitude?" Yes, they were indeed monsters, in league with the bandits accompanying the royal family to Paris. Each soldier had a loaf of bread stuck on to the end of his bayonet. The guards' heads were still on pikes. Carts followed, full of sacks of flour, and fish-wives decorated with garlands of leaves. And, instead of the cry "Vive le Roi", it was now "Vive la Nation".

They went at a snail's pace. Instead of doing the journey in one and a half hours, they did not reach Paris until ten o'clock that night—eight and a half hours. As they passed in front of the terrace of Montreuil, Elisabeth leaned forward to glance at the home she had called her "little jewel". With a sad smile, the King said: "You are greeting Montreuil?" She replied: "Sire, I am saying good-bye."

She was never to see it again.

It is easy to imagine the feelings of the cowherd Jacques and the rest of her household, as they watched the royal coach disappear into the distance.

Inside the coach—and Elisabeth always hated being imprisoned inside coaches—the little Dauphin kept wailing: "*Maman*, I'm hungry."

When they reached the Champs-Elysées, the procession was watched by Chateaubriand. Afterwards, he described it in his 'Mémoires d'Outretombe': "The king's carriages followed: they rolled in the darkness of dusk surrounded by a forest of pikes and bayonets. Rag-pickers in tatters, butchers with blood-spattered aprons around their thighs, with unsheathed knives at hip, shirt-sleeves rolled up, walked by the carriage doors; other black satyrs had climbed on to the roof; others were clinging to the lackeys' foot-boards or to the coachman's seat. Gun and pistol shots were being fired; everybody crying 'Here is the baker, the baker's wife and the little journeyman baker'."

The heads of the two murdered bodyguards had been curled and powdered by a Sèvres hairdresser.

. . . . .

Behind them, the vast palace of Versailles, empty for the first time since 1715. No sound but that of doors being locked, floors being washed clean of blood, windows closed, shutters bolted (those wonderful white and gold shutters with their perfect carving). The clocks chimed in the desolate rooms. In the Queen's bedchamber, so nearly a scene of carnage, the clock tinkled its delicate tune of harps and flutes which she was never to hear again.

The monarchy was dead.

. . . . .

J. M. Thompson says in "The French Revolution": "In 1789, nearly all respectable authorities . . . wished to retain the monarchy. But they thought of it as stock on which republican institutions could be grafted. Only if the stock proved repugnant to this process, would they consent to root it up. The number of deputies who were not monarchists could have been counted on one hand."

.   .   .   .   .   .

When the King and his family arrived at the Tuileries palace at ten-thirty, the Dauphin was asleep. The poor child had to be wakened. This whole sad story is interspersed with the broken sleep of two children, the weariness of young creatures pushed about from pillar to post.

How black this palace seemed, in strange contrast to the brightly lit streets. As she stepped into the entrance of the Pavillon de Flore, Marie-Antoinette began to cry. Elisabeth said: "*Ma sœur*, are you not feeling well?" "I'm cold," replied Marie-Antoinctte. "I feel I'm going into a vault."

And indeed, Chateaubriand called the place a jail. Several days later, the Queen's secretary, Monsieur Augeard, said to her bluntly: "Your Majesty is a prisoner."

They were prisoners in that they could not go to other royal residences, lest they made this a pretext for escape; they dared not receive old friends too often, lest they compromise them; also their palace was guarded day and night. But in one sense, they appeared deceptively free: they had not yet been deposed, and they could write letters, which they smuggled out—not realizing that many of them were seized. They were behind bars, though these bars were still gilded.

CHAPTER XVII

The palace of the Tuileries

THE Dauphin, brought up in charming surroundings, said: "*Maman*, everything is ugly here." The carved woodwork was decaying with damp, the tapestries were faded and ragged, the furniture was of Louis XIV's time, and some of the chair seats had mouldered. The vast state apartments had not been heated since the time of Louis XV's childhood.

Autumn closed in, damp, dark and rainy. Elisabeth, who had been lodged on the ground floor, soon asked to be moved to the first floor, because some fish-wives climbed into her rooms through the windows and frightened her. They did not mean ill; indeed, they blessed her as she breakfasted at her window, and called out, "Isn't she beautiful." She was always nicknamed "the Sainte Geneviève of the royal family". But Elisabeth was not used to this yet, and she had been badly shaken that last morning at Versailles.

Soon, some semblance of court life was restored. Ladies came to pay their court, dressed in white, with white ribbons, and carrying bunches of the traditional lilies. Mass was said in the Chapel Royal. (The delightful picture by Hubert Robert shows the royal family hearing Mass, in an improvised state room, with mythological tapestries on the walls. Elisabeth is in white, kneeling on a prie-Dieu, holding her missal.) On Thursdays, there was a public dinner, in full dress, as of old. The faithful Princesse de Lamballe, who, like a true friend, had refused to emigrate, insisted on staying to serve the Queen although the future looked black for the Queen's friends. She occupied the ground floor of the Pavillon de Flore, and there, for the Queen, she entertained new people, like social-climbing Madame Necker, who had certainly never been invited at Versailles. But the whole tone and atmosphere was different: that gaiety, that respectful deference had vanished. And the subjects of conversation were certainly new: no

longer the latest play, the modish head-dress, or the raciest scandal, but
plans for the new Necker hospital, in which there would never be
more than one patient in each bed, and for which Madame Necker,
Protestant though she was, would not employ lay nurses, but asked for
nuns from the Superior of St. Vincent de Paul. They also discussed the
formation of a philanthropic society for helping the poor. So many
servants were out of work, with their masters in exile or ruined. The
streets of Paris were flooded with them. All the luxury trades had
fallen into a decline.

Now that the Polignacs were gone, and the d'Artois too, with
Mesdames Tantes safely at Bellevue, the Queen and Elisabeth were
drawn more closely together in friendship. Whatever she felt privately, Elisabeth struggled to preserve outward self-control. Her
letters are full of this longing to keep calm. Together they worked on
an immense piece of embroidery in *gros-point* for the throne-room.
On a dark-brown foundation, they scattered brightly tinted sprays of
roses, marguerites and convolvulus, shaded in their natural tints.[1] When
two women are sharing a piece of needlework, they can talk quite
simply and naturally. Elisabeth had that rare and enchanting gift of
making light of her own troubles and taking those of her friends to
heart. One day the Queen said to her: "I saw Jacques driving up to
bring you your cream to-day, *ma sœur*. How is your Montreuil . . .?"

"All is well, *ma sœur*. My best cow is expecting to calve, and so is
Madame Jacques. The cowherd comes every day, and they are all so
devoted. I wish I could say the same of those monsters at Versailles!"

"Yes, alas!"

"However, who knows: better days may come. I'm keeping up
everything at Montreuil as if I were returning there in the near future.
Coupry, Marie and Madame de Coudray come and see me sometimes
and keep me in touch. The drawing-room was being furnished as I
left: it promises to be very pleasant. I forget whether you saw my little
closet at the end? It's very pretty. My library is nearly finished. As for

[1] At the Restoration, Madame Royale, then Duchesse d'Angoulême, gave two
pieces for the Chapelle Expiatoire built over the site of the first tomb of her parents,
another piece to the Princesse Louise de Bourbon-Condé at the Temple, where she
was Abbess of a convent of Benedictine nuns, and a third portion to the Church of
Sainte Geneviève.

N

the chapel, I've left Corille to work at it alone, so you can imagine if the work goes on quickly. It is even out of charity for him that I have allowed him to put a little plaster there. Talking of the library, my book-boxes have come. Do you want to borrow any books?"

"Thank you, let me look at what you've got: my book-boxes have arrived, also, but they can find nowhere to put them."

Together they went to the Pavillon de Flore and examined the shelves. Here is a selection of the 100 books (taken from the list at the end of Beauchesne). The works of Cicero, Seneca, Horace and Plutarch. Treatise on Friendship, by M. de Sacy. Gibbon's "Decline and Fall". Sacy's Bible, in 31 volumes. St. Augustine's "Confessions". The bishop of Saint-Malo on the Holy Angels. Treatise on True and Solid Piety, by St. François de Sales. Fénélon, on the Existence of God. Fénélon on the Education of Girls. The Spirit of Saint Teresa, culled from her writings. Mascaron's funeral sermons. Mezenguy, Lives of the Saints. Nine volumes of the Lives of the Fathers of the Desert.

After glancing at them rapidly, the Queen sighed: "My eyes are hurting: I think I had better save them for the embroidery."

Elisabeth had many resources. She began to paint again, sitting by the window overlooking the Seine. She wrote to Angélique de Bombelles: "This amuses, occupies and distracts me, and I assure you that one needs all that." She painted nature scenes: this young girl passionately loved woods and hills, and her greatest deprivation was to be cooped up without privacy or exercise. One can hear the yearning in her voice when she writes to the Abbé de Lubersac: ". . . but distract yourself by the beauties which fill the town in which you are living. After having admired the sublime hand which formed these immense rocks and these torrents which could have drawn you into their abyss, admire the industry which God has given to man . . ."

She walked as much as she could in the Tuileries gardens, in all weathers. It was a habit, a necessity of her active nature, and the only way she could keep fit. Her letters to absent friends are full of these walks. She went to the chapel each day and received Holy Communion very often. She said the whole Office of the Paris Breviary. She copied many prayers and put them into a blue morocco folder which was found after the loot of the palace. She read to the children, or sat with them when they were listening to Molière's "Bourgeois Gentilhomme". She played draughts with them (*reversi*). In one letter, we get a delightful picture, which shows what a loving and beloved aunt she was.

"I announce to you, Madame Bombe, that I write to you to employ my time. I am among three children,[1] one more talkative than the other. They have just played a sad game of *reversi*, in which they emulated one another in cheating and playing badly. When I say they were cheating, it is . . . that this was not true, but my niece, who was on my shoulder, was dictating to me . . ."

In the evenings, she tried to make the King play billiards with her, for he was feeling the lack of exercise. She wrote long letters to her absent friends, full of gaiety and worldly wisdom. Her interest in the teething troubles of their children is all the more touching, when we think of how her own heart was grieving with anxiety at the fate of her country. She also—rather unwisely—wrote to the Comte d'Artois in Turin, bewailing the King's lack of firmness. She always put too much trust in this prince whose moral behaviour was causing scandal all over Europe. (He was living openly on his father-in-law's estates with his mistress, Madame de Polastron.)

It was very easy for the Polignacs, safely installed in a Venetian palace, to judge of the French political situation from a distance. It was so simple for the Comte d'Artois to criticise his brother. He did him untold harm by forming an "emigration party" whose only thought was retaliation, and whose members were not at all in tune with the new ideas with which the King was trying to grapple.

La Fayette's troops formed the King's bodyguards. There was trouble at once. The Comte d'Hézecques tells us that: "These apostles of equality, refused for a long time to receive from the hands of the pages, the trains of the princess's gowns, which they had to take, according to etiquette, as they went into the closet or the chapel."

A man told Monsieur de la Boissière, a lawyer, that at the Queen's Mass he had sworn to make Elisabeth lower her eyes; we are told: ". . . he succeeded. This august princess lowered her eyes, bent her head on her muff and it was no doubt to hide the tears which his insult made her shed."

[1] The third was little Pauline de Tourzel.

Comte Ferrand tells us: "Nearly every afternoon, during her stay at the Tuileries, she went to the chapel. To get there, she had to cross the guard-rooms. Their remarks, their jokes, their sarcasms, often interspersed with impudence and impiety, did not stop her. Their spite increased when they saw she was indifferent to their derision; but their audacity was forced to lower its eyes before her. She seemed to vanquish them, less by the pride of her glance than by the influence of her virtue."

When at last she was able to ride again, there was trouble. The officer who guarded her, hearing that she was not in the habit of lending her horses to him and his like, was so furious, that he wanted to cut the shafts of her carriage before she went out one day. She writes to Angélique: "Happily I had gone when they formed this little plot; but, to revenge himself for this, the next day, he clapped himself down on my page's horse, without even saying so much as, God bless you!" This man was punished, however—he was a bad lot whom the others wanted to get rid of.

Monsieur Lenotre assures us that Elisabeth never feared to go down to the stables herself to see that good order prevailed.

But these early slights, whether from guards or officers, were but a prelude of what awaited her. . . .

CHAPTER XVIII

The horizon darkens

THE Parisian newspapers encouraged the guards in their insolent attitude towards the royal family by passages like these: "You will have to be ready to obey with religious punctuality, the orders of a man, the caprices of a woman; . . . present arms, that is render the finest homage that one can exact from a free citizen at the passing of a Marie-Antoinette, of an Elisabeth, or a little royal princess, modelled already on her mother and on her aunt."

Towards the end of 1790, Hébert, in his infamous newspaper "Père Duchesne", began blaming the King for refusing to sanction the civil constitution of the clergy. By the end of December, fearing schism, the King gave his sanction.

The era of religious persecution was dawning. Many historians have overlooked the important fact that the Revolution was a satanic affair as well as a political upheaval. Its partisans would begin by crushing the clergy as the upholders of truth. Even in our own so-called enlightened age, the communists imprison and torture arch-bishops and priests before anybody else.

The new bill ruled that all bishops and clergy should in future be appointed by local election. It also prescribed that, before admission to his office, every beneficed priest must make a solemn oath to uphold the constitution decreed by the National Assembly and accepted by the King.

This meant, among other things, that the Pope would have nothing to do with the election of bishops, and that elected clergy would be under the thumb of their electors, who might include any kind of non-Catholics; in Alsace, for example, there would be a Protestant majority.

On the day decreed by the Assembly for the clergy to make this solemn oath in their churches, there were scenes all over Paris, anticipating the terrible schism that was to split the French people in two.

Albert Sorel says that the King sanctioned the decree with the secret intention of taking it back as soon as he had recovered the necessary strength. Elisabeth wrote to Madame de Raigecourt: ". . . my conscience and my good sense tell me that one should never promise what one has no intention of keeping."

When at last the Pope pronounced against the civil constitution of the clergy, the King retracted, and civil war became imminent.

On January the 17th, 1791, on the day after the oath was sworn in many Paris churches, Elisabeth wrote to Madame de Raigecourt to tell her of the riot at St. Sulpice. The church was full of brigands, chairs were thrown and the organist pulled out all his stops to drown the voices of the non-juring priests. The same Bacchanalia at St. Roch.

In early February, Mesdames Tantes came from Bellevue to say that they were fleeing to Rome as soon as possible, so that they might practise their religion in freedom. Like all faithful Catholics, they would not hear Mass in a church where there was a juring priest. Behind closed doors, speaking in whispers lest they be overheard by a spying servant at the key-hole, they did their best to persuade their niece to join them in secret.

"Elisabeth, *ma petite*, come with us: you have remained at the Tuileries long enough. You must now think of your own soul. Can you bear to be deprived of the Sacraments for an indefinite time? Come with us to the Holy City; the Pope will welcome us, we will pray together for our country at all the great shrines and at the tombs of the martyrs."

Elisabeth looked at the two old ladies, who seemed like ghosts from the past, Tante Victoire, white, fat and flabby, always echoing her sister, Tante Adélaïde, tall, commanding and shrivelled, laying down the law in her bass voice. No, they would never understand, if she told them it was her duty to watch by the Queen and her children: they would not think "the Austrian woman" worth her sacrifice. So she appealed to them by the memory of Tante Louise, their Carmelite sister who had died in 1787. "I'm sure Tante Louise would have thought it pluckier of me to stay on. I am young. Don't you remember her last words as she lay dying: 'To paradise, quickly, at the gallop'?"

Elisabeth said herself that, seen from afar, an act of chivalry glows brightly, but it is a very different tale to carry out one's daily duty in all its petty details. To begin with, she was conscious that the King and Queen kept her out of all their confabulations, as if they did not trust her discretion. They stopped talking directly she came into a room, and this was very hard to bear. Yes, it would have been lovely in Rome, in early spring, in the sunshine, right away from everything; a new life, freedom, ah freedom. . . . Instead, there were the sneers and studied insults of the guards, and ever-growing loneliness. The ranks of her ladies were thinning. They all had such good excuses for leaving Paris. And then, almost daily, she listened to the tales of woe which her Montreuil caretakers brought to her about the estate. In the kitchen gardens, the espaliers failed, the peaches rotted, the grapes, they said, were eaten by birds and insects. The walls needed repairing and people were always climbing over to steal. The house was in a bad state of repair. The botanical garden was smothered in briars. At her farm, there remained only five cows, one horse and several hens. The bailiff had tried to make some profit from one of her adjoining out-houses, which was empty, by selling or letting it, but he had been baulked by its bad condition. Yes, it was obvious that her servants were not proving very trustworthy, and there was nothing she could do about it. But oh, what was all that compared to the sufferings of those around her? The ladies of St. Cyr, whom she visited in secret, were trembling for the fate of their institution. The peasants on their estate, who owed them everything, were very menacing in their be-haviour. The ladies wept when Elisabeth tried to comfort them. They trembled at the threat that their aristocratic house, nurtured, so to speak, within the ermine folds of the royal mantle, should now be turned into a state school, forced to take in the daughters of the butcher, the baker, the candlestick-maker. They would have to teach stately courtesies to little *"bourgeoises"* with no background and no traditions. Oh shades of Madame de Maintenon. . . .

Elisabeth now received daily calls for help from starving priests who would not take the oath. She had founded an Association among her friends, which aimed, among other things, at giving financial help to these brave men. Many were thus enabled to flee, many came to England, and were so hospitably received by the golden-hearted

Protestants, that one cannot but be convinced that God rewarded this country by giving the Faith to so many of its people.[1]

Elisabeth sent to the Cathedral of Chartres, "a golden Heart of Jesus joined to the Heart of Mary", on behalf of the Association. She had written a vow to the Immaculate Heart of Mary to obtain the conservation of religion in the kingdom. Of Our Lady, she wrote: "She is a good mother who will not abandon us." As a true Bourbon, she had the traditional devotion of her family to Our Lady and to the Sacred Heart of Jesus. As the troubles increased, she spoke of Christ's heart more and more, and composed many prayers.

.   .   .   .   .

And so Mesdames Tantes, the patronesses of Beaumarchais, the calumniators of the Queen, left for Rome without their niece on the night of February the 19th. A few hours later, the mob invaded Bellevue, and the fish-wives slept in the downy beds. But God who is not mocked, and who punishes the slanderer, perhaps even more severely than the adulterer, did not give the aunts the repose they sought in Italy. Hounded from place to place, in mid-winter, through the fortunes of war, they died within eight months of one another, unlamented, unhonoured, having done as much as the Lamottes and the Robespierres to destroy the nobles of their country—that land in which they had never been more than parasites.

.   .   .   .   .

On the following Easter Day, April the 24th, the King and Queen were enjoined by the Assembly, to go to Saint Germain l'Auxerrois, the parish church of the palace, and hear the Mass said by the new juring priest. Elisabeth stoutly refused to go to this schismatic Mass and was loudly criticised in consequence. The president of the Assembly then exhorted the King to keep away from the Dauphin any "suspect persons". No insinuations could have been clearer.

[1] Even the fishmongers of Billingsgate used to give away their fish very cheaply to the priests who came to buy on Fridays.

Religious persecutions began in earnest. All through that Lent of 1791, scandalous scenes took place on Sundays, outside churches; women were publicly beaten, children trodden underfoot, old men insulted. It was safer to stay indoors until Monday morning. The memory of the Sundays of long ago seemed very remote and nebulous —the Mass in the Chapel Royal at Versailles, the children's dances at Petit Trianon, the crowds, strolling in the gardens on summer evenings, listening to the music. And now, what a contrast! The people of Paris, badly housed, and therefore more inclined to wander about the streets, filled the Tuileries gardens. The terraces which had been the favourite meeting place of Parisian society were crowded by rough, coarse patriots wearing tricolour *cocardes*. It was quite impossible for Elisabeth to go out, even dangerous to peep out of her windows.

And yet, the troubles of others came before her own. A Comte d'Albigiac, an officer of her bodyguard, wrote to Madame de Raigecourt on April the 16th, 1791, after seeing Elisabeth: "All really afflicted hearts . . . rally around her; she consoles them . . . fortifies them by her welcome. For my part, she has overwhelmed me, and if a familiar expression could be reconciled with my deep respect, I would say she has caressed me." He goes on to say how prodigiously changed the Queen was: ". . . not thinner, but worse than that, withered, aged, . . . by adversity."

Elisabeth continued to guide her young friend Démon, who had left her in the summer of 1790, because she was expecting a child, and her husband said it would be safer to leave Paris. Elisabeth had to insist on her departure, for Démon found the sacrifice of leaving her princess almost too great. On August the 29th Elisabeth wrote to her: ". . . Perhaps you will meet there some Parisians whose reputation is not very good; . . . order your course on reason, so that no one can gossip about you. . . . Above all, *mon cœur*, try to please your husband; although you have never spoken to me about him, I know him well enough to be aware that he has some good qualities, but that he may have others which will not please you as much. Make it a rule never to insist on these, and above all never to allow anyone to talk to you about them; you owe it to him, you owe it to yourself. Try to fix his affections. Make his house agreeable to him . . . you will thus win his confidence;

and if ever you really possess them, with the wit which Heaven has given you and a little skill, you will do all you want."

Or again: ". . . Ah, is there any happiness greater than to be always at peace with one's conscience? Keep that happiness, and you will see that the torments of life are very small, compared with those borne by people given up to all the passions. May the piety of your mother-in-law not disgust you with it. . . . I am very glad that your husband knows his faults; but I should be displeased that you point them out to him by joking or otherwise. Forgive me, *mon cœur*, for all my gossip, but I love you too much, not to tell you all I think would lead to your happiness."

Again: ". . . a woman must sacrifice everything so that peace may reign" (in her home). Later she said: ". . . your husband has less intelligence than you, which gives you a great advantage over him, because if you want to take the trouble, you can forestall the scenes he might make. . . . Agree gently, and never pronounce that sentence: 'you are wrong'. A husband, still young and lively, must always detest it." She also points out, that as the husband has always been led with ill-temper and outbursts of rage (by her famous mother-in-law), he now needed an absolutely contrary régime.

To Madame de Raigecourt about her child: ". . . learn to hold a child, for from the first day you will smother him, if you have no more talent than you had for Stani. . . . How wise you are, *mon cœur*, to seek friendship only with reasonable women! Nothing more dangerous for a young person, than women who have not got very good principles, nothing leads so quickly to their perdition. . . ."

.   .   .   .   .   .

About October the 13th, 1790, Rage left for Trèves, for she was expecting another child.

Rage needed much cheering, when she got to Trèves, and Elisabeth had to remind her that she was going to give her unborn child an incurable foundation of melancholy if she did not control herself.

"Sufficient unto the day is the evil thereof," she says.

To her "Bombelinette", Elisabeth wrote from Saint-Cloud, to

say she was in a wretched temper, because she was eaten by gnats. She enquired about Diane de Polignac in exile, hoping that she had become devout. She says: "This Revolution is and always will be for me the mystery of the Holy Trinity."

.   .   .   .   .

When Mesdames Tantes went into exile, they took with them the Abbé Madier, who had been Elisabeth's confessor from childhood. Providence sent her another and a very saintly one, too. She had hoped for someone "neither too gentle, nor too severe". She found someone who was to be a true fatherly guide in the troublous times ahead— the Abbé Edgeworth de Firmont, of Irish origin, recommended by the Superior of the *Missions Etrangères*. He was an heroic creature who stayed on in Paris, sometimes in hiding, in order to help souls. It is amazing that he was allowed to see his illustrious penitent, undisturbed, sometimes coming to the Tuileries as often as three times a week. In his picture, he looks very distinguished and refined, with Celtic bonework, sensitive eyelids over deeply sunk eyes; in all, a firm, spiritual face. He was of a calibre to understand the girl who had made a vow of perfection at fifteen, and who had offered her life for her brother and his family. He appreciated this young woman, who was a blend of innocence and worldly wisdom. Here was someone who had created her own "climate" of holiness in her own little circle, in one of the most corrupt courts of history. With time, he grew to venerate her. His great regret, at the end of his life, was that he had been obliged to burn her letters, as they might have been dangerous to keep.

Elisabeth loved his simplicity, his serence countenance, and the winning charm of his manners.

He wrote: ". . . I soon became her friend, and she trusted me utterly."

In March 1791, on the eve of religious persecution, Elisabeth wrote to Rage: "I went to confession yesterday, and I was very pleased with him. He has intelligence, gentleness, a great knowledge of the human heart. . . . You can imagine that your princess was greatly embarrassed.

. . . Just think of it, Madame de Navarre showed him into my closet without warning me. I was not in my box; we both remained equally sheepish, looking at one another, I not knowing what to say. In the end, I went to fetch my hood . . . I came back and got into my confessional. I was not embarrassed long and I don't think I shall be embarrassed any more.

". . . in all that one does, it is good to consult those whom Heaven has given you as spiritual guides."

One thing she omits to tell us, about this "box", as she calls it. After the terrible day of August the 10th, 1792, the Duke of Bedford visited Elisabeth's room in the Tuileries, and he saw a wooden firescreen by the chimney which, when unfolded, became a light, portable confessional. But instead of a cushion for the princess to kneel on, there was an unevenly carved piece of yellow and black marble, most torturing to the knees. She had a true Carmelite spirit of penance.

Later in the month, she wrote again to Rage: ". . . I am still very pleased with my new acquaintance; he wants to know thoroughly what one is thinking, and it is not a dry knowledge; it helps one greatly to correct oneself."

In May she wrote: "I feel that I needed to address myself to someone who would shake up (as you say) my soul. I see that, all perfect as I thought I was, I would at least have spent several centuries in Purgatory, if Heaven had not put order in all this." She says her director is enlightened: ". . . Knowing me already better than I know myself, and who does not want to leave me to stagnate in my apathy." ". . . He understands what I say to him and always presents me with an efficacious remedy for the ills which I tell him of."

There is no doubt that the Abbé Edgeworth was sent into her life precisely when she needed him most. He trained her in valour, for the dark days ahead.

Before the era of religious persecution began, in March, 1790, Elisabeth had written to Bombe: "However, if the times of religious persecutions were to come back, ah! I would ask Heaven to take me out of the world before it began, for I do not feel at all in possession of the courage to bear them."

But by January, 1791, she was writing to Rage: "I have no taste for martyrdom, but I feel that I would be very glad to have the certitude to suffer it, rather than forsake the least tenet of my faith." By March, 1791, with her new director, her courage had grown by leaps and bounds, and she wrote to Rage: "When God speaks, a Catholic knows only His voice."

On July the 12th, 1790, the civil constitution of the clergy had been voted in the Assembly. The leaders, many of whom were Protestants, Jansenists or atheists, definitely wanted to cause a schism between Rome and France.

In a word, the Assembly had been vexed by the admirable resignation of the French clergy when its property had been confiscated. If they had hoped to engineer revolts, they were disappointed, so they tried other provoking tactics. They attempted to make them swear to uphold the civil constitution of the clergy; in a word, to do what communists try to do—put the Church in the power and under the legislation of the state, on pain of destitution. In November, 1790, Elisabeth had written to Bombe: ". . . you cannot imagine the consternation on everyone's faces. . . . Let us think that His Heart suffers more than His anger is aroused. It depends on us to console Him."

About that time there appeared "Père Duchesne", a scurrilous newspaper whose every other word was an oath or an obscenity. This was edited by Hébert, who, the following year, was to marry Mlle Goupil, a nun of the Conception Convent, in the Rue Saint-Honoré. She was the only one of 24 nuns who had wanted to leave her cloister in June, 1790, when the new laws opened its doors. Someone has expressed surprise that a man who was always urging the mobs to whip nuns, should have married a nun. P. d'Estréc has explained it in this wise: "As a matter of fact, Hébert, who was however neither unconscious nor mentally sick, experienced the sadism particular to ultra-revolutionaries who are intoxicated at the sight of these women, superior by birth, by beauty, and by fortune, and pushed by them under the knife of the guillotine. Just see with what impatient voluptuousness he longs for the execution of the 'Austrian tigress', and of the 'grosse babet', etc.

"And this feeling of cruel curiosity assuredly must have haunted him the day he learnt the past of Françoise Goupil, one of those nuns on whom he called down so often the brutal outrages of the populace. By one of these contrasts which can only be explained by the delirium of the senses, he wanted to get under the immaculate veil, to penetrate the mystery of that sacred character which he had scoffed at so indignantly."

P. d'Estrée goes on to say that Hébert hated in the priest, the born enemy of the Revolution. "He hated him . . . with that cold calculated ferocity of the master tormentor who knows how to make his victim suffer. . . ."

Naturally, when Elisabeth's staunch loyalty to the Pope and respect for the priesthood became known, filthy libels flowed, not only from Hébert's pen, but from others, dipped in the vitriolic ink of hatred, and redolent of the sewer. Thus F. Dantalle wrote of Elisabeth: ". . . this female, as malicious as she is pretty . . . eats also many white macaronis (allusion to the Sacred Host and to Elisabeth's frequent Communions) . . ." Later, he calls her "*cette mauvaise carogne*" (this dirty slut) and asks: "By whom is she kept, this '*guenon*' ('she ape')."

On April the 13th, 1791, Pope Pius VI enjoined the members of the French clergy who had sworn the civic oath, to retract within 40 days. To receive Easter Communion at their hands was to associate oneself with their rebellion and give a scandalous example to the faithful. Elisabeth threw herself at her brother's feet and implored him not to sanction the law against the non-juring priests. After his initial hesitations, Louis XVI steadily refused to approve a decree for the deportation of priests.

(On May the 3rd, the Pope's effigy was burnt at the Palais Royal.)

Elisabeth obeyed the Pope's order instantly. Comte Fleury tells us that on Easter Day she never left her suite. "Her absence was commented on in lively fashion by the revolutionary public, insults and threats were heard under her windows."

She was to write on May the 11th to Rage: ". . . in moments of crisis, God overwhelmed me with kindnesses. I suffered a great deal during Holy Week; but once the moment is past, I calm myself."

How her mind must have gone back to a memorable Holy Week, long ago, spent with Madame de Mackau, to the "O Filii" sung in her parish church, St. Symphorien of Montreuil, to all the ceremonies of

Holy Week at the chapel of Versailles, particularly those of Holy Thursday. Twelve freshly scrubbed little children each holding an enormous bouquet of rare flowers, dressed in red gowns, all sat in a row. To represent Christ washing the feet of the disciples, they had their feet washed and dried by the King's brothers, and then the King would kiss them.

Afterwards a meal was served for them. The Prince de Condé, master of the King's house, would lead the procession, carrying a stick studded with diamonds, and a superb bouquet. Each child was given twelve dishes. In the afternoon, the Queen and the princesses would repeat the ceremony for twelve little girls.

Elisabeth wondered if ungrateful Versailles ever remembered those days and missed them, as she did now.

When the Papal Nuncio, Monseigneur de Salamon, wrote to the Papal Secretary of State, on January the 16th, 1792, after visiting Elisabeth at the Tuileries, he said: ". . . it seemed as if an angel spoke through her lips."

The King was now as staunch as his sister about non-juring priests. His firmness eventually led to the terrible days of June the 20th, August the 10th and . . . final imprisonment in the Temple. Indeed, when the Pope pronounced his allocution, *Quare lacrimae*, after the King's death, he stated that Louis XVI had been immolated by those who hated the Faith.

CHAPTER XIX

Nuns and priests in hiding

MIRABEAU had said: "We must de-Christianise France."
J. M. Thompson in his excellent history of the French
Revolution does not stress that the revolutionaries professed a religion
of hatred, and that, after the King's return from Varennes, they were
filled by an evil spirit over which they had less and less control. Just as
religious persecution in our times has taught us that priests and bishops
are the first to be attacked, for they are the last upholders of the
stronghold of Faith, so, strangely enough, the mob leaders attacking
the Tuileries on August 10th said to Louis XVI, "Hand us over the
priests you are hiding in your cellars and we will leave you alone."

So very few authors speak at all of what happened to priests and
nuns during the Revolution, that it would be illuminating to pause
and track down these victims to their obscure hiding places, even
though it means anticipating a little chronologically. To this day,
there are still, in old Paris houses, niches behind sliding panels where
men crouched in the dark for weeks on end, afraid of being betrayed
by a servant, and having food brought up to them occasionally by
their terrified hosts. In the Rue Cassette, there was a block of flats with
several staircases. The *concierge*, a real Cerberus, kept a watchful eye on
the comings and goings of his tenants. In September, 1792, a flat had
been let to eight ladies. Odd that the porter had no suspicions about
them. One of them was a Visitation nun from the Rue du Bac, and the
seven others were Carmelites from the Rue de Grenelle, who, alas,
were eventually brought to the Conciergerie and then to the Salpêtrière, where they stayed with prostitutes till the 9th Thermidor.
Another flat in the same building was let to an eccentric who called
himself Joseph Mercier (it was really the Père de la Clorivière in disguise). Once a week, a drawing-master came to give lessons to the
eight ladies. The doors were locked, a chest of drawers served as an

altar, Mass was said, the Office recited. There was Benediction of the Blessed Sacrament, and sometimes the nuns would sing in a low humming voice. If an alert were given—quickly, the ciborium and the ivory statue of the Virgin were whisked away, and the chapel became a bedroom again.

The Père de la Clorivière laughed at danger. At all hours of the day, he left his dwelling with consecrated Hosts in a silken sachet hidden against his heart. Another priest from St. Nicolas-des-Champs had sewn inside each of his waistcoats two little pockets carefully concealed in the lining, to hold consecrated Hosts and the box of Holy Oils.

At 134 Rue de Tournon, the Prior of the Carthusians of Paris had taken refuge. In the Rue Mouffetard, Mademoiselle de Soyecourt, in religion Sœur Camille de l'Enfant Jésus, had grouped a few Carmelites from the Rue de Grenelle in a little pavilion between the courtyard and the garden. They would fill volumes, the adventures of this frail and aristocratic young lady who had never been expected to survive the days of her novitiate, and who lived through the Reign of Terror in disguise, and eventually re-established her Order. The director of the Autun Seminary, l'Abbé Magnin, was an old clothes dealer: this profession allowed him to penetrate different houses unchallenged and bring help to many of the faithful in hiding. In the end he had the great consolation of being able to bring Holy Communion to Marie-Antoinette immediately before her execution. An ancient Benedictine monk of the Blancs-Manteaux tried to earn his living with literary work, but when his pen failed to feed him, he turned apothecary and utilised different secret prescriptions which he possessed, amongst which were an ointment, known to this day, an eye lotion, and an elixir for the stomach. The Papal Nuncio, Monseigneur de Salamon, who had a great esteem for Madame Elisabeth, escaped the September Massacres. A friend of his, Mademoiselle Girard, managed to find him a horrible attic without a roof, open to all weathers, which he reached by a ladder. He possessed three planks, an old straw mattress, a rickety table and two chairs. This priest was a most practical man. He bought himself a little oven, a saucepan, some vegetables and a spot of butter. Even when he took refuge in a deserted kiosk in the Bois de

Boulogne, he carried his pathetic little oven under his arm and lived as a vegetarian. Through the means of one saucepan and the grace of God, communications with Rome continued uninterrupted throughout the Reign of Terror.

In contemporary accounts, one is impressed by the fact that the ordinary, decent, obscure people of Paris had not given up their religion at all. One icy-cold Christmas night, the Church of St. Etienne-du-Mont was crowded out with more than a thousand parishioners, determined to hear Midnight Mass. Needless to say, the National Assembly did not approve of these nocturnal gatherings, and the procurator said: "One may say that Jesus was the head of the *Sans Culottes* of Judea and that under this title I am sure He would pitilessly have forbidden Midnight Mass, that reminder of Egyptian orgies." The French love their national feasts. Imagine the horror of the little people when their favourite feast of the Epiphany was called "*La Fête des Sans Culottes*". On that day, at the Château de la Muette, Monsieur de Trudaine mysteriously invited a few intimate friends. He locked the door and took the traditional cake or *galette* out of his portfolio. The meal was served in a remote corner of the château, far away from the servants. The guests drank to the health of the royal prisoners by signs. Of the twelve guests, only two survived the Reign of Terror.

The Mont Valérien became a refuge for persecuted Christians, because its woody slopes were quite hard to penetrate. There were still several private chapels in the Faubourg St. Germain.

The French were devoted to the Feast of Corpus Christi. They soon began to miss their processions in honour of the Blessed Sacrament. In one church, the priest in charge climbed into the pulpit and asked the crowd what they wanted. They replied with one voice: "To make the procession." The commissionnaire from the National Assembly had to bow before the will of the people. Two women from the flower markets preceded the dais, scattering flowers on the way, soldiers forming a protective guard. The parishioners carrying banners, and singing devoutly, followed on foot. When they passed a section of the Municipal Guard, the soldiers thereof presented arms and saluted the Sacred Host by beating their drums. At the Halles, in great haste the women decorated the houses, men and women fell on their knees in adoration, and some men let off guns as a sign of rejoicing.

It was in outlying districts in which workmen lived that the feast was celebrated most brilliantly. A police officer declared that light had not yet penetrated from the centre to the extremities! In the Saint Marceau quarter, all the houses were bedecked with flowers, and the workers at the Gobelins factory brought out the most admirable tapestries of Scriptural scenes. When, however, it became more and more unsafe to have these processions, the flower women were the first to mourn. A man said, "This morning at the Halles I saw a head flower woman crying because they had suppressed the Corpus Christi processions. Every year she made her little packet with two women who earned enough for a fortnight. There are no dressmakers, stuff merchants, decorators, who do not curse the existence of all those who have helped towards the suppression."

A priest who was returning from burying the dead in the church-yard, accidentally, with his silver cross, knocked up against a drunken street porter bent under his burden. He started swearing at the priest. "Hush," said his friend who was accompanying him, "it's the Good God." "Bah," replied the porter, "the Good God, there is no more God." And around these two citizens having a blasphemous quarrel, the passers-by doffed their hats, made the sign of the cross and prayed. In the church of Sainte Geneviève and elsewhere, street porters offered crucifixes and little statues at the shrine. At cross-roads, hawkers could still be heard, singing the pious songs of long ago, and when one such man was imprudent enough to sing of Sainte Geneviève as a *"Comtesse de grande noblesse"*, a servant maid in the auditorium took to her heels. A priest was bringing Viaticum to a poor man and had to go through the Halles. Six armed *sans-culottes*, apparently from the dregs of the people, gave him military honours, accompanied him to the door of the dying man and waited to escort him back to church. Everybody was kneeling.

The good Abbé of St. Nicolas-des-Champs was betrayed on October 7th, 1793, by a woman to whom he had been kind and who had heard his Masses. The police broke into his room, opened the ward-robes and found the chalice and all the things necessary to bring

Viaticum to the sick—altar linen, missal, two boxes of Hosts which the *sans-culottes* called "these baubles of superstition". They even found a paper with a black mark on it, and underneath the words: "Blood of Louis XVI."

The Père de la Clorivière quite soon had to leave his old room in the Rue Cassette, and go and hide in a house on the hoarding of which was written "empty lodging". The police never suspected that he was in there, hidden in a wall niche, spending his days reading, writing and praying. He said his Mass and reserved the Blessed Sacrament. At night he would furtively slip out to take the air, eat a hasty meal and speak a few words with a spiritual daughter of his, who later became the foundress of the Daughters of the Heart of Mary.

On October 17th, 1793, the day after the execution of Marie-Antoinette, the Sisters of Charity were denounced because they had asked for passports. When their cell was searched, there was an uproar; they found in the nuns' ample habits an almanach with effigies of Louis XVI and Marie-Antoinette, reliquaries, and images of the Sacred Heart.

One was not safe, even with one's closest relations. An old man of eighty, Monsieur Pierre Broquet, ex-chaplain of Notre Dame, was given a lodging by an unbelieving nephew who kept a bar. This nephew wanted to prevent his uncle from leaving the house to hear Mass at St. Germain l'Auxerrois, or from going to help some parishioners in hiding. One day the uncle got into a terrible temper and left the house in his dressing gown, without hat or shoes. When the nephew heard of this, he tried to shake off his responsibility by betraying him. And poor old Monsieur Broquet was sent to the scaffold.

On the 17th Brumaire, an actress Mademoiselle Aubry was chosen to impersonate the goddess of Reason in Notre Dame. It must have been a horrible sight, with all her assistants in white tunics and the national colours around their waists, going up and down a mountain. At the end of the performance, great applause from the congregation, and Mademoiselle Aubry, forgetting that she was supposed to be immortal, turned back and dropped a curtsey to the delirious crowds. Afterwards, she went with her maidens to the Convention. It was a pathetic sight in the narrow streets of Paris, for it was pouring with rain and the wind blew tempestuously. The road was a swamp. The musicians, soldiers, fish-wives, the operatic corps de ballet—all were shivering, their wigs had become uncurled, rouge streamed down their cheeks, their white Grecian robes were dripping with mud.

Monsieur Lenotre, with his fascinating way of wanting to know what happened after the end of a story, traced somewhere the fate of this unknown little actress. One seems to remember that she died, ill and all alone, in an obscure Paris attic.

And then, one day, amid a howling mob, six chariots brought to the Convention all the marvellous silver and goldsmith work of the ancient abbey of St. Denis, where the Kings of France had been buried.

Until then, even after the violation of the royal tombs, the basilica's treasury had remained untouched, locked up in high wardrobes. A Benedictine monk protected the reliquaries, crosses, crowns, statues, sacred vessels of gold and silver and silver-gilt, of crystal and ivory, chalices glittering with jewels and enamel work. He lived in two little rooms next to the Treasury, and never left them for a second. How heart-broken he must have felt when the patriots broke down the door and started smashing everything up. The basilica very soon resembled a deserted stone-mason's yard for old building materials. The next day, three men slipped noiselessly along the aisles and went to the Chapelle des Lépreux where there was a funeral vault belonging to the Pastourelle family. This had been left intact by the revolutionaries, and it was used to hide all the sacred relics which had been carefully wrapped up in separate cloths and assembled in a single coffer.

Needless to say, many things were stolen in sacristies. In old clothes shops, one could see a priceless chasuble hanging next to a pair of trousers, and in antique shops, altar frontals were displayed next to bath-tubs. On the hands of the presidents of revolutionary committees glowed the emeralds which had once decorated monstrances. These Jacobins were practical fellows, for plenty of them got their wives to make velvet trousers for them out of stolen copes, or shifts from the albs of choir boys.

At the abbaye de St. Germain-des-Près, they were able to save the relic of the True Cross, bequeathed by Anne de Gonzague, which to-day is preserved at Notre Dame. Paris on that day saw a hideous carnival procession—drummers and soldiers in priestly robes, dalmatics, copes, velvet and brocade chasubles embroidered with gold and silver thread. When they opened the shrine of Sainte Geneviève, the patroness of Paris, they found a coffin made of very thick oak, wrapped up in white lambskin held together with iron bands. Inside that coffin were twenty sachets full of ashes and a phial containing some dried brown liquid, which the label said was the blood of St. Peter. And then, carefully wrapped up in a resinous cloth, some human bones and a skull. A parchment left no doubt at all that these were the venerated remains of Sainte Geneviève. The officials decided that "this trumpery rubbish" should be burnt immediately on the Place de Grève, "to expiate the crime of having served to propagate error and to pay for the luxury of so many idlers".

Mercier has a horrible description of these orgies: "The actors who took part in them were still tipsy with the brandy which they had drunk in the chalices after eating mackerels on patens. Astride on donkeys, whose hind-quarters were concealed by chasubles, they would stop at pub doors holding out sacred vases for the pub keepers to fill them three times in succession."

. . . . .

In the Rue de Lille lived a bewigged man who had a high forehead, blue eyes and a long nose. He was an old Theatine monk who, since the dispersal of his community, lived with two old maids, Louise and Jeanne Tessier. A servant called Marguerite Bussier looked after them, and she it was who eventually betrayed them. She was a fanatic who was always drinking brandy, and very talkative when she was drunk. She wanted to dominate her employer completely and was terribly jealous of the Tessier sisters whom she regarded as her rivals. She was intensely curious, always opening drawers and letters and listening at doors. She went even so far as to make a hole in the wall, so that she could hear more clearly and see all that was going on. The Theatine monk still saw friends of the royal house and the Spanish Ambassador, and used to go to the Rue de l'Université to say his Mass. Marguerite Bussier, sick with jealousy, betrayed him.

Even to the very old, the Revolution was pitiless—for example, tracking down an old canon of seventy-two, hiding in the Rue des Lavandières-Ste-Opportune, who sometimes heard the confessions of his old penitents. It was ruthless to the seventy-one-year-old Abbess of the Benedictine nuns of Montmartre, Madame de Montmorency-Laval, who had been able to preserve the kernel of her old community. Anxiety had aged her terribly: her hair was grey, her face very thin, she was very deaf, and half paralysed. She could not hold herself upright or speak, and yet this poor old lady was declared a dangerous enemy of the Revolution and was arrested on May the 10th, 1794, the very day on which Elisabeth was guillotined.

CHAPTER XX

The flight to Varennes

THE events[1] of the early part of 1791, having shown the King that he and his family could no longer practise their Faith in freedom, he secretly decided, without leaving the kingdom, to get away from the tyranny of the National Assembly, which had now ceased to be representative of France, and to take flight eastwards.

As the King and Queen no longer discussed their private affairs with her, Elisabeth was not told of the plan of escape for Varennes until the very day—June the 20th. So she was unable to warn the Abbé Edgeworth; indeed she had been forbidden to tell a soul.

There had been other plans for escape at various times, but in one, from Saint-Cloud, which augured well, the King had suddenly changed his mind, and ordered the carriages to turn homewards again.

On May the 21st, a spying maid-servant sent a report to the Assembly about the Queen. Her suspicions had been aroused, because she had seen a travelling dressing-case, ordered from a cabinet-maker, and she had caught the Queen in the act of packing up her diamonds in wool, on a sofa. But the Assembly, trusting in the many soldiers who guarded the palace, inside and out, apparently did not take the woman seriously. One wonders if the coachmen near the royal stables noticed the brand-new dark-green travelling coach with yellow wheels, white velvet upholstery and green taffeta blinds, which was stabled by a Swedish gentleman who lived at no. 17 Rue de Matignon. There it was, waiting, loaded with luggage and provisions. The Comte Axel Fersen had seen to everything—the *bœuf à la mode*, the cold veal, the sack of money for the relays, a bottle of still champagne, and five bottles of water. There must have been some gossip and surmise, in that quarter haunted by palace coachmen and grooms. Oh, if only the

[1] A brief chronological table of the main course of the Revolution will be found in the appendix.

fugitives had taken a light one-horse chaise, as the Comte and Comtesse de Provence had done, and travelled separately, in proper disguises, with no luggage at all. Even Léonard, the Queen's hairdresser, came too, and it seems that his unpunctuality added to the general delay. One goes through every step of that disastrous flight, trying to re-organise it properly, but one is baulked at every turn, by the feeling that Axel Fersen, forceful though he was, and an excellent organiser, could never have imposed his will and his more sensible plans on the shifty, lethargic, crassly imprudent King, and on the obstinate Queen. Marie-Antoinette even took the royal governess and the governess's daughter, and, in a separate carriage, two maids, not to speak of trunks full of clothing. At every turn, it looks as if fate were against them: but in reality, this is an example of fate being determined by character. The Comte de Provence never told his wife they were fleeing till the very day. And they got away with it. Can one imagine the King being as strong-minded and ruthless? They had a good chance, they so very nearly reached their goal, but no . . . they spoilt everything by allowing the King to show himself at the relays, where he was recognised. The weight of the lumbering coach must have delayed them immensely—that berline carrying all that luggage, and six human beings, not counting the coachmen and grooms.

.   .   .   .

When she had been told, Elisabeth went to her room and locked the door, saying she wanted to rest. Quietly she got out her maps and plotted the route to Montmédy, eastwards, near the frontier and near Luxembourg. First, the porte Clichy, then Claye, Meaux, Fromentières, Chaintrix, Châlons, Pont-de-Somme-Vesle, Sainte-Menehould, Clermont, Varennes, and then . . . Montmédy. She had no diamonds to pack, as she had already sold them for the benefit of persecuted priests. What a blessing it would be, to practise one's religion freely again. And who knows what good things would follow, when the King had put a great distance between himself and that National Assembly, which, as she so wittily said to a friend, loved liberty so much that it thought it was its own prerogative.

She had been told by the Queen to take nothing, not even the smallest parcel: "I can lend you anything you need from my trunks." She put into one place in her wardrobe, a large grey travelling hat trimmed with a falling gauze in the manner of a veil and a simple morning dress. She packed a supply of handkerchiefs into one of the inner hanging pockets of her petticoat. Then, to prepare for a broken night, she lay down and went to sleep.

.   .   .   .   .

What a nerve-racking day of waiting. The Queen was heard to murmur: "We are nearing the terrible quarter of an hour." She had gone to Mass at 12.30. At 5.15, she took the children for a ride in the carriage, to the Boutin garden, at Tivoli, where they had tea. She drew her daughter apart for a moment and whispered that she must not say a word, but she was going to wake her that night: they were leaving Paris, and she must be very quiet and very obedient. At seven, they returned to the château.

At nine, the royal family supped together. At nine-thirty, they went back to the Queen's drawing-room. Hardly were the doors shut, but they all drew together and talked in low voices. Elisabeth gave the Comte de Provence a little holy picture to preserve him in his flight— he was leaving at midnight. She was never to see him again.

At ten o'clock, the Queen slipped silently upstairs to wake her children. Madame de Tourzel dressed Madame Royale in a brown dress patterned with little yellow and white flowers. Pauline de Tourzel had made a girl's dress for the Dauphin and he was given a bonnet.

"How charming you look," whispered his sister. "Charles, what do you think we are going to do?" The poor little boy, heavy with sleep, replied, "We're going to act in a play, as we are disguised." "Sh . . . don't talk. Don't breathe. On tiptoe. . . ."

At ten-thirty, the Queen came up again and led them through a door which was not in use, and with beating hearts they went through many empty echoing rooms. They reached the courtyard. A shadow moved forward. It was the Comte Fersen in a coachman's great coat. He took the Dauphin by the hand, Madame de Tourzel took the girls, and, keeping close to the shadows of a row of carriages, they made for the Cour Royale, where the Queen put her children into an old cab. Then she went back to her drawing-room. It was ten forty-five. The rest of the evening was spent in the usual, gloomy, monotonous way. At their ordinary bedtime, they went to their rooms, escorted by their servants. Elisabeth went to the Pavillon de Flore, accompanied by a captain of the National Guard who left her at her door. He heard her push the bolts and saw the footman on guard place a mattress across the threshold of the door. She let her maids prepare her for the night, reminding them to wake her for Mass at eight the next morning. When they had gone, she slipped out of bed again and dressed noiselessly. Then she lifted a tapestry which hid a cupboard, got into it, pushed open its movable back, using a flexible key, then crept furtively down some steps to a deserted gallery. By the glow of a shaded night light, she made her way to a door which was not ordinarily used, and then out into the courtyard and street.

In the meantime, Fersen had driven the royal children along the quay of the Tuileries, across the Place Louis XV (now Place de la Concorde), and returned by the Rue Saint-Honoré to the Rue de l'Echelle, where he halted in front of the Hôtel Gaillerbois. There they waited for the others. At eleven-fifteen they got a fright, because La Fayette passed them on his way to the King's *coucher*. Madame de Tourzel hid the Dauphin in her skirts, but no one was recognised. The Rue de l'Echelle, being so near the royal stables, was the quarter for harness-makers and cabbies.

There was plenty of coming and going to divert suspicion. When things got quieter, Fersen, who had been behaving like a coachman for the last three-quarters of an hour, noticed a veiled woman sitting on a stone bench at the door of the Hôtel de la Vallière and thought he recognised Elisabeth. Fortunately she had not lost her way, for one of her squires, Monsieur de Saint-Pardoux, had brought her. She had never walked in the Paris streets before. Fersen went past her with the gait of a man who is loitering and said in a low voice, "You're expected." She did not hear the first time, and he had to say it again. She rose, got into the cab and trod on the Dauphin in the dark. He was plucky enough not to utter a cry.

The King came soon after, in a brown suit and a bottle green coat—for the night was fresh. Then there was a dreadful long wait for the Queen. At last she appeared, all in a fluster: "What do you think. La Fayette's coach passed so close to me, that I could have flicked the wheels with my switch. I darted into one of the dark alleys in the Place du Carrousel[1] and lost my way. I can't tell you what I felt like, knowing that you were all waiting for me."

At last, after a long détour through the sleeping city, they reached the Saint Martin barrier at two in the morning. Another precious quarter of an hour was wasted looking for the berline, which was waiting further down the road with its four horses. The cab drew alongside, door to door; the fugitives got in and installed themselves in the spacious berline. At two-thirty, Fersen took his place between the coachmen, Moustiers and Malden, and drove off at terrific speed. When they had passed the Clichy barrier, the King began to augur well for the success of the flight. This would have been the right moment to give this monarch a strong dose of opium, and keep him out of sight for the rest of the journey. Hide him under the women's cloaks. . . .

"Look," whispered Elisabeth, "you see those clouds in the distance? The dawn is breaking."

"Faster, faster," muttered Fersen to Balthasar his postilion, feeling that every minute counted, after all these delays. In half an hour, they were at Bondy, where six horses were harnessed. "Good-bye, Madame de Korff," said Fersen to the Queen. This Russian lady, a friend of Fersen's, had lent her name and passport. It is a thousand pities that the King did not allow Fersen to accompany them further. He gave him a rendezvous two days later, at Montmédy.

After Bondy, they all breathed more freely. It was arranged, laughingly, that Madame de Tourzel was the mistress, the Queen her governess, under the name of Madame Rochet, the King her steward (Durand), Madame Elisabeth the lady-companion, Rosalie. The royal children, two little girls called Amélie and Aglaée. Alas, when the critical moment came, none of them thought of playing their parts.

[1] In those days a slum of mediaeval houses and unlit, tortuous lanes.

A little before six, they relayed at Meaux, without incidents. After this, Elisabeth and the Queen put up their veils and all began to attack the provisions, without forks or plates, on bread, like hunters.

Elisabeth peeped through the little back window: "Look, there's a man on horseback following us."

He shadowed them for some time and they all felt apprehensive. However, after a while, he disappeared and they forgot him. They reached Montmirail at eleven o'clock. The King got out at two relays. At the second one, which was probably Fromentières, he was encircled by beggars. (First fatal mistake.) The children, in need of movement and air, walked up a steep incline. Towards two o'clock, Chaintrix. Here, recognised and lovingly greeted by loyal subjects, they allowed themselves to be surrounded. They unfortunately stopped an hour—*a whole hour*—with the hospitable master of the post-stage. That was the worst mistake of all.

They left at three and reached Châlons at four-thirty. Here, everybody recognised them. Many people praised God at sight of the King and Queen, and wished them all luck on their flight. The news spread in the countryside.

Another misfortune: more precious time lost, because the horses of the first two postilions fell, so that they only left Châlons at four-forty-five. At Pont-de-Somme-Vesle, they had expected to find a detachment of forty hussars under the command of Choiseul. The royal family peered through the windows, looking for the pelisses of "celestial blue" with white facings, of these hussars, but they could see nothing. Alas, Choiseul had been obliged to retreat with his soldiers, for news of the King's passage had been indiscreetly communicated to them, and the soldiers had been surrounded by bands of menacing peasants. The Queen shivered when she realised that something was amiss.

At Sainte-Menehould, things began to go seriously wrong. Thirty dragoons, waiting under the command of M. D'Andoins, attracted the curiosity of passers-by, because they instinctively saluted the royal family. A small crowd collected. M. D'Andoins was overheard saying to Moustiers, "Go, hurry, you are lost if you don't hurry."

Alas and alack, the master of the post-stage, Drouet, was just at that very minute returning from the fields. Like the others, he glanced at the heavy berline, and, seeing the pile of luggage, told the postilions not to kill the horses. Just as the berline rumbled away, the rumour spread among the crowd that the royal family was fleeing. According to Dr. Vast, Louis XVI heard the lugubrious and menacing sound of the tocsin pealing loudly, just as he was driving away.

Drouet and an employee of the "district" called Guillaume, were dispatched by the town-council to pursue the fugitives. (Hilaire Belloc has described this race in matchless and breath-taking prose.) At nine o'clock, in pitch darkness, Drouet and Guillaume mounted the only two remaining horses, and galloped off to Clermont.

In the meantime, the royal berline was rumbling steadily through the silent forest of the Argonne, and finally reached Clermont. There, another blow, the 180 dragoons under Colonel de Damas were not there, for their presence had disturbed the people. Monsieur de Damas himself was waiting in front of the posting station, where he prudently affected indifference; but the King and Queen very unwisely showed satisfaction at seeing him. The King questioned him, but the Queen discreetly cut short this conversation. The crowds did not fail to notice with what respect Monsieur de Damas saluted the travellers. They had spied on all his movements, began gossiping, and their suspicions were conveyed to the municipal authorities.

The whole plot was ruined by one small sentence of three words. As Moustiers got into the driver's seat, the chaise containing the maids passed by, and he cried to its postilion, "The Varennes road!"

Those three words tolled the knell of the monarchy.

The postilions, returning to Sainte-Menehould, were therefore able to inform Drouet, when they met him: "Yes, he's taken the Varennes road, not the Verdun road." Thus Drouet took the short cut and did not pass through Clermont.

When the berline had passed Clermont, the fugitives began to feel quite safe; indeed, they were all fast asleep. Monsieur Lenotre writes: "It is tragic, this bit of road from Clermont to Varennes; on it one is irresistibly drawn to thinking of those poor folk, tracked down like wild animals, and who, broken with fatigue, had gone to sleep, reassured."

In the woods above, running parallel with the road, Drouet and Guillaume are galloping like madmen, meeting at each cross-road the exhausted, grumbling hussars of the Duc de Choiseul.

At ten-forty-five, the two pursuers reached Varennes where the two roads converged.

The royal family cannot find the relay. And not a sign of the sixty hussars who were supposed to be waiting there. The King gets out and bangs on the door of a house.

The travellers held council. "Better go to the Auberge du Grand Monarque, beyond the bridge at the other end of the town, refresh the horses and go on."

"No, impossible," cried the postilions emphatically. "Our regulations authorise us to refuse to double the post. Anyway, beyond Varennes, we don't know the road."

CHAPTER XXI

Caught

DROUET, a little ahead of them in the main street, had seen from a distance the lanterns of the two carriages, which were huddled, as if they were cowering against the houses, and he'd even heard the argument between Moustiers and the postilions who were refusing to go any further.

Instantly, he put everyone on the alert, and barricaded the bridge with a furniture van.

As the berline passed, Sauce, a grocer and parish attorney, woke up. Hearing of the situation, he woke his children and ordered them to run through the town screaming: "Fire! Fire!"

The carriage was stopped and surrounded by armed men, under the vaulted passage-way of the Church of Saint-Gengoult. Passports were asked for. All was in order, and most of the men agreed that the travellers should be allowed to go on. But here, Drouet began: "How dare you be such fools, you idiots, it's your responsibility, you can't let them pass, it's the royal family, I tell you. If you let them slip through to a foreign country, you'll be guilty of the crime of betraying the nation." He was so set, so insistent, so furious, that he overruled public opinion.

"We are lost," thought Elisabeth inside the carriage.

Sauce the grocer turned up. He'd never seen the royal family before. "We'll stamp the passports to-morrow," he said.

"Nonsense, my good man, this is ridiculous. We wish to go on now."

Sauce kept repeating, "To-morrow morning, we'll see."

By then a crowd had collected, and the tocsin was sounded. Sauce said, "Come into my house."

This grocer's shop was a narrow hovel. And so these poor souls who had been used to the white and gold woodwork of Versailles and the Cupids of Petit Trianon were herded into the back room of the grocer's shop, among the ill-smelling tallow candles and the tubs of pickled cucumbers.

They had hardly been there an hour, but a cry rang through the little town: "The hussars! Here are the hussars!"

Here were their saviours at last; they had come through the woods from Pont-de-Somme-Vesle. Choiseul harangued his men: "You must deliver the King and Queen, or die, and thus you will acquire immortal glory."

But the exhausted and hungry hussars did not budge. *They did not understand French.* Incredible! What organisation! . . .

Sauce, still worrying because he could not recognise the royal family, suddenly had an inspiration. He knew a judge called Destez, who had married at Versailles and had often seen the royal family.

He sent a message: "Come along and tell me whether you recognise them." Madame Destez came too. They pushed past the two peasants armed with pitchforks who were guarding the shop door.

Destez opened the door into Sauce's shop. He hesitated a moment and, bending the knee before the King—the Judas—he said: "Ah! Sire."

Suddenly, very moved, the King confessed: "All right, then, yes, I am your King!" The rest is so sickening, that it is difficult to describe calmly. The King drew the grocer Sauce and the judge Destez to him, and *embraced them.* . . .

At each kiss, he became more maudlin; all the onlookers were in floods of tears. The Queen was in a state of extreme agitation. Madame Destez says cunningly that when the Queen and Elisabeth were recognised, "they sulked" (*font la mine*). The Queen was very nervous, and Elisabeth patient and resigned.

(Is it not Madame Swetchine who defined resignation as putting God between yourself and your sorrow?)

Choiseul, Goguelat and Damas—all three had come to the King and proposed to push back the crowd with a cavalry charge and clear a passage way in the street. "Unnecessary," said the King. "The municipal authorities have promised to let me reach Montmédy, on condition I postpone my departure till dawn."

P

Three dragoons in olive green uniforms, rose-coloured facings and white breeches now guarded the shop door.

The hussars, commanded by Goguelat, refused to obey, and were calling out in their own jargon, "Long live the Nation!" Sauce wandered to and fro, pale, haggard and lethargic. Radet (the future general) offered to take the King out by the back door and hide him in the woods, but he refused. The multitude outside cried out: "To Paris. To Paris, or we will shoot into the carriage."

Just then, the grand-mother of Sauce the grocer, an old woman of over eighty who had been born in the reign of Louis XIV and had a loyal French heart, dragged herself from the neighbouring village, leaning on a stick, and reached the shop. After curtseying in her peasant fashion to the King and Queen, she went over to the bed where the royal children were sleeping and wanted to bless them, "but bursting into sobs, she fell on her knees by the bed, and hiding her wrinkled face in the bed clothes, she wept long and bitterly.

"Such were the farewells which ancient France made to the noble race of her Kings, in the person of this poor child who was never to reign."[1]

The National Assembly had sent Romeuf, La Fayette's aide-de-camp, and Bayon, charging them to bring back the fugitives as quickly as possible. Romeuf went up to where the children were sleeping, and, bursting into tears, handed a paper to the King. He read: "There is no longer a King of France." The Queen snatched the document and threw it on the floor, exclaiming: "I don't want it to sully my children." Murmurs in the room, "as if something very holy had been profaned".

Louis XVI, still hoping to see Bouillé's troops, pleaded: "Let us just stay on till eleven o'clock." Romeuf gave way, but Bayon treacherously went out into the street and stirred up the mob by saying: "They don't want to go. Bouillé is coming, they're waiting for him. . . ." The crowd, terrified of these "assassins", screamed out: "We'll drag them by the feet into the carriage."

The Queen, in a terrible state, pleaded with Madame Sauce, but this woman wanted to protect her own husband. It was by now seven-

[1] From "Madame Elisabeth de France" by E. M. du L.

thirty in the morning. At last, the royal family was forced to leave the house and get back into the coach.

It lumbered along so slowly, that a dragoon could see them all quite clearly. He saluted the King, who returned his greeting, but with an air of prostration, an inexpressible expression of suffering. Another eye-witness says that Madame Elisabeth was exceptionally firm, and kept her presence of mind in an admirable way.

The young Comte de Sérent, sent by Bouillé to prevent the King from leaving Varennes, got there just too late. His cry of "God save the King" nearly cost him his life. He was rewarded by a smile from the Queen.

The whole countryside was determined not to miss a single scene of this exciting drama. The peasants were drunk with excitement. Six thousand men, of whom 200 were mounted, and 1,000 women and children escorted the berline on its return journey.

At the precise moment of departure, Bouillé and his troops arrived. But it was too late. . . .

The weather was sultry and heavy. The carriage, with its windows down, was shrouded in a cloud of dust. The mob, which always loves to kick a dog when it is down, was crowing with delight at the stricken appearance of the captives. It took three hours to do three leagues.

At Sainte-Menehould, the mayor offered them food in the Hôtel-de-Ville. M. Lenotre tells us (according to private information) that the King was bathed in sweat and seemed harassed; the dresses of the Queen and Madame Elisabeth were grey with dust. Madame Royale could hardly keep upright, and the Dauphin was asleep in his chair. But the crowd, still afraid that the royal family was waiting for Bouillé, kept shrieking: "We are betrayed. To Châlons! To Châlons!"

"All right, let's go," said the King. On his way out, he caught sight of prisoners peering at him from behind the bars of the town jail. He took ten *louis* from his pocket, to which the Queen added five, and asked the mayor to distribute this sum to the prisoners. He had a fellow feeling for men behind bars.

At three o'clock, they left again under a burning sky. They were hemmed in by the mob which had been drinking since early morning.

The Comte de Dampierre tried several times to protest against the revolting horror of the mob's uproar, by saluting the King and Queen. He was clubbed to death with cudgels and mattocks and then shot. His body was thrown into a ditch. "What is that noise of shooting?" asked the King.

"Nothing, it's a madman they are killing."

Passing by Notre Dame-de-l'Epine, the crowds broke all the presbytery windows.

They reached Châlons at eleven o'clock at night—Châlons, where twenty-one years ago Marie-Antoinette had halted as a young Archduchess, coming to France for the first time. The daughters of the women who had greeted her then must have been nurtured in a tradition of love for her, for they brought her baskets full of bouquets and respectfully offered to serve her.

At one in the morning, supper was served, and at two the children were put to bed. The King and Queen and Madame Elisabeth kept watch all night and had feverish discussions. "Supposing the good people of Reims, from the city of coronations, joined forces with the loyal subjects of Châlons?" Someone begged the King to make use of a secret staircase behind a partition, elude the sentries and escape: join Bouillé's army. But he would not.

The next day, Thursday, was the Feast of Corpus Christi. The King said he wanted to go to Mass at ten o'clock and that he would leave after luncheon. The priest was just going to begin Mass, when the "good people of Reims" knocked down the sentries and invaded the staircase leading to the chapel, crying out, "Capet is fat enough for what we want to do with him, we are going to make cords with the guts of Louis and Antoinette, and belts with their skins. . . ." Others clamoured for their hearts and livers to cook them and eat them.

So much for "my good people of Reims".

As Elisabeth had said once at Versailles, during times like these, bandits suddenly drop down from nowhere, and one had not even seen them coming. It was almost uncanny.

Mass was interrupted again and again. No time for a meal afterwards. The berline was pushed, almost lifted, by the crowd. At midday the prisoners left.

This was the most terrible stage of the whole journey. It took four hours to travel the five leagues from Matougues to Epernay. At Chouilly, the loyal peasants saw with horror that the wretches around the berline were shaking their fists at the prisoners and spitting at the King's face. He remained impassive, while the Queen and Elisabeth wept with indignation.

At five o'clock, at Epernay, they stopped in front of the Hôtel de Rohan—ill-omened name. Imprecations, cat-calls, pikes and axes brandished, and a thunder of howls and insults.

A young soldier, Cazotte, managed to fight his way to the berline and said in German to the Queen, looking straight into her eyes: "Despise this fury, God is above all." He protected them as they got out, and Madame d'Armaillé says that, had it not been for him, "the Queen would have been assassinated. Madame Elisabeth placed herself before her and risked grave dangers." The Dauphin put his arms around Cazotte's neck: The soldier's eyes were streaming with tears, for the poor child's clothes had been torn by the mobs.

Gradually the resignation of the royal family calmed the populace. A voice was heard saying: "But all the same, they look very kind." This, however, did not last long: the diabolical elements got control again. When the Queen appeared on the footboard, a woman threw her this ominous farewell: "Get along with you, *ma petite*, we'll show you tricks worth two of these."

Towards seven o'clock in the evening, in gruelling heat, near the hamlet of Cave, the carriage was met by the envoys from the National Assembly. Latour-Maubourg a royalist, Pétion a constitutionalist, and Barnave a republican.

To protect the prisoners from the mob, Barnave and Pétion got into the berline. Pétion, who wrote an account, tells us that the King, the Queen, and the royal prince were at the back of the carriage, Elisabeth, Madame de Tourzel and Madame in front. The Queen took the prince on her knees. Barnave got in between the King and the Queen. Madame de Tourzel took Madame between her knees, and so Pétion sat between Elisabeth and Madame de Tourzel.

Let us give him a chance to speak.

". . . no dignity in this conversation, and above all I did not notice, on any of their faces, that grandeur which misfortune often imprints on elevated souls.

"The first cackling over, I noted simplicity and a 'family' air which pleased me . . . there was ease and domestic *bonhomie*. The Queen called Madame Elisabeth '*ma petite sœur*'. Madame Elisabeth did the same. . . . The Queen danced the prince up and down on her knees.

". . . I examined the clothes of the travellers. Impossible to be more shabby. The King wore a suit of brown drugget and some very dirty linen: the women had very common little morning dresses."

Jérôme Pétion, aged thirty-three, was a mediocre lawyer from Chartres who, since 1789, had taken his seat at the Assembly as a member of the Tiers-Etat.[1] Mercier says: "Pétion had a proud counten-ance, quite a good-looking face, an affable glance, a gentle eloquence. . . . But his manners were affected, his eyes were cunning; there was in his features something specious which repelled confidence. Inseparable friend of Robespierre, their principles were so similar and their intimacy so marked, that they were called the two fingers of a hand."

A. Savine says: "Puffed-up by popularity, this overwhelmingly conceited personage that was Pétion, thought only of strutting and showing off, and he had just enough intelligence to notice that he was being chaffed. . . . The fop adopts a majestic silliness.

"Without principles, without morals, enemy of the court and of the great, infatuated with himself, eaten up by a thirst for gold and celebrity. . . ."

Pétion said he knew all about their flight, and that their carriage had been driven by a Swede called . . . And as he feigned inability to recall Fersen's name, the Queen said haughtily: "I am not in the habit of knowing the names of hired coachmen."

Cazotte tells us: " . . . It was Madame Elisabeth who kept up the conversation. To the reproaches which the deputies made about some proceedings at court, her answers were so clear, so candid, so sincere, and showed so much instruction, so much energy, so much

---

[1] Tiers-Etat. It will be remembered that the country was supposed to be repre-sented by the clergy, the nobility and the middle classes or "tiers-état".

affection for the people, in a princess in whom Barnave had seen until then, only a proud and ignorant woman, that the opinions of this deputy underwent a powerful revolution."

After he had heard Elisabeth speak for some time, Barnave was so impressed, that his feelings and his behaviour changed.

Pétion, however, was convinced that Elisabeth had fallen in love with him. Let us listen to his silliness:

". . . Madame Elisabeth foxed me with melting eyes, with that languishing air which unhappiness gives and which inspires a lively interest. . . . The moon began to shine softly. . . . She sometimes interrupted her words, in such a manner as to agitate me. I replied . . . with a kind of austerity. . . . She must have seen that the most seductive temptations were useless. I noticed a certain cooling off, a certain severity, which women often show when their pride is wounded."

Could anything be more fatuous! Poor owl from Chartres, blinking in the sunlight of a girl's goodness. Pétion who has handed down nothing to posterity but these impressions, in which he had the bad taste to imagine that a princess of the royal house of France was smitten with his charms! The whole thing could be comic, if it were not rather pathetic.

When Elisabeth's arm touched his in the overcrowded carriage, he imagined that she was overcome by tender emotions which she did not even take the trouble to conceal. Weber tells us that he then began making ambiguous remarks. Elisabeth pretended she had not heard them.

However, when he dared to joke against religion, Elisabeth broke her contemptuous silence and took him up forcefully and in a lively fashion. The Queen was astonished at the "eloquence, logic and force of reasoning which her sister-in-law displayed on this occasion". He twisted the Dauphin's curls around his finger so tightly, that the exhausted child wept. The Queen took him away, saying that her son was not used to treatment of this sort. Then, brusquely, Pétion asked Elisabeth for a glass and got her to fill it with water; he never even troubled to thank her.

At Dormans, they stopped outside the Hôtel du Louvre at eleven o'clock at night.

After supper, a lemonade seller, carrying refreshments, came into the room where the royal family was sitting. The boy presented his tray to Elisabeth. She lifted her eyes and recognised him. She'd met him before. He said he was the son-in-law of the mayor of Dormans, who owned this hotel, and they had both concocted a plan of escape. The King refused to entertain this, saying he was counting on his "good city of Paris". The young man went out again.

The captives opened Elisabeth's prayer book at random, and found a psalm which proved to be a source of consolation.

Friday, June the 24th, at six o'clock, under a burning sun, they got into the berline again.

Every attempt to pull down the spring roller blind had been met by murmurs from the crowd. The Queen said, "One must show firmness," but in the end she was obliged to put it up herself.

Two o'clock, la Ferté-sous-Jouarre. A clamouring crowd was waiting for them. The mayor, Régnard de l'Isle, had asked by courier that the royal family should come to his house, a pretty place overlooking the Marne. Pétion walked with Elisabeth on the terrace before dinner. ". . . I spoke to her of all the intrigues, of all the court manœuvres, with the dignity of a free mind, the disdain of a wise one. . . . I should not be surprised if she had a beautiful and good soul, though greatly imbued with the prejudices of birth and spoilt by the vices of a court education."

Madame Royale says that her aunt felt ill during the whole of dinner. The meals, according to Pétion, were "splendid"; according to Madame de Tourzel, "simple but properly served". The mayor's wife, from delicacy of feeling, did not want to eat with the royal family, so she disguised herself as a cook and served them with respect and zeal. When Marie-Antoinette asked her whether this charming house had a mistress, she replied with all the courtesy of old France, "I was its mistress, Madame, before the coming of your Majesty."

At five o'clock they left. Pétion then talked to the Queen. "I cannot say with what energy, with what abundancy of *soul*, I spoke; I was spurred by the idea . . . that the Queen would remember this moment's conversation."

He then told them that a beautiful calm had reigned in Paris, at the news of the King's flight. . . . "I thought I noticed that they (the Queen and Elisabeth) were nettled about that." How feline of him to do this. . . .

Suddenly, screams outside the carriage. A poor village curé, who had wanted to get near the King to speak to him, was set upon by the cannibals. Barnave leaped to his feet, crying: "Tigers, have you ceased being Frenchmen? Nation of brave men, have you become a people of assassins?"

Barnave nearly threw himself out of the carriage window in his excitement, and Elisabeth kept him in by clutching at his coat tails! Madame Campan tells us in her memoirs how the Queen used to say that "the pious Elisabeth" holding Barnave back by the coat tails seemed to her such a surprising sight. Madame Campan also expresses how shocked she was by Pétion's outrageous manners, his "republican ruggedness", for he ate and drank in the King's berline in a dirty fashion, throwing chicken bones out of the window, at the risk of hitting the King in the face; and when Elisabeth poured him out some wine, he just lifted the glass without saying a word, to indicate that he'd had enough. This offensive tone was calculated, for this man had received some education. Barnave was revolted by it all.

Odious people can often be quite fascinating to watch. Probably Pétion did much to distract the afflicted family from their wretchedness.

The berline reached Meaux at eight o'clock at night. Lenotre says: "The Parisian element of swaggerers, guzzlers and tipplers, mingled already its note of licence with the tumult which greeted the prisoners. Along the Faubourg Saint Nicolas, the welcome was the same —noisy, sniggering and insulting."

The berline often came to a standstill, then advanced slowly, by fits and starts. All this under a leaden sky, in a stifling and stormy atmosphere.

National Guards were clinging to the crumbling sculptures of the cathedral of Meaux.

By torchlight, they went into the bishop's house. It was not properly furnished, for a constitutional bishop, Monscigneur Thuin, had just replaced Monseigneur de Polignac. The bishop apologized to the King for his makeshift hospitality. Louis XVI most aptly replied: "When one is not '*chez soi*' (in one's own place) one is dispensed from excusing oneself."

Some of the china and linen had to be borrowed.

The Queen began feeling more and more anxious about the reception they would get in Paris on the morrow.

On Saturday, June the 25th, by five o'clock in the morning, they were all up. The royal family was served with a dish of eggs, some cream, sugar and light rolls. The journey lasted thirteen hours, in terrible heat, under a fiery sky, in clouds of thick grey dust. In the wood of Bondy, a band of brigands and termagants, profiting by a quarrel between the grenadiers and the Parisian guards, slipped close up to the berline and cynically insulted the Queen. The Dauphin was frightened and started crying out. His mother drew him to her and her eyes filled with tears.

At three o'clock, they reached Pantin, a suburb of Paris, and suddenly the crowd became dead silent. The orders for the day were that "whosoever applauds the King would be beaten, whoever insults him would be hanged".

The berline crept like a tortoise, for patriots were covering its roof and clinging to its sides. At the Pavillon de Monceau, the King took a glass of wine. Then the rabble started down the Champs-Elysées, which were lined by the National Guards presenting arms with their butt-ends reversed, as for a funeral. After passing the Place Louis XV, the carriage went into the alley in the middle of the Tuileries gardens and then stopped at the steps leading into the château.

At once, a cry: "The guards, death for the guards!" The National Guards were powerless to control the mob. Moustiers, the coachman, climbed down first and only reached the vestibule of the palace after receiving many wounds. Madame Royale says: "When we had got out of the carriage, we were nearly carried by the enormous crowd which filled the staircase."

It was seven o'clock at night. The exhausted members of the royal family went to their apartments. Pétion, half dead with fatigue, asked Elisabeth for a drink, and she sent for some beer.

Madame de Tourzel, fearing she would have to pay for her loyalty, sent a message to Elisabeth to ask for the book she had promised her, and she received "Meditations on Death".

Cazotte tells us that the Queen, covered in dust, had asked for a bath when she returned to her bed-chamber, but she could not induce her guard to leave her alone. "Forget that I am Queen, and remember that I am a woman," she said. She was answered by an indelicate joke and an ironical smile.

Madame Campan saw the Queen soon after the catastrophe. "In a single night, her hair had gone completely white, like that of a woman of seventy."

CHAPTER XXII

After Varennes

"OUR home life here is hell," wrote the Queen to Fersen on October the 31st. It is easy to imagine the recriminations which ensued on their return to the Tuileries. "If only you hadn't let the crowds seen you at the posting stations," the Queen kept saying to the King, "if only you had sat quietly in the carriage and kept your head back. But no, you must act a part, you with your trust in human nature, and your 'good people of Reims' and your 'good people of Paris'." One must admit that if the Queen and Elisabeth attacked the King on his return, he deserved it all. "If only the flight had been organised by me," the Queen would say.

"I like that," the King would reply. "And it is you who insisted on taking two maids, Léonard, and that quantity of trunks." Elisabeth tried to smoothe them both down. "Well, it's no use crying over spilt milk. Every night I go over the flight in my mind, again and again, trying to put my finger on the exact moment where we went wrong. And I feel that everything was against us."

"And yet the Provences were able to escape. . . ." "Ah," said Louis, holding his trump card, "because my brother never told his wife beforehand." The Queen flushed scarlet, the imperial nose became pinched with anger, she held her head proudly and looked down contemptuously at her husband. "And if we hadn't had to take so many provisions for *you*, my dear, that would have lightened the load considerably. All you thought about was the next meal." Even a worm will turn. The King replied: "And if you hadn't been caught packing your diamonds, my dear . . ."

At this point, Elisabeth intervened. "Well, it's all over now, and we must admit that it had its funny side. For example, when Pétion was throwing chicken bones out of the window and almost hitting me on the nose." The Queen laughed: "And that idiotic moment when you were clinging on to Barnave's coat tails, to prevent him from falling out of the window."

Elisabeth sighed. "Alas for Monsieur de Dampierre. I cannot bear to think of his fate."

The Queen said: "I can still hear his screams as he was being clubbed." She turned to the King and said violently: "So this is what happens to your subjects when you refuse to protect them, you with your constant cry of 'I will not shed a drop of French blood'."

With a weary gesture of resignation and despair, the King went out of the room, only to fall over a sentry who had been listening to the whole quarrel through the key-hole. Indeed, the constant espionage, the lack of privacy, helped to set the captives on edge, though the physical and nervous reaction from that terrible week of flight was bad enough. The prison walls began to close in still further. Mass in the chapel was stopped, because it was too far from the royal suites, and the National Assembly feared that the family would try to escape again. So a wooden altar was put up in another room.

The officer in charge of the Queen quite calmly installed himself in an armchair in her bedroom. She was obliged to put up a screen in order to dress. At night, she was woken several times by soldiers coming in to see whether she were still there. In terrible heat, they never left the palace for six weeks. The gardens were more private, now, for they were locked to strangers. "This large, sad garden," as Elisabeth called it.

The Bourbon princes, safely out of France, were all for calling in foreign aid. The Queen was against it. Baron Hué in his "*Souvenirs*", tells us that the Queen told him one day in the Tuileries gardens: "The King and I have just refused the help of 60,000 men which the Emperor, my brother, proposed to send to us in France. . . . The assistance of strangers, however friendly they may seem, is a temerity. . . ."

Other writers prove to us, too, that both the King and Queen were opposed to armed intervention by the *émigrés*. The peoples of Europe, watching the Coblentz *émigrés*, saw nothing but frivolity—everyone out for himself: nobody was interested in the common weal.

The Prince de Tarente, himself an *émigré*, speaks of the exiled

French courtiers leaving Turin and going to Coblentz: "At Turin, their bragging, their boasting, their inconsequence, began to lower them in the esteem of European powers."

As M. Jules Mazé has said: "It was strange, this court of Coblentz where two princes played at being king, and who, both married, had for queens their mistresses, the Comte de Provence, Madame de Balbi, the Comte d'Artois, Madame de Polastron. There was no love lost between the two princes; the two mistresses detested one another. Madame de Balbi, very proud of belonging to the elder of the brothers, to the one who was nearest the throne, stayed in a country house near the town. There she presided over a circle where the Comte d'Artois and his society were vilified. There the lord of the place became intoxicated with flatteries; sometimes, courtiers, after a meal accompanied by generous wines, went so far as to embellish manifestations of their enthusiasm with the magical word 'Sire'. Then the prince would make a vague gesture of smiling protest and murmur: 'My dear friends, I beg you, let us not anticipate.'

"Madame de Polastron, known for the maliciousness of her viper's tongue, had nicknamed Madame de Balbi the 'white queen' in a most transparent allusion to the impotence of the Comte de Provence."

Marie-Antoinette mistrusted them and their mad ambitions. She knew they would not hesitate to aggravate the King's perils. She had put her brother, the Emperor, on his guard, and he disdainfully nicknamed them *"les jeunes messieurs"*—'the young gentlemen'. Seeing Elisabeth's blind faith in the Comte d'Artois, the Queen thought it wiser never to confide in her during that period. She wrote to Fersen, after Varennes: "My sister is so indiscreet, surrounded by intriguers, and, above all, dominated by her brothers outside (France), that it is impossible for us to speak to one another, or we would quarrel all day."

This is strange, for, at that time, Elisabeth's letters show how conciliating she was. She was a peace-maker, always loyally trying to point out her sister-in-law's good points to her brothers. (Apparently, we learn that one of d'Artois' complaints against the Queen had been her reckless extravagance. He seemed to forget Bagatelle, that jewel of a château he had built for a wager.) Elisabeth wrote: "One thing could really affect me deeply: that a coolness should be created in a family which I sincerely love."

Léonard, the hairdresser, a veritable mischief-maker, went so far as to say that the Queen was jealous of Elisabeth's youth and beauty. This is just as ridiculous as Madame de la Tour du Pin's story, that the Queen at Versailles had envied young women with dazzling complexions.

In July, Elisabeth wrote to Rage: "Ah, *mon cœur*, happy the man, who, in full possession of his soul, only sees God and eternity. . . .

". . . I have even preserved some gaiety. Yesterday I laughed a lot as I recalled the ridiculous anecdotes of our journey." But the shock had been great, and she spoke of it once or twice to her intimate friends. However, the nightmare of the flight had taught her a lesson in detachment. She wrote to Bombe: "We are not created to live happy in this world." Now, after hoping in plots and plans, she felt more and more drawn to trusting only in God's providence for His children.

And still, she continued to be concerned about the headaches and ear-aches of her friends, and the weaning and teething troubles of their babies! "Rub Henry's gums very hard, so that his teeth will grow fast and he will let you sleep."

Fears of poison increased their miseries at the end of that fateful 1791. Madame Campan tells us of a former Palais Royal pastry-cook, a fierce revolutionary who made no secret of his belief that the King should be killed off. He found employment in the Tuileries kitchens. Thenceforward, they ate no pastry, and hid their morsels under the dining-table.

The sentries themselves got nervy. On the terrace of the Feuillants, a sentry mistook some falling chestnuts for bullets and began shooting. Elisabeth also told Bombe of a night sentry who had fallen asleep, and who, screaming in a nightmare, caused pendemonium in the entire palace.

.   .   .   .   .

Winter drew near, and at once the princess's thoughts turned from family troubles to anxiety about the Paris poor, who were facing greater hardships than ever. On November the 8th, 1791, she wrote to Bombe: ". . . If you want to know, it's terribly cold (_un froid de loup_) . . . especially since the last three days. There is already enough ice on the ponds to fill the ice-houses. If the winter is as cold as it promises to be, I don't know what will become of the poor. . . ."

With the civil list reduced and unemployed servants wandering about because their masters were abroad, the numbers of the poor increased enormously, and Elisabeth was deluged with begging letters. She entrusted her first maid, Madame de Navarre, with the task of investigation. A charitable lady from the parish of the Madeleine de la Ville-l'Evêque wrote the following letter: "By Madame's order, I went to the joiner of No. 9. We went up together; it's all true: the man is dying, the woman very ill, the three children huddled in straw; they have nothing to cover themselves with and cannot go down to beg, naked. . . . The joiner's wife gave them a little soup. It is in a garret of the Rue Roquépine that these unfortunate people are moaning."

(As Elisabeth had once written before the Revolution: "Although our century prides itself a great deal on sensibility, it consists infinitely more in words than in feelings.")

Elisabeth had a help-mate in the angelic little Dauphin. She seems to have inspired him with love of the poor. One day, he was found locking coins away safely in a small money box. His father said: "Well, Charles, are you hoarding money like a miser?" At the word "miser", the child blushed, then he said, "No, I'm saving for the _Enfants Trouvés_ (home for lost children). Oh, if you only knew how much they needed help."

Seven-year-old Charles, "_ce chou d'amour_", as his mother called him, was a great consolation, not only to his parents, but to his aunt. The page, Comte d'Hézecques, wrote: "All who came near him, will always remember with happiness, the candour of his face, the beauty of his complexion, his long fair hair, and especially his charming attention, as when in Paris he followed with his eyes, his parents' slightest movements, to know when to smile or to greet . . ."

This little boy simply adored his mother. His one ambition was to give her bouquets of flowers from his own garden. He grew some "immortelles", or everlasting plants, for her feast day, because he wanted her to be immortal. He refused to give her "soucis" or marsh-marigolds, for she had enough cares. ("*Soucis*" were cares.) One day when he was listening to her singing, he went off into such a day-dream that his aunt said: "Really, Charles, you've fallen asleep." He quickly replied: "How could one fall asleep when *Maman-Reine* is singing?"

Q

CHAPTER XXIII

The fatal year

JUNE the 20th, 1792. The anniversary of the flight to Varennes—a month ill-fated for the Bourbons, just as the Ides of March for Julius Caesar. The mob invaded the Tuileries. Elisabeth stayed with the King and was quickly surrounded. Horace Walpole wrote of all this to Miss Hannah Moore: he had an admiration for this princess whom he called "an heroic virgin saint", and "the angelic Madame Elisabeth". "In this deluge of triumphant enormities, what traits of the sublime and beautiful may be gleaned! Did you hear of Madame Elisabeth the king's sister? a saint like yourself." Horace Walpole tells us that the viragos, mistaking her for the Queen, yelled out: ". . . Here is that bitch, that Austrian woman! . . ." and were proceding to violence. Somebody, to save her, screamed out: "It is not the Queen, it is . . ." The princess said: "Ah! my God, do not undeceive them."

At seven-forty-five in the evening, worn out by heat, tumult and anxiety, the members of the royal family were re-united again. Brigands had rushed into every cranny of the palace, even up to attics and on to roofs, shrieking for the Queen. Rooms were sacked, doors and panelling smashed, locks picked and wrenched off.

A woman of the people said naïvely: "Nothing could be done to-day, their Sainte Geneviève was there."

When a deputation appeared on the morrow, the little Dauphin asked his mother: "Isn't yesterday finished?"

The mills of that royal martyrdom ground very slowly: each month brought an increase in studied insolence, from men who should have known better. Bertrand de Molleville tells us that "Cahier de Gerville treated Madame Elisabeth with revolting brutality. She had asked him to go and see her half an hour before the council meeting. She wanted to speak to him in favour of an unhappy nun who had been recommended to her, and in whose plight she took the liveliest interest. Cahier de Gerville interrupted Madame Elisabeth before she had finished what she wanted to say, and he answered her in the driest possible manner: 'It is very astonishing, Madame, that you hold a minister's time in such low esteem, and make me lose half an hour to hear you speak about a nun; I have much other business besides that of nuns . . .'

"The good Madame Elisabeth, whose ears were so little accustomed to such hard, coarse tones, was so thunderstruck, that she let the minister go without saying a single word."

On July the 14th, 1792, the Feast of the Federation took place in the Champ-de-Mars. Madame de Staël who was present said that she would never forget the expression on the Queen's face: ". . . her eyes were worn with weeping, the splendour of her dress, the dignity of her bearing, contrasted with the retinue by which she was surrounded."

Weber says: "In my eyes, Madame Elisabeth looked as ever, like an angel . . . and the Dauphin was as beautiful as love."

Madame de Staël sent someone to the King with a plan of escape she had concocted. She had bought a property at Lamotte, on the coast of Normandy, and went there two or three times a week in a berline, always accompanied by the same people. As soon as the postilions and the masters of the posting stations had got accustomed to this, and no longer looked in closely at the windows, she suggested that the royal family should come and take the place of these persons.

The offer was refused.

. . . . .

August the 10th. The sack of the Tuileries. The clumsy manifesto of the Duc de Brunswick unleashed that fateful day and set fire to the barrel of gunpowder. He said that if the King and Queen were attacked, he would exercise "an exemplary and unforgettable vengeance, by delivering up Paris to military execution and complete destruction". Prussian belief in the efficacy of threats which infuriated the Parisians. This manifesto, which offered a pretext for aggression, was made known on July the 28th. Under the leadership of Danton, the 48 "sections"[1] of Paris voted for the King's downfall. On the 30th, the confederates arrived from Marseilles.

[1] In 1790, the city had been divided into forty-eight sections.

Through an emissary, the King secretly sounded Pétion—by now mayor of Paris. This was the reply of Pétion and his friends: they demanded 800,000 francs to divide amongst themselves, and they pledged their word to employ all the means in their power to ward off the "*coup*" which was being prepared.

On August the 9th, it was very hot. Elisabeth wrote to Bombe—her last letter—and made the King play billiards. She saw the Abbé Edgeworth—also for the last time. At midnight, the tocsin was rung, first at the Cordeliers, and then all over Paris. Pétion went into the King's bed-chamber, "looking false" says an eye-witness. And well he might, for, in spite of accepting those 800,000 francs, he had purposely kept the King's bodyguard short of ammunition. The members of the royal family got up and met in one room. Soon, they were joined by an élite of loyal noblemen, disguised as commoners, and hiding arms on their persons. They had rushed out to defend the King. They went to the open windows to listen to the alarm-bells, and each named the church whose bell he thought he recognised. Ah! Paris churches which for centuries had delighted the saints, bells which had summoned to prayer some of the greatest men and women in history—soon, they were doomed to a long silence. (A bishop of Tulle once said: "The land of France keeps in her breast the dust of millions of hearts, who beat in unison with the Heart of Christ.") Elisabeth wrote: "It is from the Heart of Jesus that people seem to await the graces which they need; the fervour of this devotion appears to redouble; the more our ills increase, the more we address our prayers to It."

The great bell of Notre Dame! Elisabeth thought at once of that "good Mother" who was the patroness of France, that Queen of Heaven to whom her ancestor Louis XIII had dedicated his kingdom. How long ago it seemed since that first February at the Tuileries, when she had gone to Mass at Notre Dame with the family, and a woman, overcoming her shyness, had distributed some little printed forms of consecration to Our Lady to the congregation.

At one o'clock in the morning, the Queen said: "Let us go and rest on a sofa in a little closet overlooking the courtyard." Madame Campan relates: ". . . Madame Elisabeth loosened several garments which hampered her, in order to lie down on the sofa; she had taken from her neckerchief, a cornelian brooch, and before putting it on the table, she showed it to me and told me to read a device engraved on it, around a sheaf of lilies. I saw these words: 'To forget offences, to forgive injuries.' 'I greatly fear,' added this virtuous princess, 'that this maxim has little influence amongst our enemies, but for that reason it must not be any the less dear to us.'"

Between four and five o'clock in the morning, one of the ring-leaders came into the room in which the princesses had again joined the King. He said: "Here is your last day: the people are stronger than you; what carnage there will be." They ran to the Dauphin's room. Just then, a sound of coach wheels was heard in the courtyard: they hurried to the window just in time to watch Pétion's coach leaving—that ignominious Judas had accepted the King's money, but had betrayed them. Elisabeth gazed at the sky which was very red. She said to the Queen who was kissing the Dauphin in his bed: *"Ma sœur,* come and see the sunrise." The Queen joined her. How far away seemed that day when Marie-Antoinette scandalised Mesdames Tantes by watching the sunrise at Marly with her gay young friends. . . . This was the last sunrise they were ever to watch from the Tuileries, or indeed anywhere, for the windows of their next prison were barricaded with planks. That crimson presaged all the blood that was to be shed that day—blood of all the Swiss Guards, blood of all the young noblemen, blood of all the servants left in the palace. There was one chestnut tree in the Tuileries gardens whose roots were so soaked with blood that, every spring, it always blossomed earlier than its fellows.

The King, the Queen and Elisabeth all visited the defence posts in the interior of the château. We are told that the Queen choked her sobs with difficulty. "Her Austrian lip, her aquiline nose . . . gave to her face an air of majesty, difficult to picture, unless one had seen it at that moment." As for Elisabeth, everyone admired her "presence of mind, the nobility and intrepidity which she showed in her least words". This angelic soul was full of sisterly tenderness. Her very glance inspired courage.

Quite soon, the situation outside got beyond control. The King and his family were persuaded to seek refuge with the National

Assembly near by. Madame de Tourzel says that "... Consternation was general when the King was seen to leave for the Assembly. The Queen followed him, holding her two children by the hand. By their sides were Madame Elisabeth, Madame la Princesse de Lamballe, who, as a relation of their Majesties, had obtained permission to follow them, and I was behind Monseigneur le Dauphin."

François de la Rochefoucauld tells us that the Queen was weeping: "... from time to time she wiped away her tears and tried to assume a radiant air which she kept for some minutes. However, as she leant for one moment against my arm, I felt her trembling all over. .... Madame Elisabeth was the calmest; she was resigned to everything. .... Madame de Lamballe said to me: 'We will never return to the Château.'" (She was murdered the following month.)

The crowd was so thick, that the Queen's purse was stolen.

Elisabeth caught sight of Weber, sobbing bitterly. She seized him and said: "Calm yourself, Weber; Weber . . . be reasonable."

Another witness tells us that they all walked on leaves which had fallen in the night and which the gardeners had just piled up into heaps. The little prince jumped into them, and amused himself by pushing the leaves on to the legs of the people ahead of him. "The leaves are falling very early," sighed Louis XVI.

On the terrace, people were shouting insults as they passed. In the passage leading to the Assembly, they were kept waiting for half an hour, because some deputies were opposed to giving them refuge from the populace.

At last the door was opened. The Queen sailed in with great dignity, looking as serene and august as if she were at a royal function at Versailles. They were shown into the "*loge du logographe*", that is to say the booth of the editor of a newspaper called "Le Logographe"—a tiny square space, with whitewashed walls which reflected the intense heat, a box only separated from the Assembly by iron railings.

In the meantime, the mob had invaded the Place Louis Quinze, the Rue Royale and the Champs-Elysées. Soon, the 300 Swiss Guards, purposely kept short of ammunition by Pétion, could hold out no longer. The massacring and pillaging began in the palace. The Swiss Guards were killed, and about 100 of the royal servants dragged out of hiding. The scene has been described often enough. The royal family, Madame de Tourzel and Madame de Lamballe could not see, but they could hear the yells, the explosions, and the strains of the funereal "*Dies Irae*" played on the chapel organ by a Savoyard; and they could smell the smoke of the fires and the burning flesh. From time to time, men tottered in, drenched in blood. Police *commissionnaires*, to camouflage their looting, would ostentatiously bring in things like the altar candlesticks, and the Ciborium. Elisabeth covered her face in horror when she saw the Sacred Hosts hurled to the ground amid mocking cries from the Assembly. At one moment, an unfaithful servant would struggle in, to make false accusations against his master, followed by a loyal nobleman who would stagger in, dying of his wounds. The royal booth was a furnace in the hot mid-day sun, and the smell of blood became sickening. Everybody was bathed in sweat. François de la Rochefoucauld went up to ask the Queen what he could do for her. "Bring me a handkerchief." Her *fichu* and handkerchief were drenched in tears and sweat. But he had given his to the Vicomte de Maillé to bandage his wounds. The inspectors of the hall, in pity, brought the children a little currant syrup.

They were in there, in that pitiable state, *for sixteen hours.*

Some of the time, the Dauphin slept on his mother's breast. Indignation and grief were portrayed on Elisabeth's features, as deputations came flooding in, calling out for the King's downfall with bloodthirsty, menacing cries. The King peered at them with his spy glasses.

At ten o'clock at night, nearly collapsing, they were led to the Feuillants—a disaffected Trappist monastery quite near. In days gone by, the white monks of St. Bernard were privileged to keep vigil for the dead of the Royal House.

The royal family crossed the garden through a sea of pikes still dripping with blood. Their way was lit by candles placed in the butt end of rifles. Cries of "Give us Louis' head. Give us the head of the infamous Antoinette."

They reached the convent. The Dauphin began to cry: "Oh, Citron, my little dog Citron, where is he? I'm sure he's been crushed in the crowd." Elisabeth said to him gently: "There, dear child, don't mourn; there are griefs more cruel; continue to love God so that He will preserve you from them."

As they had no linen at all, the wife of the English Ambassador, the Countess of Sutherland who had a son the same age as the Dauphin, sent some clothes. Several kind people offered a few things for the others.

The King, who alone had eaten on this day, went to sleep and snored soundly. This disconcerting calm of Louis XVI! All night long, bandits shrieked outside his windows: "Throw us down his head, or we'll come up." Sometimes, they even tried to climb up to the windows, crying, "Let's shorten fat Veto." Each time Elisabeth peeped at them, it was like seeing a menagerie of wild beasts, suddenly roaring when you appeared before their bars. Blood-stained clothes of the Swiss Guards were stuck on the ends of pikes, for banners. Faces were convulsed with fury: these were not all Frenchmen—they were the foreigners who always poured into Paris at times of revolution, to live on the spoils of blood. One never saw those people in times of peace.

And the royal family had to pass through that throng four times a day, for three more days. Once, the Queen and Elisabeth, recognising some servants, greeted them with a bow. But one of them cried out: "No good putting on those gracious airs, you won't have long to wait." Another decently dressed citizen started hurling obscenities at Elisabeth as she passed. And once, quite a respectable young man got close up to the Queen, cocked a snook at her and shrieked: "Infamous Antoinette, you wanted to make the Austrians bathe in our blood; you'll pay for this with your head."

Others shouted, "*Hé*, got some priests in your pockets, to say private Masses for you, *Hé*!"

The first night, the Queen, in her green-papered cell, wept till six o'clock. She was tormented with anxiety about the fate of the women left behind in the palace. When she fell into broken slumber, Elisabeth called the children quietly and helped them to dress. "Don't make a sound: *Maman-Reine* is asleep." When it was time to leave, the children gently woke their mother with caresses.

When the Duc de Choiseul and other gentlemen said farewell to the King, they induced him to accept all the gold and the paper money they had on their persons.

At last they were told that they were going to be taken to the Temple. The Queen trembled, and whispered to Madame de Tourzel: "You will see, they will put us in the tower, and they will make it a veritable prison. I have always had such a horror of that tower, that a thousand times I begged the Comte d'Artois to have it pulled down; it must surely have been a foreboding of all that we would suffer there. . . . You will see if I am not mistaken. . . ."

On the evening of August the 13th, at 7.15, they were taken away in two carriages accompanied by officials who ostentatiously kept their hats on, and who addressed the King as *Monsieur*. By a refinement of cruelty, they passed by the Place Vendôme, to show him the equestrian statue of Louis XIV, thrown from its pedestal, broken to bits and trodden underfoot by the mob. "That's how we treat tyrants," cried the people.

They reached the Temple as night was falling. The battlements of the mediaeval towers were all lit up.

"Probably we will be housed in the Prior's palace where d'Artois lodged when he was in Paris," said the King.

The drawing-room was quite modern, with tall windows, and light woodwork. The Princesse de Conti used to give English tea parties there, and Mozart played to them as a child. "Yes, I think they'll put us there."[1]

"I doubt it," said the Queen.

On August the 10th, Monsieur Berthélemy, the Keeper of the Archives of the Order of Malta in the Tower of the Temple, had heard the cannon of the Tuileries, but as he was a very selfish little man, ensconced in his creature comforts, like a snug angora cat, he did not allow it to worry him unduly. True, the times were troublesome, very troublesome, but when a man has the privilege of occupying the little tower left empty by the death of the Prince de Conti, who had used it for his assignations with actresses, he does not allow re-

[1] See Ollivier's picture in the Louvre: "Le thé à l'Anglaise chez la Princesse de Conti."

volutions to disturb his sleep. Monsieur Berthélemy furnished the three floors with exquisite taste—marquetry work, and gorgeous silk damask. His large study on the first floor, next to his library, was hung with yellow silk bordered with crimson. The drawing-room on the floor above was hung with azure, and the armchairs—"les fauteuils à la reine"—were in blue and white silk damask, the footstools heart shaped, the larger armchairs or "*bergères*" were "*couleur prune de Monsieur*" (fortunate Monsieur who had escaped to Brussels). His bedroom, next to the drawing-room, was draped with white stuff embossed with flowers. He had a Boulle bureau, and a writing-table in rosewood. He had collected some charming though slightly *risqué* engravings—"Diana's bath", the "*Coucher*" of Van Loo, "La Chaste Suzanne", and, on a marble console, a delicate *biscuit de Sèvres* group, "Venus whipping Cupid with a bunch of roses". On the third floor was his *pièce de résistance* of which he was justly proud—a bathroom, entirely surrounded with mirrors, in which the circular sofa was covered with lilac taffeta trimmed with fringes.

Everywhere were light-coloured carpets, decorative porcelain, rosewood corner-cupboards, and heavy silver candelabra. His windows looked on to a vast park. The sun flooded his bedroom in the morning and his drawing-room in the evening. Yes, with such a *pied à terre*, an expert cook, and many beautifully bound books, a man could not complain. Not that Monsieur Berthélemy was a hermit. Oh, no. He enjoyed his intimate little supper parties in well-chosen company, when he and his guests would sing gaily until the small hours of "*l'œil vif et fripon de Catherine*"—the bright and roguish eye of Catherine, and such like carefree ditties.

So, on August the 10th, the honourable Keeper of the Archives heard the cannon of the Tuileries, and no doubt congratulated himself on being quite safe. On Monday, the 13th, at eight in the evening, he noticed some workmen; on enquiring who they were, he was told curtly that they were preparing the royal family's supper in the main building, which was called the Prior's palace. "Yes; no doubt," he said to himself, "they have had to move from the Tuileries." If they were going to stay in the palace, he would probably go and pay them his court. He remembered that the last time the Queen had been on the premises was when she had come to Paris to give thanks at Notre Dame for the birth of her last little boy. The Comte d'Artois, who made the palace his *pied à terre* when he was in Paris, had entertained her there in the evening, much to the scandal of the pious.

Two hours later, at ten o'clock at night, Monsieur Berthélemy heard a noise of footsteps on his stairs. "You must evacuate from here within an hour." "Why, what's happening?" "You've got to move." "To move?" "The Capet family is coming here." "For one night?" "For ever—*prison perpétuelle*." "But the palace is the Temple." "The palace is not secure enough." The little man tried not to have hysterics. In a few moments his precious carpets were covered with filth, for it was raining outside. Some of his furniture was put out in the rain before being hurled helter-skelter into the disaffected Temple church. Alas, in that brief hour, he only had time to move the contents of the first floor and the wine cellar. He was trying to push his way upstairs to get to the second floor when he was thrown back by the inexorable guard. He saw the royal family and their suites enter his lair. But he didn't think of them very much; he wandered about all night, trying to borrow a bed and some linen. The following morning, wretchedly installed, in a horrible hovel of the Rue des Prêtres St. Paul, behind the church of St. Louis, in a street that was sordid, tortuous and dirty, he read in the morning newspapers that Louis XVI was reading the books in his library and sleeping in his bed. Then he heard that the King had taken down his engravings, as he thought they were unsuitable for the eyes of his young daughter.

Poor little Monsieur Berthélemy spent the rest of his life trying to get compensation from indifferent bureaucrats. His furniture is now in a Paris museum, and the bed with its dilapidated cretonne cover, lined with taffeta, the bed which was used by Elisabeth, is still there.

PART III

The Chalice

CHAPTER XXIV

The Temple prison

WITH premeditated viciousness, the officials had played a practical joke. They let their victims think that they would be lodged in the Prior's palace. The great drawing-room was all candle-lit. Lying on a sofa was a rough man holding forth on the bliss of equality for all men. The King was listening. He asked him: "What is your profession?"

"Cobbler," replied the man.

It was Simon—the man who, more than any other, was employed to cause the little Dauphin's slow death by neglect and ill-treatment.

At ten o'clock, supper was served. At eleven o'clock, François Hué and the royal servants were told to take their effects—so few of them —and follow the municipal officers. By lantern-light, they led the way up a narrow winding corkscrew staircase. Soon, the royal victims were told they would be temporarily housed in the small tower.

Here briefly was the lay-out of the rooms. The ground floor— porter's lodge. First floor—antechamber, dining-room, and small library. Second floor—room for Madame de Lamballe, another— former billiard room—for Madame de Tourzel and the Dauphin, another for the Queen and Madame Royale. A privy. A sentry's den. Third floor—a guard-room. A kitchen in which slept Elisabeth and Pauline de Tourzel. A room where some spying servants called Tison were installed later. The King's bedroom, a tiny reading room; a lair for Hué and Cléry, serving the royal family.

When Madame de Lamballe and the Tourzels left, Elisabeth moved down into the Dauphin's room, which she shared with Madame Royale, and the Queen took the Dauphin in with her.

The privy served for the municipal authorities, the royal family and the soldiers. When Elisabeth moved down, everyone had to cross her room to get to it.

The old kitchen in which Elisabeth spent her first night was indescribably filthy, with smelly cooking utensils lying about. Her dressing-table was a stone on which laundry was scrubbed, next to the ovens. Her camp bed was very small. There was a buffet for earthenware pottery which was still covered with grease. Monsieur Berthélemy must have employed a sluttish cook.

The guards next door sang and talked till dawn: it was impossible to sleep.

Quietly, so as not to wake little Pauline, Elisabeth said her Office for the Vigil of the Feast of the Assumption. She knew it by heart, from having said it for the last eleven years. In the morning, she rose, washed in cold water, and tried to turn herself out as neatly as if she had been tended by Madame de Navarre and her other maids. Then she helped Pauline with her toilet.

"I've only got this one dress, Madame," said the child. "All my other things were pillaged."

"Never mind," said Elisabeth, rolling her curls with a rounded wooden ruler, "I'll cut down a dress of mine to your size."

This task, at which the three royal ladies worked, was soon interrupted, for at midnight of August the 19th–20th, the Tourzels and the Princesse de Lamballe were taken away to the Prison de la Force. The parting was heart-rending. "Take care of Madame de Lamballe," whispered the Queen to her governess. Elisabeth kissed them and spoke encouraging words to them. They were never to meet again.

No maids had been allotted to the princesses, and there were no servants to do any scrubbing or cleaning of rooms. This is strange when one thinks of the large staff in the kitchens, far away across the gardens. To us, in these days, trained by long adversity to become not only independent of good service, but even to surpass our former servants in the perfection and finish of our work, it is difficult to realise that there once existed women who never did anything for themselves. They had been dressed and washed by maids, their curls were rolled by the hairdresser, their chemises had been handed to them by ladies-in-waiting. They would not have known how to dust and sweep a room, or make a bed. (What laughter on that day at Madame

Adélaïde's, when they had given Adèle de Boigne a doll's bed and made it up themselves!)

Elisabeth's time-table was as follows. She rose at six. She and her niece helped each other to dress. Elisabeth tried to teach Madame Royale to be independent of help, and this literally saved her life, when she was later condemned to solitary confinement. Hué came and did their curls. At nine o'clock, they all went up to the King's room for breakfast. At first, this was opulent—coffee, chocolate, double cream, cold syrup, barley water, milk bread, fine white rolls, sugar. The King did not take anything, and he did not sit down. The remains of the breakfast went to fifteen other people. Tison and his wife—of whom we shall hear later—watched through a glass panel during the whole meal. The royal ladies wore morning dresses of white bombasine or dimity, and simple linen bonnets, trimmed with narrow lace edging. At ten o'clock, they all went down to the Queen's room. The King taught his son his lessons: (Corneille. Racine. Geography. Maps.) The Queen instructed her daughter. Elisabeth gave Madame Royale lessons in drawing and arithmetic, music and religion. A soldier peered over the child's shoulder when she did mathematics, thinking she was inventing a code for plots. At mid-day, the ladies went into Elisabeth's room to change into day clothes—brown linen dresses patterned with flowers.[1] Once or twice, they were unable to change, because a soldier would come in and refuse to budge. At one o'clock, they all went into the garden for exercise. At two, luncheon, of which they ate most soberly. The Queen drank only water from Ville d'Avray, the King always added much water to his wine and only had one glass of liqueur. He never failed to put Cléry's meal aside in the antechamber stove, pointing out the best dishes to him. Luncheon was followed by a game of piquet or back-gammon. At four, the King had a snooze, while the princesses read quietly, so as not to disturb him. When he woke, Cléry gave the prince his handwriting lesson. Afterwards, this good devoted servant took him to Elisabeth's room for a game of ball or shuttlecock. Then they all gathered together round a table, and, until

---

[1] Among objects asked for by Elisabeth, who had practically nothing: cambric cuffs for dresses, cambric chemises, white and grey silk stockings, grey shoes, a pair of Chinese clogs, a hat—"castor noir en jockey".

R

eight o'clock, the Queen or Elisabeth read aloud something which would amuse and interest the children. At seven, they would pause a little to hear the news cried in the streets. Sometimes, tears came to Elisabeth's eyes, for some unknown friend would play the air of "*Pauvre Jacques*" on the hurdy-gurdy. Jacques of Montreuil—how anxious he must be about her now. . . .

During the five months he was at the Temple, the King read 257 volumes. The ladies read, among other things, "Cecilia" and "Evelina". The King ordered the 14 volumes of the Paris Missal and Breviary, and Elisabeth 14 prayer books. The children had their supper in Elisabeth's room, while the King asked them riddles from the "*Mercure de France*", which he'd found in Monsieur Berthélemy's library. Cléry undressed the Dauphin, the Queen heard his prayers—he would pray for Madame de Tourzel and Madame de Lamballe in a whisper if a guard were listening. At nine, the King supped, while the Queen and Elisabeth stayed in turns with the Dauphin. After supper, the King took his wife's hand and his sister's, as he wished them good night, received the kisses of his children, and would go to his closet and read till midnight. The royal ladies retired to their rooms.

This time-table lasted till September the 30th, 1792.

Hué speaks of the great privations in body, bed and table linen endured by the captives. The prince's sheets were full of holes. The King's only suit of clothes got so threadbare, that Elisabeth often sat up a great part of the night to mend it.

The walk time was a torture. The workmen who were building the walls up higher, sang the "*Ça Ira*" as loudly as possible when they saw the royal prisoners.

> Ah! ça ira, ça ira, ça ira.
> Pierrot et Margot chant'nt à la quinquette.
> Ah! ça ira, ça ira, ça ira.
> Réjouissons-nous, le bon temps viendra;
> Le peuple français, jadis *a quia*,
> L'aristocrate dit: *mea culpa*.
> Ah! ça ira, ça ira, ça ira.
> Le clergé regrette le bien qu'il a,
>
> (and so on)

The red-bonneted porters Rocher and Risbey, waiting in their den, always puffed tobacco smoke from their pipes right into the faces of the prisoners, as they bent their heads to go through the low wicket-gate. Rocher used to say: "Marie-Antoinette was putting on her proud airs, but I forced her to come down a peg or two. Her daughter and Elisabeth curtsey to me in spite of themselves: the gate is so low, that, to pass, they are obliged to bend down in front of me. I always puff smoke from my pipe on to that Elisabeth." Hué tells us how Rocher would rattle his bunch of keys and make the prisoners wait a long time, on purpose, then open the doors with tremendous clanging. The guards would gather round him, guffaw with laughter at each whiff of smoke, and make coarse jests. Sometimes they would bring chairs, in order to relish this spectacle at leisure. The chairs blocked the very narrow passage and this added to the general fun. The royal ladies did the only thing possible under the circumstances: pretended they had not noticed. With a little training, one can assume quite a feasible air of slightly contemptuous indifference which only maddens the torturers more than ever.

Then the royal party walked up and down the chestnut alley. Elisabeth would take a book in order to achieve a little seclusion. The gunners danced and sang revolutionary songs and chalked insults on the tower walls: "Madame Veto will dance thus." Once, a workman boasted that he could cut off the Queen's head with his tools: Pétion, oddly enough, had him arrested.

Cléry speaks of a young guard in the garden whose cheeks were wet with tears of pity. Under cover of finding quoits for the prince's games, Cléry tried to pick up a message this guard had dropped, but he was told by one of the officers that he must not speak to the sentries.

Another municipal soldier called Goret managed to convey his sympathy to the afflicted family. He wrote that, as he was trying to read while guarding the family indoors, the Queen said: "Come nearer to us, Monsieur, you will see better to read." Elisabeth, who was playing chess with the King, appeared amused at his embarrassment and said gaily to the King: "Come along, *Monsieur le roi*, your turn now." She seemed to read into Goret's thoughts. Indeed, she was so shrewd in summing up the character of each different guard on duty, that Prudhomme says: "This little prude is a demon of unbelievable restlessness. She goes up and down more than a hundred times a day from her room to her sister-in-law's. . . . One cannot be too strictly on one's guard . . . her lynx eyes . . . read one's thoughts, penetrate to the bottom of one's soul. . . . One must begin by studying all her movements to ward off seduction. . . ."

Goret tells us how Elisabeth was leaning on the arm of his chair, and singing a light melody. When her niece appeared, she invited her to join in, but the little princess was too proud, too much on her dignity. She lacked her aunt's simple *bonhomie*. Elisabeth seemed a little peeked and said to the Queen: "Your daughter is obstinate, very obstinate, I assure you, my sister."

This is the only indication one gets that Madame Royale was not always a very pleasant little girl. Indeed, when she grew to womanhood, although she was sound morally, she was totally lacking in the charm and grace which had been her mother's.

The Tisons, who eventually did the heavy work, and who were really sent to spy, were a sinister couple. He was naturally hard and suspicious, and like all men of his class, full of prejudices against the royal family. He was as false and crafty as a fox: he could even go into slobbering, maudlin ecstasies over the charms of the Dauphin, if it suited his purpose. His wife appeared gentle and compassionate on the surface. The Commune held the whip-hand over them, by forbidding them to have their beloved fifteen-year-old daughter with them. Therefore, the Tisons were jealous when they saw the King and Queen enjoy the society of their own children. Furthermore, they realised that if anything went wrong, they would lose their daughter. They knew that the Commune was ruthless. All these things made them terribly watchful. If ever Elisabeth glanced towards the glass partition, she would see two pairs of eyes, full of hate, peering through. Those Tisons were like an infestation. One has met people like that: in some inexplicable way, they seem to be in several places at once in a house: there is no escaping them, even with bolts and bars.

Elisabeth took refuge in her prayers. One day, Hué, coming into her room to do some housework, found the princess on her knees. His first impulse was to withdraw, but she said: "Stay, carry on with your occupations, it won't disturb me." This was the prayer which she had adapted to her own needs from "The perfect adorer of the Sacred Heart of Jesus", by Gabriel Nicollet (1772). Her additions are in parentheses.

"What will happen to me to-day, O my God? (I know not). All that I know, is that nothing will happen to me which you have not foreseen from all eternity. That suffices me, O my God (to be at peace). I adore your eternal designs. I submit to them with all my heart: I want all, I accept all, I make a sacrifice of all to you. I unite this sacrifice to that of your dear Son, my Saviour, asking you by his sacred Heart and by his infinite merits, for patience (in our ills) and the perfect submission which is your due, to all that you want and permit."

Madame Royale relates that in the Great Tower, "My Aunt prayed often in the day; she said her Office every day, read many holy books and made long meditations. She and my father kept the feasts and abstinences ordained by the Church."

·   ·   ·   ·   ·   ·

Among the servants, Turgy worked in the kitchens. He it was who, on October the 6th, 1789, had opened the door connecting the secret passage which led from the Queen's room to the King's. The Queen, thinking the mob was coming at any moment, knocked desperately for five minutes before he heard.

Cléry, who had been the Dauphin's valet, asked Pétion for permission to continue his service, and was admitted on August the 26th. He was solely occupied with the young prince, and at night he rolled the King's locks. Hué had to provide all the things the royal family needed, and therefore he was the victim of constant, petty persecution. The King tried to cheer him on. One night, at bedtime, he said to him: "You have had a great deal to suffer to-day. Well, for my sake, continue to bear all, don't answer back."

One evening, the princess, who had been eight days without women, asked Cléry whether he could comb their curls. He replied: "I will do all to be of service to you." The officer on guard said arrogantly: "Be more circumspect in your answers."

These guards never missed an opportunity of tormenting their victims. If ever they found scurrilous articles in the papers against the royal family, they took care to place them in evidence on the chimney-piece or the table. Hébert, for example, would write this about Elisabeth: ". . . I was forgetting the sister of Madame Veto; she's a fat wanton, quite well set up, and who appears to have a good appetite; it's a pity, damn it all, that she's descended from such a race, she looks more like a plump miller's wife than an erstwhile princess; she must have been begotten by some sturdy fellow from the markets or by a great churl. . . ."

CHAPTER XXV

The September Massacres and the King's death

ON September the 2nd, the workmen who had been demolishing the buildings around the Tower and raising the surrounding wall, suddenly became more insulting than ever. They threw stones at the King walking in the garden, and yelled insults at him. Elisabeth looked up at a woman who had written in large letters on a piece of cardboard "Verdun is taken". "*Maman reine! Maman reine!*" cried the little Dauphin, as the cannon boomed in the distance, the tocsin sounded and drums were beaten.

The September Massacres had begun.

The Princesse de Lamballe suffered a terrible fate on the following day. Her naked corpse with the guts streaming out on to the pavement was dragged along the street, with its stomach in the mud. Her chemise was stained with blood. The head was put on a pike and taken to a hairdresser's. The trembling assistant was forced to wash the fair hair and to use his curling tongs. The creatures who went by the name of women were in the meantime going through the pathetic contents of her pockets, and the clothes left in a heap. "Hi, what's this?" shrieked an elderly harpy. "Some holy mumbo jumbo, I warrant." "Hi, you old whore, let me have a peep." And they pored over a picture of a flaming heart surrounded with thorns and pierced with a dagger, round which was written, "Cor Jésu, salva nos, perimus." The account of what they did to her body is so satanic that the historian Lenotre has to describe it in Latin. One man had blood upon his lips after eating her heart, which he said was most delicious. The woman who had seized the image from her pocket screeched out, "Fat lot of use her picture of the heart did her!" In truth the princess could have shared the battle cry of Henry IV: "You tremble, carcass, if you knew where I lead you to." The juxtaposition of this death-scene with her former life makes too violent a "*clair-obscur*".

At three o'clock in the afternoon, terrible screams outside the Temple windows. The guard behaved very well: he shut both door and window and drew the curtains in the Queen's room. Cléry went to sit with the Tisons, when suddenly, a head appeared at the window, on the end of a pike. Tison's wife gave a piercing scream. The assassins, thinking they'd recognised the Queen's voice, burst into frenzied laughter. It was the veritable cacophony of Hades.

It was the head of Madame de Lamballe, which, though still bleeding, was not disfigured.

Cléry ran to the King, trying to conceal his terror. Suddenly, some guards came in, insisting that the royal family should appear at the window. The municipal soldiers were opposed to this. One of them, trailing a great sword, said roughly to the Queen: "They want to hide the head of la Lamballe from you, which they were bringing you, to show you how the people take vengeance on their tyrants; I advise you to appear if you do not want the people to come up here."

The Queen fainted. Cléry and Elisabeth helped to carry her in to an armchair. The poor children burst into tears and sought by caresses to restore their mother to consciousness.

The shouting went on until five o'clock. The beating of drums sounded all night long. And that September, as Madame Royale wrote later, the weather was "of dazzling loveliness and rarely has one seen so radiant a sun lighting so sombre a drama".

Elisabeth, realising that the sight of many little objects which had belonged to the unhappy princess, only upset the Queen, told Cléry to collect them and give them to the victim's first maid. But they never reached her.

On September the 4th, at 4 p.m., trumpets sounded, and Lubin came to read aloud to the royal family the official decree abolishing the monarchy in France. Hébert was among the crowd, but he was disappointed if he thought he'd make his victims wince. The King continued to read, as if nothing had happened, Elisabeth went on with her embroidery, quite unconcerned, and the Queen appeared calm and dignified.

This was too much for Hébert, for when he wrote an article for his

"Père Duchesne", he said that the Austrian woman had had the vapours, and that "fat Elisabeth went off to cry in a corner".

. . . .

When some new linen appeared at the Tower, it was found that the sewing-women had marked it all with initials and crowns. The guards forced the royal ladies to unpick the lot.

On September the 29th, a long, unpleasant search took place, to deprive the prisoners of all writing materials. The little princess and the Queen managed to hide some pencils.

Some nights, when the Queen was going to bed, the guards would not leave the room until repeated demands had been made. They put a malicious interpretation on all her gestures, words and looks, and even on her silences.

In spite of this, the royal family always spoke with courtesy and gentleness to the guards. One of them, Verdier, records of the royal ladies: "I found them affable, simple and even gay." When they had been there some time, some guards were greeted with the words, "We are very pleased to see you." The Dauphin was the charmer of the group. His little ways, his beauty, liveliness and intelligence, fascinated those demagogues. He had such lovely golden hair, laughing eyes, a clear voice and a wide-awake look. Hébert himself told Pache: "I have seen the little child of the Tower—he is as beautiful as the day, very intelligent, acts his kingly part to perfection; I enjoy playing a game of draughts with him; the day before yesterday, he was asking me whether the people were still unhappy. 'What a great pity,' he answered, after I had said 'Yes'."

He would run about in the antechamber, playing at shuttlecock, or at bowls, totally unabashed by the guards.

A little later, Chaumette, the procurator of the Commune,[1] had a bright idea: he would nominate Simon the Dauphin's preceptor— Simon the cobbler whom the King had met on his first night at the Temple, lounging on a sofa and babbling about equality. As Monsieur

[1] J. M. Thompson says of Anaxegoras Chaumette that he was idealistic and envious, and "showed how dangerous Rousseauism might be to little minds".

Lenotre has said: "This man was ignorant, a blunderer, absolutely unlettered, incapable of writing one line correctly, and possessing only one quality which could justify the decision of his protector Chaumette: the necessary passivity to make of him the most pliable, the most docile instrument. In a word, Simon would never have been nominated, if he had not been Chaumette's tool."

Royalist writers have tended to exaggerate Simon's cruelty—he was really stupid to the point of imbecility. His simplicity amused the princesses, as on the day he told them about his wife who was ill at the Hôtel-Dieu: "It is a pleasure actually to see those ladies of the Hôtel-Dieu, they take good care of the sick; I wish you could see them, to-day they are dressed like my wife, like you ladies, no better, no worse."

The princesses laughed, totally unsuspecting that he was destined to cause many tears to flow. Lenotre describes him: "Physically, Simon was a robust man, in spite of his 56 years, a little hard of hearing, with features both brutal and sottish, wide-open eyes, like those of people who find it hard to understand what you are saying. His hair was flat, his head always covered with an old round soft hat; for best, he wore a cloth suit, 'couleur de la nation', lined with scarlet."

One day, when the Queen saw him running into the royal apartments, covered in sweat, she said kindly to him: "You're very hot, Monsieur Simon, would you like a little wine?" "Madame," he replied proudly, "I don't drink like this with just anybody."

"Everybody at the Temple laughed quietly at his stupidity and his self-importance; he even inspired his colleagues with a sort of pity; but he was not feared. . . ."

On the day the prisoners were transferred to the Great Tower, it was Simon who confiscated their writing materials and rulers.

The bonnet maker, his colleague, was hissed when he reported to the general council, about the Queen and Elisabeth: "They were so voluptuous that there is no prostitute in the Rue Saint-Jean-Saint-Denis who can compare with them." Which shows that the cess-pools of scurrility had not yet flooded the whole of Paris.

On October the 26th, the royal family was moved to the Great Tower, which had walls seven feet thick. There was something sinister about this place which filled them all with foreboding. Even the children lost their liveliness. The windows, with their thick iron bars, were shaded outside, so that the place was dark. Goret says: "I always thought that a powerful occult force had a hand in all this." The large room on each floor had been hastily partitioned into four small rooms. On the second floor, a privy, the King's room with its closet, an antechamber, Cléry's room, and a dark narrow room without a fireplace which served as a dining-room.

On the third floor, a room for the Queen and Madame Royale, one for the Tisons, and one for Elisabeth. The privy for that floor was reached by going through Elisabeth's room. Through that privy, one could go up to the roof by a narrow spiral staircase. The chimneys of the stoves smoked. Some of the furniture of Elisabeth's room is in a Paris museum—her iron bedstead, with its *toile de Jouy* bedspread lined with green taffeta, its chintz-covered chairs, its walnut dressing-table. There was a mirror over the chimney-piece, and two silvered torches. The wallpaper was yellow and rather common-looking. It could not have been pleasant to be next door to the Tisons. Cléry tells us how the woman was obsequious and sly, and helped the ladies with their toilet. Tison, always gloomy and acrimonious, prepared the table for breakfast in the antechamber. Lepître writes that he was "deceitful and spiteful" and knew how to compose his looks. ". . . His wife modelled herself on him, but she was propelled more by fear of her husband than by her own inclinations." One must remember that she had experienced a severe shock on seeing the Princesse de Lamballe's head, and this was finally to unbalance her altogether. (At the Musée Grevin in Paris—in a kind of Chamber of Horrors in waxworks—one could see a representation of the whole scene, in slow motion, and it made one's blood run cold.) The proximity of the Tisons must have done much to undermine the morale of the prisoners, for it was constant, relentless, not intermittent, like the presence of the guards. Some of these, however, were bad enough for sheer coarseness; Lechenard, a tailor, drank half a bottle of liqueur at one gulp, and his room, the next day, gave such proof of his intemperance, that when the Queen went through it in the morning, she just had time to cry out to Elisabeth: "*Ma sœur*, do not leave your room." And, one day, a stonemason, Mercereau, in the filthiest clothes, lay down on the silk sofa on which the Queen usually sat, and justified this licence by the principle of equality. One could overlook all this in a workman, but it was unpardonable, coming insolently and of set purpose from men of excellent education; they used to place their armchairs in front of the fireplace and stick their feet on the fire-dogs in such a way that the princesses could not get near the fire. At meals, when they tasted the food before the family, they would open the rolls and poke their dirty fingers inside; and when the linen returned from the laundresses, they had each article unfolded under their very noses.

One day, the Queen said to Turgy: "I've broken my comb. Please buy me another." The poet Dorat-Palmezeaux, *chevalier* of Cubières who was on guard, said: "Buy her a horn one, box-wood would be too good for her. . . ." Turgy and the Queen talked sadly of this afterwards, and Turgy, who had known Versailles, said to her: "Madame, there were many people who looked as if they were paying their court to the royal family, but it was only because of the treasury." The Queen replied: "You are right, Turgy."

(Oh Polignacs, oh Esterhazys, Vaudreuils. . . .)

The little Dauphin was always very anxious to know who would be on guard for the day. If it were a decent fellow, he would run to the Queen and say: "*Maman*, to-day it is Monsieur So-and-So." He was never frightened of these men, and used to go up to them without the least sign of timidity. For his age—and he was only eight—he was singularly precocious: for example, Cléry said that, for fear of saddening his adored parents, he never spoke of the Tuileries and Versailles. Goret tells us that even in a prison, he was still taught courtesy, for when the child passed him one day without greeting him, the Queen said to him severely: "My son, come back and greet Monsieur as you pass by him." The prisoners showed the Dauphin a good example in their manners with the guards: Lepître wrote: "It is, however, difficult to imagine with what gentleness and courtesy the Queen and the princesses asked them for the smallest thing."

A newspaper of the times, no doubt gleaning its information from a *commissaire*, gives one a little glimpse of the family at meals. The Dauphin, one day, was gazing at an apple with longing. Elisabeth said:

"You look as if you wanted that apple and you don't ask for it." "My aunt," he replied in serious tones, "my character is frank and firm: if I had wanted that apple, I would have asked for it the self-same instant."

The Queen was very musical—in Vienna, Mozart had been her playfellow, and later, in France she protected Glück. Once, she told two pleasant guards, Lepître and Jacquetot, that she wanted to continue giving music lessons to her daughter, but that the spinet was out of tune, and she could not get anyone to do something about it. Lepître and Jacquetot sent an express note to a tuner that same evening. Then they all looked through a few pieces of music which were on top of it, and they found one called "The Queen of France". Marie-Antoinette said: "How times have changed." The guards could not restrain a few tears.

.   .   .   .   .

Winter closed in. The old tower was very damp, and before long they all fell ill in turn. The King, first, with an inflammation, then Elisabeth with very bad toothache. Everybody caught colds, the Dauphin got whooping cough, and faithful Cléry was bowled over by an attack of rheumatic fever.

The Commune, hearing that the King was seriously ill, and fearing that its victim would be released by death, sent him Le Monnier, his first physician. He came twice a day for a week. It is easy to picture Elisabeth's emotion on seeing her old botany-master, her neighbour of Montreuil days, again. They were unable to speak, but his mere presence must have meant much to her.

Elisabeth, who had a bad cold, deprived herself of remedies which she surreptitiously gave to Cléry. The whole family came to visit him every day. One night, towards eleven o'clock, Cléry went to the King's room to prepare his bed, when the Dauphin, who should have been asleep long ago, said to him in a whisper: "My aunt gave me a little box for you, and I did not want to go to sleep without giving it to you; it is time you came, for my eyes have already closed several time." And he gave him a box of ipecacuanha pastilles. Cléry's eyes filled with tears. The Dauphin, noticing it, kissed him, and, two minutes later, was fast asleep.

Cléry was so touched by the kindness of his masters, that he begged the King's pardon for several little things about which he reproached himself, in his service.

The Christ-like gentleness and charity of that little family did much to win hardened hearts. One day, on December the 9th, after that spell of illness, when they were all feeling very low, a young Gascon, Toulan from Toulouse, came on guard duty. He did not inspire confidence, for he'd taken part in the days of July the 14th and October the 6th, 1789, and had attacked the Tuileries on August the 10th. Like many Gascons, he was talkative, bombastic, lively and bold.

Two days in the presence of the Bourbons sufficed to change his whole political outlook. From then on, he became their devoted slave. Of all the men who served the captives at great personal risk to themselves, he distinguished himself by his immense zeal. He won for himself the nickname "Fidèle". They soon found that under all the Gascon garrulity there was great "*finesse*". He did all in his power to make their imprisonment bearable.

"H'm, don't like the look of that Gascon," muttered Tison, peering through his glass partition. "Better keep an eye on 'im. He's gazing at Elisabeth with adoring eyes."

"Oh, I think he's all right," said Madame Tison. She was very weary, and the place got on her nerves. Tison cuffed her on the head.

"Do as I say and don't argue. I know a bad patriot when I see one. And don't snivel, or I'll give you a taste of the broom-handle. Hard enough being shut up in here all day, watching the mincings and mouthings of those aristos, without having trouble with you."

Madame Tison began to weep. "What gets me down is that they're allowed their children with them all the time, and we . . . we can't even have our own daughter in for the day, on Sundays."

"That's just it, and that's why I'm telling you to keep a sharp look-out for what you can glean on the other side. If anything important escapes our notice, we'll never see our daughter again. Never can tell: they'll be propping *her* head up on a pike, like the *ci-devant* Lamballe. . . ."

"Help!" screamed Madame Tison, white with terror. She glanced sideways at the window. She was always doing that.

"Stop your bawling, will you?" And he gave her another cuff on the head.

.   .   .   .   .

But Toulan was sharp enough to outwit the Tisons for a time. When he thought he was being watched, he assumed a mask of republicanism which the keenest eye could not have pierced.

Soon the captives were searched again and deprived of scissors, knives, razors. In fact, they were treated like prisoners who are presumed criminals. One day, Elisabeth was mending the King's jacket: and as she had no scissors, she cut the thread with her teeth. "What a contrast," said the King, gazing at her tenderly. "You were short of nothing in your pretty house at Montreuil."

"Ah! *mon frère*," she replied, "can I have any regrets, when I share your misfortunes!"

Soon their nails began to grow so long, that they asked if they could borrow some scissors. This was solemnly debated by the council and a lot of red tape had to be swallowed and documents signed.

In early December, the King was taken to the Convention to be tried. It was raining when he got into the courtyard. He was seen to glance up at the Tower he had just left.

Elisabeth managed to send a message to him by a slip of paper which she let down to his window, giving him the address of the Abbé Edgeworth de Firmont, in case he were allowed a confessor. By some special Providence, all the letters which Elisabeth wrote to her confessor reached him safely, without being intercepted. The King told Malesherbes, his advocate, about the Abbé, and asked him to deliver the note.

Christmas Day. No Mass, no celebrations, no presents. Elisabeth's thoughts turned to the lovely Midnight Masses at Versailles, at which she had so longed to make her Communion, but in vain. She recalled Bombe, and her delight at the Sèvres porcelain she had given her one Christmas; the poor at Montreuil, who always had their share in

Christmas cheer; Bombon prancing around the room; Aunt Louise at Carmel, who had died one December; Carmelites who dance round at Christmastide recreation, holding the Child Jesus in their arms. . . .

Yes, she had wanted to live with God in a cell, and He had granted her her heart's desire. There was all in this Temple which could lead a Christian to Paradise—penance, mortification, humiliation. . . . Still, she missed Midnight Mass sorely.

And so did many good souls in Paris. And when Chaumette, the procurator of the Commune, decreed that there would be no Midnight Mass, there were riots in many of the Paris churches, and the soldiers were beaten up. Indeed, one boy called Beugneou, a master mason, turned up at the Temple for guard duty with his face scarred. He laughed at his misadventure, for he was a good fellow. "Yes, it was the market women of Saint Eustache who greeted me like this."

That Christmas Day, Louis XVI, all alone—for he had been separated from his family—wrote his admirable testament in which he begged his sister to continue lavishing her tenderness on his children, and to be a mother to them, if they lost their own. He implored his children, in his memory, to look upon his sister as a second mother.

He said that his children, the Queen and his sister, had brought "much enchantment" to his days, and that his sister's life had been nothing but "affection, devotion and courage".

The trial ended. He was condemned to death. Paris learnt the news on Thursday morning, January the 17th. His family only knew when they heard the street criers near the Temple. He was to be guillotined on Monday, January the 21st—the anniversary of the day he had sent his wedding ring to his wife.

On Sunday evening, the 20th, the King waited in the narrow fireless dining-room. The door opened, and his family came in to say farewell. The princesses were in white muslin dresses. (Much later, Cléry wrote a detailed description of the whole scene for Madame Vigée Le Brun, so that she could paint a picture of it, but she never had the courage to undertake it.)

For nearly two hours, the members of that poor little family sobbed in each other's arms. The King was seated with his young son at his knees, and his daughter before him. The Queen was on his left,

Elisabeth on his right. All were leaning towards him, and they frequently embraced him. Afterwards, his daughter wrote: "He wept because of our grief, not because of his death."

Between ten and ten-thirty, the King rose. The Queen was in such a state of collapse that she could hardly hold herself up. The Dauphin clung to his parents' hands, kissed them and bathed them with tears. Then the King said gently: "Adieu. Rest assured that I will see you again to-morrow morning at seven o'clock." And he dragged himself away. Madame Royale fainted, and Elisabeth and Cléry supported her.

That night, Elisabeth and her niece pulled their mattresses into the Queen's room, so that she would not be alone. At six, someone knocked. They had come to borrow Madame Tison's missal for the King's Mass. The family waited in vain for the King to come at seven, as he had promised. The little Dauphin rushed wildly to the guards. "Let me pass, *Messieurs*, let me pass."

"Where do you want to go?"

"To speak to the people, so that they will not put my father to death. In God's name, let me pass!"

But the jailers were adamant, and the distracted child rushed to his mother's arms.

In the Paris streets, eye-witness after eye-witness has testified that silence and terror prevailed everywhere. A dull stupor reigned in the city.

"Dense crowds all along the way, not one cry, not one insult. An immense silence, compact with horror, anxiety, shame and dismay. . . . The sun had withheld its light to this execrable day, marked with the sign of Cain."[1]

And as the King's head fell, the Abbé de Firmont, who had accompanied him in his closed carriage, cried out: "Son of Saint Louis, ascend to Heaven."

And so died a good king, a victim of the sins of Louis XIV and Louis XV. He was a martyr to his religious convictions, for he had said that if ever he came into power again, he would do his utmost to re-establish the Catholic Faith in France.

At about ten o'clock, the Queen wanted the children to take a little

[1] Charrnuau, "Une famille de brigands en 1793."

food, but they refused. Soon after, they heard the guns. Elisabeth looking Heaven-wards exclaimed, 'The monsters, so they're satisfied now!' Then, the beating of the drum, and the frenzied cries of the Temple guards, drowned the sobs of the Dauphin and the piercing screams of his sister.

The boy was clinging to his mother's knees. Gently she disengaged herself, and following ancient and immemorial custom, she curtsied to the new King, Louis XVII.

. . . . . .

That night, the Queen and Elisabeth could not sleep. They spoke to one another in the darkness of the January night. Surprised at hearing sounds at such an hour, the Tison woman rapped sharply at the door to find out what was happening. Elisabeth, half opening the door, said gently: "For pity's sake, let us weep in peace."

CHAPTER XXVI

After the King's death

THE bereaved family went into mourning. The Queen and Elisabeth had become so thin that they were almost unrecognisable. Little Marie-Thérèse's body was covered with ulcers and she was threatened with grave ill-health. Goret, the kindly guard, finding them in this state of great affliction, discovered that they had not been out to take any exercise for some time. He made them see the necessity of getting fresh air, particularly for the sake of the young princess. "We don't want to pass by the door which my husband crossed for the last time," said the Queen. Goret thought for a moment. "I know! There is a circular gallery at the top of the Tower. I'll have some chairs put there. It's narrow and there's a parapet, but at any rate, you will see the sky." They agreed, although heads appeared at all the windows around, and groups of staring people formed in the streets.

Meals were less splendidly served than in the King's time. Men who had done guard-duty at the Temple, and had not complained (largely because of the good food), now started lamenting at the waste of their time. One man publicly protested that it was ridiculous to see men elected by the people of Paris serve as valets to Madame Capet.

As the King's rooms were sealed, the prisoners and their guards—eight people in all—had to crowd into four small rooms. The constant proximity became quite nerve-racking. Four little rooms on the third floor. The Queen and her two children in one room. Elisabeth in another, the Tisons in a third, and the two guards in an ante-chamber, where they remained day and night.

In February, Toulan, the faithful Gascon, conceived a plan of escape. He had himself inscribed for guard duty with Lepître, and spoke to the Queen and Elisabeth in whispers, when the Tisons had gone to bed. "At five-thirty each evening, a man, accompanied by his two children, comes to the tower to clean and light the lamps and reflectors. He always leaves well before seven. I've examined the children's clothes carefully, and I can have them copied. We will put the young King into a basket covered with table napkins. Turgy will carry it down, as if it were all in the course of his duties, and the Queen, disguised as a municipal officer, will appear at the wicket-gate, to see that I'm allowed to pass. She will follow a few minutes later." (It must be remembered that the Queen and Elisabeth had become alarmingly thin.) "Then Madame Royale will come, disguised as the lamp-lighter's son, led by Monsieur Ricard in the lamp-lighter's clothes, preceded by Madame Elisabeth, also in the uniform of a municipal officer. I've studied this man's appearance closely—an old wig, an obliterating hat and a rough wide shirt, dirty face and hands will complete her travesty."

"But where to you propose that we change? And what about the Tisons?"

"I've thought of all that. You can all dress up in the little turret next to the Queen's room: the Tisons never go there. At a quarter to seven, knowing their love for my Spanish snuff, which I've often given them, I will offer them a pinch, taking care to add beforehand a narcotic so powerful that they'll fall asleep instantly and only wake seven or eight hours later."

"But what about the sentries outside?"

"No fear of them. I simply wave my identity card at them from a distance, they are reassured by my tricolour scarf, and they never bother to budge. We will then go to Rue de la Corderie, where Monsieur de . . . would be waiting for us. If your Majesty would order supper for nine-thirty that night, instead of seven-thirty, we will have got five hours' start. In a good berline. . . ."

"What!" exclaimed the Queen. "Never! Remember Varennes. It must be three cabs, and we must all go separately."

"But supposing one of them breaks down? Suspicions would be aroused when the others catch up and wait until repairs are effected."

Lepître, who wrote his account of all this in 1817 with such gusto, did not mention that in 1793 he was much cooler and more calculating. Indeed, his faint-heartedness caused the failure of the plot, because he refused to provide the passports, although he was President of the

Commission for issuing passports. Lenotre points out that this Lepître, who makes himself out to be such a hero, had exacted financial remuneration from the Queen, to compensate him for any loss resulting from the escape of the prisoners. But, at the Restoration, when rewards loomed in the offing for those who had served the royal family, guards and others were apt to lose their heads a little, and paint their adventures with heroic quill.

Everything, at length, was fixed for March the 8th. They hoped to reach Normandy, and then set sail for England, for they had enough money.

Alas, *just one day too late*. One day only. On March the 7th, there was an uprising in Paris, following the news of the evacuation of Aix-la-Chapelle. Sugar and coffee were pillaged in shops. The royal family was more closely guarded, and the passport office was told to deliver passports with great circumspection. It was at this point that Lepître had refused to provide passports.

"Escape alone," said Elisabeth to the Queen. "We are safe enough: it is you who are threatened by the revolutionaries."

Marie-Antoinette hesitated for a moment. "No, I couldn't leave the children. We must not be parted."

.   .   .   .   .

So another plan of escape failed, a plan which had every chance of success. It has all the flavour of the Scarlet Pimpernel's exploits. And those twilit evenings in early March would have been so propitious for slipping out of Paris. The lessons learnt at Varennes would have served the Queen in good stead, and, with Marie-Antoinette at the head of affairs, unencumbered by the vacillations of her late-lamented spouse, there was real hope. The hospitable English had every chance of welcoming the stricken family. And in good time, the charming little prince would have been crowned at Reims as Louis XVII in place of his horrible old uncle who had just declared himself regent of the kingdom. Alas and alack. . . .

The royal ladies took refuge in needlework. The Vicomte Jean de Blois possessed a piece of embroidery done by Elisabeth at the Temple:

it was a pansy on violet silk, in the form of a death's head, with this device: "*Elle est mon unique pensée*" (This is my sole thought). One day, Elisabeth asked two of the friendly guards—Lepître and Toulan —whether they could not bring her some cotton and knitting needles. They forgot, and then were much embarrassed when the princesses thanked them ironically for having kept their word. Lepître tells us: "Madame Elisabeth had begun what one calls a stocking, when she asked me my opinion of her work. I could not prevent myself from smiling, when I saw the width of this so-called stocking, and I told her that probably it was a bonnet she had wanted to make. 'All right, then, a bonnet,' she replied, 'and it will be for you.' She finished it during the day and gave it to me when we were going, ordering me to give to the poor the sum which a bonnet might cost at that time. I obeyed scrupulously, and it cost me the small sum of 10 francs in paper money."

However, the Tisons were still on the watch. It was their denunci-ations which led to the dismissal of Toulan and other faithful guards. The authorities goaded the Tisons to their betrayals, by prolonging the separation from their only daughter. Tison's envious fury knew no bounds when he saw a stranger allowed in to bring various necessities to Elisabeth, a prisoner, while he, a free man and loyal citizen, was not even permitted to see his own daughter. So he began to talk, and forced his wife to do the same. After discovering a drop of sealing wax on a candlestick of Elisabeth's, they said they were sure that the prisoners were in correspondence with the enemy, and that the guards were providing them with writing materials. They signed their denunciation on the 19th of April. The next day, they were allowed to see their daughter.

That very day, the searches began in earnest. In the middle of the night, Hébert appeared with his confederates, dragged the Dauphin rudely out of bed and searched his mattress. His mother took him into her arms, for he was shivering with cold. The search continued till four in the morning. Amongst other things, they found on Madame Royale an image of the Sacred Heart of Jesus, and a prayer for France.

Nothing incriminating, and the men were furious for looking ridiculous.

Then started a new era of rudeness and insolence from the Tisons. One day, when these two had been sharply reprimanded by Vincent, a *commissionnaire* on duty, the Tisons thought that the Dauphin had been telling tales. They burst into the Queen's room and poured forth recriminations against the child. "Spy! Informer!" Marie-Antoinette replied with dignity. "I would have you know that no member of our family ever stabs in the back, and I am not the kind of person to tolerate it." (This must have flicked the Tison woman on the raw, for she was an arch-informer.) So she and her husband vomited imprecations against the Queen and heaped curses on her child. At last they left the room, but not before Tison had heard Elisabeth say gently to the indignant Queen: "They're in a temper, forgive them." He returned like a madman and bawled: "Forgive them! Ah, I like that! And what do you think we are? Do you forget that it is the people alone who have the right to forgive?"

.   .   .   .   .

One more plot for escape, concocted by the Baron de Batz. This time the conspirators decided to dispense with the Queen's consent. The Baron had recruited thirty enterprising royalists under Cortey, a captain of the National Guard. These men were to occupy the Temple sentry posts on a night when the municipal Michonis, who was in the plot, would be the police superintendent of the Tower. He would undertake to unlock the doors, warn the prisoners, who, dressed in military hats and coats, and armed with guns, would leave towards midnight on a false patrol; the two children, well surrounded by the soldiers, would pass unnoticed. Several faithful royalists, posted in the vicinity, would quickly take them to a lonely house in the neighbourhood of Brie-Comte-Robert, where they would remain hidden.

On the night fixed for the escape, every man was at his post, as arranged. Everything promised to work like a charm, and Cortey was just about to give his men the signal to start, when suddenly he saw Simon the cobbler running towards him as fast as he could pelt. "Ah, here you are," he said to Cortey, "if I had not seen you here, I would not feel at ease." He had the prisoners' room opened, to see if they were still there, and sent Michonis away to the Hôtel-de-Ville. Simon took his place and gave the alarm.

Simon had been warned by an anonymous note: "Michonis will betray this night; watch!"

One's only surmise is that the Tison woman had revealed the plot to Simon. The last hope of saving the royal family had vanished.

How bitter her remorse was to be. . . .

CHAPTER XXVII

The Queen's tragedy

THE execrable public prosecutor, Fouquier-Tinville, looking like a cormorant in a feathered tricorne, sat ruminating on how best to debase the monarchy in the eyes of the people. "Can't have a repetition of the show-down on January the 21st. Not an insult. Dead silence. No, let's rake up something really exciting, and we'll see to it that the widow Capet gets a good Carnival procession on her way to the guillotine." His eye fell on a copy of the libellous pamphlet written by the Lamotte creature, of Necklace fame. He searched it avidly. It was full of filthy accusations against the Queen. It spoke of her Lesbian tendencies, her many lovers, her bastards, and then . . . other unspeakable unnatural practices. And here, he lighted on something so nauseating that one's pen refuses to name it. Suffice it to say that at the precise moment that Fouquier-Tinville concocted his vilest accusation against the Queen, an accusation which involved the moral corruption of her son, he committed the vilest, the most Satanic crime of the whole Revolution, and one which was to bring down God's wrath on the French people. It is base enough to turn a child against its mother, but when in cold blood a man corrupts this child's body and mind, he deserves the millstone promised in the Bible for those who "scandalise those little ones".

An unfortunate accident to the young prince played into Fouquier-Tinville's hands. The child had been "riding a cock-horse" on a stick in the manner of children, and he had injured himself. Somewhat alarmed by the resulting hernia, the Queen said she wanted to consult doctor Hippolyte Pipelet, a well-known specialist and truss-maker, living in the Rue Mazarine. Only after repeatedly insisting did she induce the authorities to send for him. He came and made a suspensory bandage.[1]

[1] All this is testified by an English agent in correspondence with Lord Grenville, who got his information from Simon. But Simon left in disgust, soon after this.

When Fouquier-Tinville heard of this, his foul imagination explored the possibilities of this accident. Why, it could serve as a theme for his insinuations. So his mother was looking after him, was she? The child could be trapped into saying all sorts of things against her. It is so easy to make innocent children say anything. Yes, a little strong liquor and a few beatings, some sleepless nights, visits from prostitutes . . . and soon the mother's moral reputation would lie in the mud. Ha! Ha! To see the proud Capet woman bow her neck in irremediable shame under her own son's affirmations. Yes, that would crush her, yes, and the populace would loathe her. He felt he could count on giving the people a good Punch and Judy show, the day she was paraded in a cart, on the way to execution. There would be rotten eggs thrown, and some women could be relied on to spit, and the tougher harlots would break through the bodyguard and strike the Austrian on her pallid face. Ah, he'd make her wince all right, he'd soon have her crawling and licking the dust. Perhaps a little judicious bleeding whilst Sanson was shearing her locks would deprive her of her aristocratic swagger at the last minute and she'd make an exhibition of herself on the scaffold: "Help, help, good people, mister executioner. Just one more minute, mister . . ."

Plomp!

. . . . .

By June the 23rd, the Dauphin was better, and went to play in the garden. His mischievous gaiety, his love for his mother, touched the most hard-hearted guards, and one of them could not resist taking him into a corner and giving him a hug.

But he fell ill again, and this time another secret admirer of his, no other than Madame Tison herself, began to feel the gnawings of remorse. This woman, whose maternal cravings had been so thwarted, realised that she had been the cause of all the trouble. Supposing now that charming child were to die for want of proper care? She sighed deeply.

"Hi, what's the matter?" shouted her husband, striking her a heavy blow on the ears. "Look, I've got some work for you. I want to tell the police that Elisabeth and the Capet woman hold a secret correspondence with Turgy. Tell 'em what you told me—that you found that some more sealing wax had dripped on to a candlestick."

"I can't. What's the good? A bit of wax proves nothing. Can't you leave them alone? What harm have they done you?"

For an answer, he started knocking her about, as only a Parisian revolutionary turnkey could.

So she betrayed them again, on June the 28th.

After that, her reason snapped. It had really all started the day they shoved that blood-stained head on a pike up to her window. She had such terrible nightmares. And then, during the day, the strain of spying on a family she believed to be innocent, her constant fear of her husband. . . . Only constant tit-bits of information would keep him quiet. The men at the top used her daughter as bait, and she and Tison lived in daily fear of losing her. And those blows on the head, and those kicks . . . No, life had slowly become one vast Inferno. And living in that dark, damp Tower, with all its doors, and its narrow spiral staircases guarded by sentries, her nights broken by the singing and shouting of drunken guards. And Tison, Tison, Tison, with his terrible fists, his terrible boots, his flaming eyes—a butcher, a butcher. And she had betrayed those three gentle courteous women in black, into his hands. No, it was too much . . . too much. . . . She began raving. She must beg their pardon. The thoughts of being cut off from their kindliness for ever was too much, too much, too much. . . .

On July the 3rd, after the young King had been forcibly separated from his mother, the woman's reason gave way entirely. It had taken one whole hour to part mother and child. And the proudest of Queens, the daughter of Emperors, had pleaded in vain with a stonemason, a perfumer, a carpenter and three other revolutionaries sent up to fetch her son away. The Tison woman shivered as she heard their insults and their threats to use violence, the wild sobs of the mother and child. (Madame Royale wrote heart-rendingly of the whole thing.) At last, towards eleven o'clock at night, the Queen got her child up, dressed him, and gave him into the men's hands, ". . . bathing him with tears as if she had foreseen that she would see him no more".

And then the footsteps echoed on the spiral staircase. A little boy's voice crying: "*Maman! Maman!*"

Madame Royale says: "My mother thought she had tasted the bitterest dregs of the cup, when she was separated from her son; . . . her desolation increased when she knew that it was Simon, the cobbler, whom she had known when he was a municipalist, who was in charge of the person of her unhappy child."

For three nights, Madame Tison tossed and turned in sleepless agony, thinking of the child, thinking of his mother, and blaming herself for her share in their misery. "Can't you stay still?" shouted Tison, kicking her.

On the morning of July the 6th, she rushed into the room where the three mourning women sat, guarded by sentries. The Queen was a stricken mother, and had that blank look of victims who have endured the acme of moral suffering, and can now feel no more. Madame Tison threw herself at her feet. "Madame, I beg your Majesty's forgiveness; I am a wretch, I am the cause of your death and of the death of Madame Elisabeth." The princesses drew her up again with great kindness and tried to console her.

Just then Turgy, followed by his assistants, brought the luncheon. Madame Tison fell at Turgy's feet and started begging his forgiveness too. Then she had horrible convulsions. It was awful to watch. It took eight men to hold her. Two days later, they carried her to the Hôtel-Dieu, where she was certified. She never reappeared at the Temple.

There is nothing in life more terrible for a young girl than the sight of dementia. It does something to one that later joys can never, never efface. That is why society protects itself by segregating the mad. If Madame Royale grew up to be rather a grim, forbidding woman, a scene such as this was responsible. It must have been ghastly for her mother and aunt to see the child exposed to the gibberings of lunacy. If Marie-Thérèse did not break down altogether, it was due to her aunt's great sanity of behaviour, her instinctive knowledge of how to heal and cheer and be astringently, though not offensively, bracing. She would make her immediately react to such horrors by sensible action, rub her hands, tempt her to eat something, talk quietly about other things.

After the meal, which they could hardly touch, the Queen and Elisabeth made enquiries about Madame Tison. They had quite forgotten how much she had made them suffer: they only saw her as an afflicted human being.

This tragedy was a thunderbolt to Tison. After witnessing the attentions lavished on his wife by the Queen and the princesses, he was so touched that he was sorry for his past behaviour and wanted to give proofs of his repentance.

. . . . . .

Now that the young King had been removed, supervision was less strict. The municipals no longer stayed in the Queen's room, though the guards came to bring meals and test the iron bars. The prisoners were kept under lock and key, day and night, so there was no question of meeting the child in the garden. One day, Elisabeth said to the Queen and her niece: "You know the little staircase which leads out of the *garde-robe*? There is a small window on that staircase which looks out on to the garden."

The Queen looked up, still not understanding. "Yes, *ma sœur*?"

"I'm going up to keep watch. Who knows, we might get a glimpse of Charles playing in the garden."

The poor mother turned pale and faint. She whispered: "We will all go, we will all go and watch. Oh, for just one tiny glimpse of him, and then I could live."

And she started weeping.

So, directly after one of the municipal visits, at a time when they knew they would be undisturbed, the three women in black went up the staircase and peered through the tiny window. The Queen cleaned the dirty pane with her handkerchief and waited, very quietly. There was nobody. The chestnut alley was deserted, that hot July day. All her soul was in her eyes, and they, alas, were so weakened by tears, that she could hardly see. Her sister held her round the waist, as if to communicate to her some of the warmth of her valiant spirit. (Before the Temple was finally demolished, oh, if walls ever echo human woes, the very stones of that little spiral staircase could surely have sweated tears, the slow, anguished tears of a mother waiting for her only son.)

They were just turning away, when Elisabeth gave a smothered cry: she had caught a glimpse of a little boy, dragging his feet in the chestnut alley, followed by several drunken soldiers.

"*Ma sœur*, there he is. Oh, my God!"

The Queen, feeling that she was going to faint, mastered herself and strained her eyes to look. They saw a sorry sight. Her son was sobbing. She could hear and see him. Suddenly, he turned to Simon and said: "I want my mother. Show me the law which ordains that we should be parted." Simon kicked him and the child fell. His mother stifled a scream. "Come away, *ma sœur*," cried Elisabeth. "Come away."

"No, no, don't make me. I must see him. Hold me up." The child rose from the ground and they heard his tormentors say: "Cry out loudly, Capet, so that you will really be heard proclaiming these words, 'The Republic is eternal'." But the little prince replied firmly, in the manner of the early child martyrs of Rome: "Nothing is eternal but God." His jailers fell on him like a pack of wolves. The boy was knocked over and kicked in the chest.[1] His mother heard and saw the blows.

The next day, Elisabeth persuaded her sister-in-law not to go up to the staircase. She made the pretext that they would be missed, during a long absence. But she could not restrain her for long. ("Love is watchful,—sleeping, slumbereth not," says Thomas à Kempis. Can a mother forget her child?) Before long, supported by Elisabeth, this stricken mother was keeping another long, sorrowful vigil. "Oh, if only my eyes were stronger. If only I had a spy glass!" And in that odd, inconsequent manner of the human mind, she recalled the magnifying glass hidden in the meshes of a fan, which she had given—so long ago—to the Comtesse du Nord. Had she been that Queen? It was a dream figure from another world. And her "*petit chou d'amour*", playing in his small private garden at Versailles and picking his daily posy for her—had he ever really been her own son?

"Oh," cried Elisabeth suddenly, "I see a boy, but it can't be Charles, he's not in mourning."

"Let me look, let me look."

Down below was the little King of France, in coloured clothes—for

[1] Mémoires de la Duchesse de Gontaut.

Simon had taken away his black ones. He had a red bonnet on his fair curls, and was wearing the revolutionary blouse. He was tottering and swaying, as if he were drunk. Indeed, he was drunk. "Sing," shouted Simon. And the poor waif sang in a strident pipe, first the "Carmagnole", then the "Marseillaise". Armed with a stick, Simon stood over him. At this point, the Queen, without a cry, fell into her sister-in-law's arms. "Don't look," said Elisabeth to her niece. But, after they had revived the Queen and taken her down, Madame Royale must have gone up again, for she tells us that her brother stood under the windows, swearing and blaspheming against God, his family and the aristocrats.

Elisabeth would not allow her sister-in-law to go up very often after that, but, alas, mothers have a sixth sense of what is happening to their children.

Nothing really had mattered so much till now: the enmity of courtiers and relatives, the Necklace affair, separation from her friends, from Fersen, her husband's death, the insults of dirty-minded men and women—these were nothing to the tortures, the subtle anguish, the Queen endured during those summer months. She was as a butterfly impaled on a pin by a master tormentor, skilled in wresting the last anguished spasm from his victim, learned in crucifying the prisoner up to the limit of his endurance, and then . . . letting him breathe again, just in time, for fear of killing him off.

On August the 2nd, at two o'clock in the morning, a terrible knocking at the door. Tison opened and was confronted by the men who'd come to escort the Queen to the Conciergerie. Tison went to Elisabeth and told her this. She took a key, put it into the lock, then leaning hard on the key, she said firmly: "Sirs, I will not open until I am sure that my sister and my niece are up and dressed."

At length, the men came in and read the decree of transfer; then they searched the Queen's pockets. It was noticed that Elisabeth did not weep, but that her face expressed contempt, grief and indignation. Just as the Queen was leaving, Elisabeth said to one of the men: "Monsieur, I ask the Committee of Public Safety to grant me a favour, and that is to allow me to share my sister's new prison; I beg you to ask this for me." This was refused. The Queen kissed her daughter again and again and told her to be brave and to look after her health. Then she left.

When she went out of the Tower, misjudging the height of the low wicket gate, she struck her head. But she did not mind: nothing could hurt her any more.

And thus for Elisabeth, in this world, concluded a friendship which had begun one May morning during her childhood. How long ago it seemed since that mad game of hide-and-seek, which the young Rouget de Lisle had watched from his hiding place. (And now, they were singing his "Marseillaise" in the streets.) And those donkey-rides at Trianon, under Madame de Marsan's very nose, or those mornings trying on Rose Bertin's new dresses, or those glorious days hunting together. Though Elisabeth's tastes and friends had been very different from the young Queen's, all the same, she had loved her, for she was generous and gay and charming, and every passing year had increased her need of affection. Elisabeth was one of those women who are most closely drawn to their friends when they are in need.

After the Queen's departure, aunt and niece were inconsolable. They spent the night in tears.

The next morning, with her usual practical foresight, Elisabeth asked that the water from Ville d'Avray, which was brought daily to the Queen, should now be sent to the Conciergerie, for Seine water always made her ill. But this request was not granted.

Elisabeth secretly wrote more notes to Turgy, asking what had happened to the English fleet and to her brothers; had France a navy on any sea, how was the Abbé (Monsieur Edgeworth de Firmont)? Had he received any news of Madame de Bombelles? How were the persons of St. Cyr?

When the Queen was put in the darkest, dampest cell in the Conciergerie, for the first ten days she was without linen. She asked for some constantly, but in vain. What a misery for a woman of refinement in hot weather! At long last, however, Elisabeth was allowed to make up a parcel for her and she did this very carefully. When the Queen opened it, she said to Madame Richard, the wife of the prison *concierge*: "By the care with which all this has been prepared, I recognise the attentions and the hand of my poor sister Elisabeth."

There were beautiful cambric chemises, pocket handkerchiefs, neckerchiefs, stockings of silk and of black floss silk, a white morning dress, several night bonnets, lengths of ribbon, and lastly, some knitting, which she was not allowed to keep.

But to return to the Temple, where Elisabeth and her niece were now alone together day and night, and never allowed to go out. The young girl would certainly have lost her reason and her physical health had not her aunt taken her in hand, and trained her to self-discipline and fortitude.

"My dear, I know the food is not very appetising now, but you must make it a duty to eat." Indeed, by September, Hébert, having decreed that the two prisoners should have nobody to serve them, also attacked the food problem. On October the 13th Turgy reported that the princesses were served with a tin bowl full of soup and a hunk of beef, a piece of coarse bread, a bottle of tavern wine. (No one was allowed to lay a table for them.) This was apparently the meal intended for the superintendents, for, when the meal prepared by Turgy for the two royal ladies appeared, it was seized on by the guards. Stringent economies of all kinds were enforced in the kitchens. Game and pastry were forbidden, and at breakfast, they had only one kind of food. Perhaps only then did the two princesses realise that meals, in the past, had been a stand-by, a pause during the day, a blessing, as God intended them to be. And now, nausea had to be overcome to avoid starvation. Perhaps they learnt that useful little trick, when one's gorge rises in the house of strangers—a sip of water to help one to get the beastliness down one's heaving gullet, without attracting attention.

The searches became more thorough. For fear of being undressed by Madame Simon, Elisabeth and Marie-Thérèse threw away pencils and writing materials which they had secreted on their persons until now. Wax tapers were taken away, to be replaced by tallow candles. (Oh, those thousands of unused tapers at Versailles, the daily perquisites of the staff—how welcome just one of them would have been now!) Silver and porcelain were confiscated, only common earthenware and tin were allowed. Except for the man who brought water and wood once a day, nobody ever came into their rooms. As they

T

now had no servants of any kind, they were obliged to make their own beds and sweep their rooms, "a thing which took a long time because we were so little accustomed to it in the beginning", said Marie-Thérèse rather pathetically. Elisabeth smiled as she recalled the eighty members of her staff, at Versailles, at Montreuil, the floors always beautifully polished, fresh flowers, meals served with every possible refinement, the bath-tub wheeled up before a blazing fire, the clean shifts daily, redolent with lavender and pot-pourri, the brilliant lighting everywhere, the fine linen sheets—and now—their sheets were taken away and replaced by others which were coarse and dirty. They were forbidden to go to the Tower (this was just as well, as it had turned out). Elisabeth asked for some ointment to heal a wound in her arm, which came after applying a cautery, but this was refused for a long time. The search parties, not finding the regulation quota of silver and china to take away—for it had been filched by their colleagues—had the baseness and silliness to accuse the royal ladies of stealing it. Even the bare necessities were confiscated, says Marie-Thérèse, by which one imagines body-linen. One man, during a search, had found Elisabeth's gold thimble, so used that it was all pierced with holes. "The Commune, great and generous, decrees that this object shall be sold to profit the indigents, and that the woman Elisabeth will be provided with a tin or ivory thimble."

On Sunday, October the 6th, Chaumette, Hébert, and five others appeared at Simon's lodging: the cobbler had arranged chairs and a table. The child-King was made to sign a statement of "certain facts" he had told Simon and his wife. His handwriting, usually so tidy in his lesson books, is so clumsy, indeed almost illegible, that it is certain he was drunk when he held that quill.

The following day, at one o'clock in the afternoon, they confronted the child with his sister. This time, Hébert was absent, but David, the painter David, was there—seething with delight at this unique opportunity to vent his spite on a family which had not fully appreciated his pictures.

When Marie-Thérèse had been fetched from her prison, in vain her aunt begged to accompany her. When the child got down to Simon's room, she saw her brother. She was kissing him tenderly, when Madame Simon snatched him away from her and pushed her into the next room.

Chaumette began the cross-examination.

Chaumette: Your name.

Madame Royale: Thérèse.

Chaumette: Speak the truth.

Madame Royale: Yes, *Monsieur*.

With prudence far above her age, she pretended ignorance of all plots in which guards were implicated. Then . . . the bombshell.

". . . Chaumette then questioned me about a thousand filthy things of which they were accusing my mother; I replied truthfully that these were not true, but infamous calumnies; they insisted very much, but I denied it all the time, thus speaking the truth."

They brought in the Dauphin, and sat him down in an armchair, where he swung his little legs which could not reach the floor. They charged him to declare whether he persisted in upholding his assertions about the indecent scenes, revealed by him the day before. He repeated his accusation and his sister obstinately denied it.[1]

This went on for *three hours*.

.   .   .   .   .

Then, seeing that the Dauphin was coming round from his drunken stupor and even kissing his sister's hand, Chaumette sent the little princess up again, with strict injunctions not to say anything to her aunt.

Then it was Elisabeth's turn. Duval, in "Souvenirs Thermidoriens", says she had a bad cold. Suddenly, she recognised David, the King's first painter, from having seen him at Versailles, and, noticing a snuff-box in his hands, she said to him gently: "Monsieur David, would you give me a pinch of snuff? I've got such a bad cold in the head." And she made as if to receive the snuff-box. David replied: "I would have you learn that you are not made to put your fingers in my snuff-box." Then he poured out a little snuff in the hollow formed by his thumb

---

[1] Lord Grenville's notes reveal that Simon said: "After the Queen's death, no more prostitutes were presented to the little King." So then, at this very time, the poor child was at the mercy of Paris harlots.

and offered it to Madame Elisabeth. She turned her back on him. After questioning her about the loyalty of some guards, and about Toulan getting news to them by pedlars near the Temple, Chaumette again uncovered his cesspool before this lily of the French court. She declared haughtily that such an infamy was too greatly beneath her, and too foreign to her to have to reply to it. Her proud dignity infuriated Chaumette, who shouted out: "Come down a peg or two; you are before your magistrates; drop your court arrogancies."

When she heard her nephew protest that he was not lying, she could not restrain her indignation, and exclaimed: "Oh! the monster." (She did not know anything of the attempts to bring about the little boy's moral degradation.)

It was obvious, however, to a guard called Goret, who has left it on record, that the obscene words had been put into the child's mouth, and he was repeating his harshly learnt lesson, parrot-fashion, without probably understanding anything of what was said; his poor head was fuddled with drink, and he was unable to see that "they" were trying to misinterpret his mother's care of him during his recent illness. But, he had four hours of this. So, lest the truth come out, the session was brought to an end. Elisabeth was taken up again, quivering with indignation, leaving the poor child with hideous memories and a nightmare of indefinable remorse, which were to drive him to a state of semi-imbecility. She was never to see her little nephew again.[1]

One can imagine the feelings of aunt and niece, when they were together again that evening. But God is the Lord of the midnight prison: so many captives, in their darkest hour, have found that God makes His presence felt to them in their cells. Dungeons, filled with such sweetness, became the very ante-rooms of Paradise. Was it not in the stinking cell of Toledo, that the great Spanish mystic, St. John of the Cross, verminous and streaming with blood from public scourgings, experienced the heights of mystical union? And Elisabeth, trained to prayer, to trust in God's Providence, soon returned to her natural climate of prayer and drew her little niece into the radiance of it.

[1] It is more than likely that he died of neglect in solitary confinement. The picture is too terrible.

CHAPTER XXVIII

Last days together

THEY knew nothing of the Queen's fate. They imagined her to be alive at the Conciergerie, awaiting trial.

In her admirable testament, written at four-thirty on the morning of October the 16th, the Queen said: "In our misfortunes, how many consolations our friendship has given us! And in happiness, one's enjoyment is doubled when one can share it with a friend; and where can one find one more tender and more dear than in one's own family? . . .

". . . Adieu, my good and tender sister; . . ."

.   .   .   .   .   .

Late that autumn, the procurator of the Commune began protesting against the enormous expenses occasioned by the prisoners. (Expense! When Elisabeth, unable to obtain fish for fast and abstinence days, contented herself with bread and coffee.) In November, the engineer Dufourny de Villiers, "in the name of Jacobin societies and of several thousands of citizens", besought the National Convention that "Capet's sister" should be sent to the Revolutionary Tribunal. He demanded that what remained of the "impure blood of kings" should be shed on the scaffold.

Now, there were three searches a day; one of them lasted four hours. The municipals were quite drunk. Marie-Thérèse writes: "One can have no idea of their remarks, of their insults and their oaths during those four hours. They took away several trifles, like hats, cards with kings on them, works engraved with arms; they left pious books, but only after having uttered a thousand blasphemies."

At the end of November, Robespierre, who wanted to save

Elisabeth, devised, as he thought, an ingenuous way of gaining popularity; he suggested that a horrible law should be passed, forcing any girl of fifteen or over, who was not married in six months, to be handed over to the public. In this case Elisabeth and Madame Royale would have been the first victims.

On November the 6th, 1793, they heard the street criers shouting of the Duc d'Orléan's execution. His last words about Louis XVI were: "I contributed to the death of an innocent man, and now it's my turn to die! But he was too good not to forgive me."

"Yes," said Elisabeth to her niece, as they sat silently in the twilight, "the last time I saw him was in May, at the procession of the States General at Versailles."

"Didn't the fish-wives cheer him and then affect a dead silence when mother passed?"

"Yes. She nearly fainted. Fortunately I was near to support her. Oh, what a traitor he was! He had it in his power to do so much good, he was so wealthy and so powerful, but no, he engineered his own destruction. A curse has always rested on the House of Orléans and its descendants."

Lord Grenville's bulletins tell us that in February, 1794, the police superintendents forced the princesses to leave their doors open always. These were locked at four each evening. But there was little sleep, for the guards sang infamous ditties the whole night long.

Again, the little Dauphin was induced to sign documents, stating that his aunt was involved in conspiracies. Before signing, they made out that little Capet said his mother feared his aunt, and his aunt was best at carrying out plots.

Then Simon came forward and declared that the two princesses were forging paper money (the noise of their game of back-gammon, which they played in the evenings).

A later letter of Madame Royale to Madame de Raigecourt in 1799 indicates that during that winter, aunt and niece often talked of her dear friends, recalling happier days.

"Aunt, tell me again all about Bombon dancing, about Jacques and his cows, about your garden at Montreuil, about Angélique de Bombelles' ball-gown, about Adalbert de Chamisot and your botany lessons, about Tante Louise' cell at the Carmelites, about your visits to Saint-Cyr, about when you were a little girl."

And so, across a river of blood, from beyond a forest of pikes and pitchforks, Elisabeth would evoke, one by one, beloved figures of the past—Démon, Rage, Bombe and Bombon, and Louise de Condé. Conjured up by her nostalgic descriptions, delicate Sèvres figurines in panniers of Lyon brocade would float through the serried ranks of *sans-culottes*, curtsey aloofly, tread a minuet to Rameau's pipes and Lulli's airs, and then disappear into the mist of the gardens of Petit Trianon. Red Phrygian bonnets and unkempt locks would vanish for a second, ousted by white powdered wigs. Elisabeth had not forgotten how to be gay. "I can't tell you how funny the Baronne d'Oberkirch was with real flowers in the glass bottles of her wig. She was so uncomfortable!" And sweet sounds were conjured up to ears wearied of shouts, insults and the strains of the *Ça Ira*. In place of prison stenches, of damp and dirt, and revolting food, Elisabeth evoked the perfumes of long ago—the wholesome effluvia of a well-kept stable; new-mown hay at Montreuil; lilies in her flower garden; incense clouds at Midnight Mass at Versailles, when the King's musicians always surpassed themselves; the lilacs at Petit Trianon, which had sent the Baronne d'Oberkirch into such ecstasies; the crisp tang of frost on a sledge ride; the invigorating, pungent odour of dead leaves, on hunting days at Fontainebleau; lavender in linen, pot-pourri. . . . And those were the days when red damask roses really smelt good. . . .

Elisabeth behaved in prison as if she were in her own drawing-room. Ernest Daudet says: ". . . she had abdicated none of the graces." She tried to train her little charge in all the discipline of a Christian gentlewoman. In any ancient civilisation, the women have got refinement ingrained in them, through long generations: it is only the *bourgeois* women whose breeding is skin-deep, who let themselves go in private, when exiled from their country and their accustomed mode of life.

Elisabeth trained Marie-Thérèse to dispense with the services of maids in every way. "She arranged my life so that each hour had its employment. The care of my room, prayer, reading, work, all was arranged. She had accustomed me to making my bed alone, to do my hair, to wash, to dress; and moreover, she had neglected nothing to maintain my health. She made me sprinkle my room with water to keep it fresh, and besides, she insisted that I walk very quickly indeed for an hour, watch in hand, to prevent spleen and stagnation."[1]

In her memoirs, the young princess says: "My aunt kept the fasts and abstinences of the Church." In fact, in Lent, she had no breakfast, although she had risen early—a bowl of coffee at luncheon, and some bread at supper-time. (One feels that Elisabeth made this an excuse for giving away her own share to the growing girl.)

"Listen, my dearest child, I want to give you a word of warning in case you and I are separated."

"Oh, *ma tante* . . ."

"There, there, we must just be prepared for all emergencies. Now, promise you will ask for a woman to be sent to you, if I go?"

"But I would so much rather be alone: supposing they sent me another Madame Tison?"

"Even that would be better than being alone. It would be some protection."

"I promise."

"Secondly, supposing you are left entirely alone, I want you to continue living by the clock, strictly to time-table. I will lend you 'La Journée du Chrétien', which you can learn off by heart, and then this small provision of wool, for your embroidery. When you've finished a piece, as beautifully as possible, admire it for a little while, then unpick it carefully and begin an entirely new pattern. Your efforts won't be wasted, because you will be acquiring greater skill all the time. And then . . . and then . . ."

"Yes, aunt, what is it?"

"I don't like stressing this, or making you nervous, but if the guards come to fetch you at night, don't unbolt the door until you are fully dressed."

"But aunt, you know how they knock and kick the door and shout curses."

"Take no notice. Don't let that upset you. Dress quickly and calmly, and then open. On no account let those men see you in bed,

[1] Told to the Duchesse de Tourzel, her former governess.

even if you are ill with a fever. Thank Heaven that we have a bolt to this door: it is the one decent thing our jailers have done for us, the one point in their favour. If we had been guarded by fishwives, or by women of the *bourgeoisie*, you can be sure that we would have been deprived of that bolt. But then, women are so subtle at debasing their fellow women."

In Elisabeth's bedroom, someone had scribbled two prayers on the walls. "Per agoniam et passionem tuam, libera nos." "Per mortem et sepulturam tuam, libera nos." ("By thine agony and passion, deliver us." "By thy death and burial, deliver us.")

Yes, she knew that death was nigh, and she made haste to do all in her power for the child, so that she could fend for herself when she had gone.

A silversmith once explained in a most illuminating way the meaning of the Biblical words, used in the office of Candlemas: "He shall come as a refiner and purifier of silver." The silversmith hangs over the boiling vat most intently, for he must take it off the fire at the *precise* moment of purification. The silver must not be refined for too long or too short a time, else it will be worthless. And how does the silversmith know when that crucial moment has arrived? Only when, for one fleeting second, he can see his own reflection in the silver.

The long training was nearing completion. A stormy childhood in which a tempestuous small girl had stamped her feet at her maids. Then, at fifteen, a vow of perfection. The sacrifice of a Carmelite vocation, to devote herself to her family. And now, one by one, the members of that family had been taken from her. Elisabeth was so thin, so diaphanous, that she was almost unrecognisable. She was fast becoming the Veronica kerchief on which Christ's suffering image was imprinted. Pride had changed to lowliness, hot temper to gentleness, the Bourbon joie-de-vivre to fasting—to what George Herbert calls: "the cleanness of sweet abstinence"—the sparkling gaiety to an even, disciplined day-to-day cheeriness which turned prison walls to gold, as if a yellowhammer were singing behind the iron bars. Even her tormentors were aware of the beauty of her patience. Lord Grenville tells us: "On March 29th, Elisabeth, having written to Solmon, who commanded the service guard, for some linen for herself and her niece, he went to her and told her the nation was tired of her demands, and that she could wash her own linen if she wanted. For six weeks they had been very badly fed, but nothing equals the heroism of Madame Elisabeth. Whatever they say or do to her, the tormentors themselves agree, in the accounts they send up to the municipality, that one never notices in her the least movement of impatience."

The Divine Craftsman had seen His own countenance reflected in the silver He had been purifying in His Crucible, and her deliverance was near. The precious metal, now molten, was soon to be fashioned into a glowing silver chalice of praise, a holy Grail.

CHAPTER XXIX

The Crucible

LENT 1794; perpetual fasting and abstinence. Then Holy Week, with its memories of Maundy Thursday and the Altar of Repose at Versailles. Easter Sunday, with its "O Filii", once sung in the simple parish church at Montreuil. May the 3rd, Feast of the Finding of the Holy Cross, and Elisabeth's thirtieth birthday. "Many happy returns of the day," cried little Madame, throwing her arms around her aunt's neck. Elisabeth smiled and said nothing. Her breviary fell from her lap. Her niece picked it up and glanced at the pages in which there were markers. Her eye caught the hymn for first Vespers, "Salve Crux sancta, salve mundi gloria." ("Hail holy Cross, hail glory of the world.")

May the 8th—the Feast of the Apparition of St. Michael Archangel.

> Tibi Christe, splendor Patris,
> Vita, virtus cordium,
> In conspectu Angelorum
> Votis, voce psallimus:
> Alternantes concrepando
> Melos damus vocibus.
>
> [To Thee, O Christ, splendour of the Father,
> Heart's life, heart's power,
> Here before the Angels' gaze
> With vows and voice we sing,
> Offering (sweet) melody
> With our voices in alternate choirs.]

Great Michael, patron-defender of France! By saying the Office daily, Elisabeth forgot her own burdens and lived in the wider life of the Church's praise. Liturgical praise is unequalled for making Catholics universal-minded. It draws them into the rhythm of the eternal spheres.

And that glorious Lauds hymn, "Christe, sanctorum decus Ange-lorum",—"Christ, the beauty of the holy angels"—that hymn associating the heavenly citizens with their suffering mortal brethren. . . . One of the Doctors of the Church says that the angels delight in helping souls to pray: how Elisabeth's constant prayer must have rejoiced them! Even those of us who often heard the late saintly Gervase Elwes sing in "The Dream of Gerontius", with Cardinal Newman's stanzas express-ing such tenderness to guardian angels—we do not think enough of these celestial guardians.

May the 9th—within the Octave of the Feast of The Holy Cross, within the Octave of the Apparition of Michael Archangel, and Elisabeth's last day at the Temple. The two princesses had supped at seven-thirty—or, at least, Marie-Thérèse had supped, but her aunt fasted, for it was a Friday. Since early spring, the authorities had deprived them even of tallow candles, so that they were obliged to go to bed at twilight. It was raining.

Towards nine o'clock, locked up in their room, Elisabeth and Marie-Thérèse were just preparing for bed before the light faded. Suddenly, frenzied knocking at the double door which separated them from the guards always on duty. It was more violent, more uncon-trolled than the usual sort of knocking, almost diabolic, and the child's blood ran cold.

Be it said to the honour of Frenchmen, Fouquier-Tinville had experienced great difficulty in finding any men in the Paris army willing to fetch Elisabeth away from the Temple and bring her to the Conciergerie. Robespierre at last unearthed a violent brute called Saralier, and he was followed by a bailiff Monet, and an artillery officer, Fontaine.

Elisabeth called out that she was putting on her dress. The men bawled, "That will not take so long," and they banged so hard that the two princesses thought the heavy door was going to give way. However, Elisabeth kept her head and only opened when she was properly dressed. They came in, with a great rattling of swords and clicking of spurs. (They addressed her by the familiar "*tu*" or "thou", which was insulting.)

"Citizeness, come down."

"And my niece?"

"She'll be dealt with later."

Elisabeth kissed Marie-Thérèse and told her she would be coming up again.

"No, citizeness, you will not be coming up again, get your bonnet and come down."

Then they started insulting her, which she endured with patience. She took her bonnet, kissed her niece again, told her to be brave and to hope in God. She was just trying to whisper something in her ear (doubtless a last injunction on how to protect her unguarded state), when one of the devils seized her by the hair and thus dragged her out of the room. In the doorway, the wife and daughters of the jailer burst into tears.

Thus was the pure victim led to the slaughter-house.

When she reached the bottom of the staircase, greatly shaken, and full of a mother's anguish for the fate of her niece, she was surrounded by more soldiers and her pockets were searched again. Amongst other little trinkets, they took away her gold watch, so that during her last hours in this world she never knew the time. The torch-light shone on her white dress among the uniforms and revolutionary blouses. We know that it was raining, because this is recorded in an unpublished diary by one Célestin Guitard, living in the Place Saint-Sulpice. (Just now, in the gentle spring rain, the lilies-of-the-valley of Montreuil would be scenting the night air. . . .)

It was then about eight o'clock.

Under heavy rain, without a cloak, Elisabeth was made to cross the Temple garden and the first courtyard. There, she was pushed into a cab and driven to the Conciergerie.

"I wonder whether I shall see my sister-in-law," she thought.

And then her heart ached with misery at remembrance of the poor little girl, left in her desolation, all alone in the dark, all alone for the first time in her life. And the Dauphin—oh, where was he?

They arrived at the Conciergerie, that fortress-like palace of Philippe-Auguste and Saint Louis, by the banks of the Seine, still grim and grey and impregnable. Its walls were so thick, that, though the turret for the torture chamber directly overlooked the street, the shrieks of the victims could never be heard by passers-by a few feet away. Many a Parisian glancing up, fearfully, with memories of poisoners like la Voisin and the Marquise de Brinvilliers, would cross himself furtively, and then hurry on his way, taking care not to look back.

First, she crossed through a double wicket gate guarded by two turnkeys, a mere hatch, a gate so low, that you had to bend almost double to get in, and step very high to cross it. Then she arrived in another room in which the *concierge* Richard presided. Richard was made much of by friends of prisoners who hoped to curry favour. Passing by him, Elisabeth said: "Perhaps I will see my sister again?"

Richard kept saying to his underlings in slang, "*Allumez le miston*," which meant, "Look under this type's nose—examine him."

She was taken to the clerks' office. This was a room divided in two by large iron bars; one half was for the clerks' records, the other half was for those condemned to death.

The cells, called "mousetraps", should have been called rat-holes. An honest citizen called Beauregard, who spent one night in such a cell, had his breeches eaten away in various places by rats, and he had to cover his nose and ears to protect them. Daylight rarely filtered in, the straw quickly decayed for want of air, and the "*griaches*" or sanitary pails exhaled such pestilential stenches that even the air in the clerks' office was befouled when a door was opened. The outside galleries, where the prisoners took cover during the day, were likewise infected with nauseating odours. Is it surprising that the prisoners, catching and passing on diseases, and unable to keep clean, preferred death to this Hades?

At ten o'clock, Elisabeth was led from the clerks' office into the Council Hall of the Revolutionary Tribunal, to undergo her first questioning: she was always addressed with the familiar "*tu*".

Judge: Your name.

Elisabeth: Elisabeth de France.

Judge: Have you, with the last tyrant, conspired against the safety and liberty of the French people?

Elisabeth: I do not know to whom you give this title, but I have never desired anything but the happiness of the French.

Judge: Have you pursued correspondence or had intelligence with the enemies, interior or exterior, of the Republic, notably with Capet's brothers and yours, and have you not provided them with financial aid?

.   .   .   .   .   .

And so on—about her diamonds, her proposed flight from Saint-Cloud, her flight to Varennes (about which she makes it crystal clear that the King never had any intention of leaving the kingdom). She forcibly denied any knowledge of the alleged secret discussions at her sister's, called "Austrian committees", discussions which were supposed to take place between midnight and 3 a.m. It must be recalled that throughout, Elisabeth thought the Queen was still in the Conciergerie, so she was very careful. As E. M. du L. has said: "The answers of Madame Elisabeth are as remarkable for their gallant frankness as for their faultless prudence."

She was told to sign her statements. She wrote "Elisabeth Marie". In the printed account of her trial, "they" were false enough to make out that she had signed "Elisabeth Capet". So much for the veracity of the republican press!

She was then taken to a cell: in the adjoining alcove slept Richard the *concierge*. When the Papal Nuncio, Mgr. de Salamon, was imprisoned there in his turn, Richard used to tell him that the Duc d'Orléans had occupied that cell, before his execution. Pointing to the bed, he would say: "Here, one after the other, vice and virtue have slept."

The first thing Elisabeth did was to enquire with the liveliest interest about the Queen's health—the Queen whom she always called her sister. She asked Richard whether he had seen her recently. He replied: "She is very well and lacks for nothing."

The Nuncio continues: "The whole night, she appeared anxious. All the time, she kept asking Richard what time it was. . . . She rose early. Richard was already up. She again asked him what time it was. Richard took out his watch to let her see the time and made it chime. She said: 'My sister had one almost like it, only she did not wind it. . . .'

She took a little chocolate, then, towards eleven o'clock, she went to the entrance of her prison. Many great ladies who were going with her to the guillotine, were already assembled there. Among others, there was Madame de Sénozan, sister of Malesherbes the minister, the King's defender; she was the best and most charitable of women. Madame Elisabeth charged Richard to present her compliments to her sister (the Queen). Then, one of these ladies, whose name I have forgotten, a duchess, I think, spoke: 'Madame,' she said to her, 'your sister has undergone the fate which we ourselves are facing.'"

Only the day before, Monsieur Chauveau-Lagarde had been told that he was to place Elisabeth's case before the revolutionary tribunal. (This gave the proceedings a false semblance of justice which did no dishonour to the partisans of equality.) But when he appeared at the prison to confer with his client, he was not allowed to see her.

The roll-call followed: the turnkeys, often drunk, and accompanied by dogs, roared the names of the accused with such mispronunciations, that they were rarely recognised by the victims. No answers. A volley of oaths, in voices so thunderous, that they struck terror into the listeners. At last, they were herded into the great hall.

On May the 10th, Chauveau-Lagarde's surprise was very great when he suddenly caught sight of Elisabeth among the other people accused before the tribunal: she was standing on the top tier of the benches. They had placed her there before all others, on purpose, to set her more in evidence. There she was, in her white dress, dominating the whole assembly, and looking perfectly calm. Fouquier-Tinville had purposely deceived Chauveau-Lagarde, when he told him that Elisabeth was not going to be judged right away. And now, it was too late: he could never speak to her in private before her trial.

This "*Grande Chambre*" of Parliament, with its half light filtering in through three high windows, and its black and white marble floor, had been famous throughout Christendom for the richness of its blue and gold Louis XII ceiling, its tapestries and fine velvet draperies sprinkled with fleur-de-lys. But all the pomp and beauty had been destroyed. The "*Grande Chambre*" was now called "*Salle de la Liberté*", the ceiling covered over, walls denuded, Louis XV's bust thrown away, and replaced by three busts—Marat, Lepeletier and Brutus, very popular at the time, because they had condemned their own children to death.

The president of the tribunal himself had denounced his own brother and father. He was one Dumas, a barrister, nicknamed Dumas-le-Rouge because of his red hair and face. First at the seminary, then with the Benedictines, he broke his vows before taking orders. His morals were more than doubtful. In 1789, he had been a creature of acute sensibilities, and had written to Madame de Lauraguais: "Humiliation is that which affects me most keenly." And yet . . . when he presided at the revolutionary tribunal, he questioned his victims with insolence, often with irony, insulting the wretches who were going to be guillotined. He even went so far as to call a notoriously valiant soldier a coward, thus inflicting on him public ignominy worse than death.

There were fifteen jurymen in this travesty of a trial. They were nicknamed "*solides*", because they had been hand-picked for this great occasion, and could be trusted to condemn. Indeed, hardly had Elisabeth's name been read out, but all the jurymen cried: "That's enough; death! death!"

Dumas sat down and gave one glance at his chief victim. There she was, very proud in the way she bore her golden head, and quite unmoved, for her cheeks were still rosy. (Several witnesses have testified that she did not turn pale that day.) He tried to quell her with a look, but she merely glanced at him with vague contempt, and turned away.

"Visibly wounded by the noble pride of a woman whose high situation, as much as whose merit, crushed him, he sought revenge in mockery, a weapon as base as it is cruel."[1]

Ah, so she thinks she'll get away with it, does she! Not on your life. He'd make her lick the dust before he'd finished. One doesn't have red hair and a red face for nothing.

Dumas: What is your name?

Elisabeth: Elisabeth-Marie.

Dumas: Your age?

Elisabeth: Thirty.

Dumas: Where were you born?

[1] Duval, "Souvenirs Thermidoriens."

U

Elisabeth: Versailles.
Dumas: Where do you live?
Elisabeth: Paris.
And so on.

Twenty-five other names were read out—nine were women. The ages of the accused ranged from twenty-one to seventy-three, and though they were mostly aristocrats, they included a chemist, a merchant, a farmer and a servant who would not betray his master. The lovely Madame de Sérilly (whose bust is in the Wallace Collection) was reprieved at the very last minute, because she was pregnant.

The accusations droned on: "Elisabeth has shared in all the crimes, she has co-operated with all the machinations and plots formed by her infamous brothers, by the vile and shameless Antoinette and all the horde of conspirators who had gathered around them. . . ." Of course, the very word *conspirators* had an electric effect in those days. The doom of the victims was a foregone conclusion.

". . . it is she who keeps up a most active correspondence with the other brother, become to-day an object of derision, an object of the contempt of despots in coalition, in whose country he has gone to lay down his imbecile and heavy nullity; it is she who wished, by the most insulting pride and disdain, to degrade and humiliate the free men who consecrated their time to guarding the tyrant. . . ."

The usual accusations began again—that she had assisted at the orgy of the guards' banquet, in October 1789, that she had taken part in court plots against the people, that she had nurtured *"le petit Capet"* in the hope that he would succeed his father on the throne. . . . To this last, she answered (doubtless with a pang in her heart), "I used to talk familiarly with this unfortunate one who was dear to me for more than one reason, and consequently I administered to him the consolations which I thought would compensate him for the loss of those who had borne him."

Then came the turn of her advocate, Chauveau-Lagarde. At the peril of his life, he spoke of Elisabeth's goodness of heart and the heroism of her friendship, and asserted that so perfect a model of all the virtues could not be an enemy of the French people. Chauveau-Lagarde was wily enough to appeal to the classical pretensions of these patriots. He speaks of the virtuous man of antiquity, "calm and immovable among the ruins of a civilisation which has just crumbled around him. This portrait of the good man . . . is an image, though an imperfect one, of the Queen and Elisabeth de France. . . ."

As she listened, did Elisabeth remember the heroes from Plutarch's Lives, introduced to her by Madame de la Ferté-Imbault?

After hearing this praise, Dumas proposed that Chauveau-Lagarde should be arrested. However, he was not imprisoned, because they wanted to make it seem as if advocates were allowed freedom of speech.

Dumas shouted at him furiously for daring to speak of the pretended virtues of the accused, and therefore corrupting public morality. Elisabeth, who was calm and, as it were, indifferent to her own danger, was moved at the perils which her defender had now incurred.

.   .   .   .   .   .

Only one witness was called to depose against all the other victims. . . .

The jury went out. After deliberating for several minutes, they returned to the hall and declared that Elisabeth and the other accused prisoners were guilty. The list of names was then read out and they were all condemned to death. Then it was ordained that their possessions were to be confiscated (O Montreuil), and acquired by the Republic, to contribute to the sustenance of impecunious widows and children.

After the sentences, seeing that Elisabeth had not even turned pale, but still held herself proudly, Fouquier-Tinville said to Dumas: "One must confess, however, that she has not uttered one complaint." To which Dumas replied with ironic gaiety: "Of what then should she complain, Elisabeth de France? Have we not formed for her to-day a court of aristocrats worthy of her? And nothing will prevent her from thinking herself still in her drawing-rooms of Versailles, when she will see herself at the foot of the holy guillotine, surrounded by all that faithful nobility."

Just then, Elisabeth spoke to Dumas and asked him for a priest to assist her at her last moments. When this was referred to Fouquier-

Tinville, he replied: "Bah! bah! She can very well die without the blessing of a capucin."

It was now one o'clock. The prisoners filed out into the room reserved for those sentenced to death: this room was long, narrow, dark, separated from the clerks' office by a door and a glass partition. Candle-ends, meshes of hair and faded ribbons trailed on the wooden benches which lined the stone walls. At once, Elisabeth was surrounded. Even in that dreadful place, she held her last court, and her companions placed her on the pedestal to which she belonged. And here, as ever before in her life, she forgot herself, and lived only for others. She saw the pale faces before her, some of them quite unresigned, and several unrepentant, cut off in the very blossom of their sins, and she pitied them. She spoke to them with great sweetness and gentleness. And her own face was so serene, that she renewed the courage of her fellows.

The Abbé Charles Magnin—a priest with an admirable face—who had consoled the Queen in her last moments, was later to tell Madame de Tarente that he had had the joy of assisting Elisabeth during the twenty-four hours that she spent at the Conciergerie. He probably saw her just then, whilst a Canon of Sens, who had been the Superior of the Carmelites of that town, gave the last consolations to some other fellow prisoners.

Fifty-seven-year-old Madame de Montmorin, who had lost practically all her family at the guillotine, could not bear to think of her son being butchered. She sobbed: "I'm quite willing to die, but I cannot see him die." A good maid called Marguerite, in the service of the Marquis de Fenouil, and who had been thrown into the Conciergerie for refusing to testify against her master, was an eye-witness to the following scene. (She knew Madame de Montmorin, who had been very kind to her invalid father.)

Elisabeth came over to Madame de Montmorin and said: "You have loved your son, and you don't want him to accompany you! You are going to find the bliss of Paradise, and you want him to remain in this world, where to-day there is nothing but torment and grief!" Madame de Montmorin stopped weeping; clasping her child in her arms she cried: "Come, come! we will go up together."

(Four years before, Elisabeth had told Rage the sublime words of a woman on learning of the death of her only son: "My God, he sees you, he loves you!")

Sixty-four-year-old Marquise de Crussol d'Amboise had been so nervous during her life-time, that she always had two women to sleep in her room: even a spider made her tremble. But this day, she lost her nervousness and acquired a new serenity through the example of the princess.

Elisabeth went from group to group, an angel of consolation in her white gown, wiping away tears, exhorting to courage and faith, pointing to the joys of eternity.

The executioner's assistants came and prepared the women's shoulders for the knife and cut off their hair. When Elisabeth's golden locks were shorn, she put a kerchief over her head and knotted it loosely under her chin. Her hands were tightly pinioned behind her. Then they were all herded into the *cour du Mai*. At four o'clock Elisabeth was put into a cart, "that bier of the living", with Mesdames de Sénozan and de Crussol d'Amboise. She talked to them the whole way from the Conciergerie to the Place Louis XV. (Did she recall that this was the anniversary of Louis XV's death?)

The rumour had spread through Paris that Elisabeth was going to the guillotine. Eye-witnesses have said that at first the crowds roared, and then suddenly fell silent, as if in consternation.

An officer of the National Guard, sword in hand, rode before the cart, inviting the people to silence. His solemn air, the feeling he gave one of being imbued with the gravity of his office, the slowness of his pace, the concentrated dolour of this herald of death, all lent poignancy to the spectacle. However timorous one might be, this whole procession was so riveting in its horror, that it was impossible to tear oneself away. The shops closed on the route, the dregs of the population emerged from their lairs, the street-criers ran about with lists of names, freshly printed. Suddenly, all along the route, the cry: "Here they are."

The journey took from three-quarters to one and a half hours.

Elisabeth's old botanist friend, Dassy, chanced to see her, and he was so greatly affected by the vision, that when he got home, he replied to his wife, who pressed him to account for his changed looks: "I've received my death-blow; I've just met and recognised in a cart . . . an angel going to the scaffold!"

Another, the Abbé Morellet, who saw her, wrote in his memoirs that her image pursued him for a long time during sleepless nights.

A celebrated scholar, a Monsieur Jomard, said, forty years later, that she was much paler than usual. (He is the only one who says that.) But, he recalled that her features were calm, and sometimes her beautiful lashes covered her gentle gaze. She was singled out among the others by her inexpressible dignity. She spoke during almost the whole journey, and never tried to hide from the gaze of the crowds. He noticed the slight toss of her head, for, her hands being tightly and painfully pinioned behind her back, the meshes of her golden hair escaped from her kerchief and kept falling forward over her face. A revolutionary witness noted that she seemed as if she were going to lead this cohort to Heaven. He adds: "I've heard it said to a famous revolutionary that, as she passed, there were great numbers of bouquets of roses in the Place Louis XV, so that the air was impregnated with their perfume." He concludes: "Nothing could paint this for you, as I saw it all. The same emotion was felt around me."

It is to Moelle, member of the Commune, who had known the princess at the Temple, that we owe some precious details: ". . . I left my home, and found myself on the downward slope of the Pont-Neuf, on the side of the quai de l'Ecole, at the moment when a white hand-kerchief which covered the princess's head, came undone and fell at the feet of the executioner standing by her side; he picked it up; when the princess refused to have it put back on her head, I saw him seize this sacred relic and appropriate it.

"Bare-headed, and by this fortuitous circumstance, distinguishable from several women who shared her fate, nothing could conceal from the multitude, the modest calm and the pious serenity of Madame Elisabeth going to her death.

". . . I try in vain to be noticed by the princess and to show her my grief. I follow her to the scaffold. There, the satellites and the victims stop. Unfastened at once from the plank to which she had been tied during the journey, and the first to stand up, the august virgin, until then withdrawn into herself, smiled angelically at her companions in death, raised her eyes to Heaven, lowered them on (the victims) and told them thus that it was in Heaven that they would meet again. . . .

"This is all I could see of this sublime and baneful scene. I did not see more. . . ."

Alas, scandal rode in the wake of sanctity. In another tumbril sat Martial de Loménie who had been consecrated Archbishop very young. He had been living in sin with his pretty cousin. And she was there too.

An eye-witness recounts that, on the way to the guillotine, seeing one of her rivals at a window, this cousin let fly at her, in a transport of triumphant and furious passion: "Yes, it's him all right, Madame, it's me all right. Have a good look! . . . Now you will never steal him from me again, he is mine, and I am going to die with him."

With the aid of an old map, it is easy to trace that last itinerary, over the Pont-Neuf, and then along the ancient Rue Saint-Honoré—the long agony of the Rue Saint-Honoré—that street which has witnessed so many scenes of French history.

Notre Dame on the right on the island, then the Oratoire, the Louvre, the Palais Royal, Saint Roch: this church, because of its raised steps, was much sought after by spectators, and they crowded there early in the day. The onlookers were at a good vantage point to spit on those unfortunate creatures whose hands were tied. Then the Tuileries palace and gardens, full of blossoming chestnut trees, a view of the Place Vendôme, without its statue, and the Rue Royale. (By looking right, she could have descried the cemetery of the Benedictine nuns, near the Madeleine, where the King and Queen had been buried.)

Every street, every building has its own memories, hallowed and heart-rending. But one senses that Elisabeth was not aware of her surroundings. Like the Carthusians whom Saint Sir Thomas More saw leaving the Tower of London for martyrdom at Tyburn, she had the joyance of one going to her bridal. She had loved God so much, she had tried to serve Him in the obscure hum-drum of every day, in the person of His poor, in overcrowded prison rooms which could so easily have become the antechambers of Hell. She had loved God in a sister-in-law with whom she had little in common and whom she had so tenderly befriended to the end. Like her father, the Dauphin, she had thought that mystical contemplation was not for princes, and so she had trodden the way of ordinary prayer, like the just man of the Scriptures, "living by faith".

At the angle of the Rue Saint-Honoré and the Rue Royale, two women asked Elisabeth to bless them.

Usually, onlookers mocked the upward glances of the victims in the tumbrils, and even mimicked the way they raised their eyes to Heaven. But this time, the dignity of the chief victim imposed veneration, and there was silence.

At last, the Place Louis XV[1] with the guillotine on a raised platform, near the seated statue of Liberty. The first sight of that blade glittering in the sunshine must have sent a shiver of fear down many a spine. There it was, smiling and ruthless, and now, there was no escape.

They say that the workmen of the Tuileries, on the terrace dominating the square, wasted an immense amount of time staring at the guillotine. At the Cabaret de la Guillotine, near by, the restaurant proprietor took care to provide for his clients a list of the day's victims, written on the back of the menu.

The first to get down from the cart, Elisabeth sat with her back to the scaffold on the wooden bench where she was to await her turn. She was to be last. The bench was under the scaffold.

Madame de Crussol, the first to be summoned, rose, curtseyed to Elisabeth and asked her permission to kiss her. Elisabeth replied: "Very willingly and with all my heart." All the women did the same, and as "E. M. du L" has so admirably put it, "thus they went to the scaffold, marked by this angelic kiss, for blessed immortality".

The men came and bowed to her when it was their turn.

It is easy to imagine what a great consolation the presence of the late King's sister must have been to them all.

Several heads had already fallen, when a man from the dregs of the populace, curious to know the identity of this person whom everyone was greeting so respectfully, elbowed his way forward to the bench and recognised her. He cried out cynically so that she could

[1] Place de la Concorde.

hear him: "It's all very well for them to carry on with these bowings and scrapings, she's dished, like the Austrian woman."

Elisabeth was reciting the De Profundis.

"Out of the depths have I cried to thee, O Lord: Lord hear my voice.
My soul hath relied on his word: my soul hath hoped in the Lord.
From the morning watch, even until night. . . ."

.   .   .   .   .

The executioner's assistants, in their crimson tunics and with red roses in their mouths, seized each victim, placed him face downwards on a wooden plank; this was lowered horizontally till the head was held down by a wooden clamp. The last thing the victim would see was the basket into which his head would fall. And then, a heavy, metallic sound and a thud as the blade crashed and yet another head fell. The blood gushed forth, and the boards became more and more slippery with the torrents of blood.

Each time that the knife fell, Calixte de Montmorin answered the roars of the mob by crying at the top of his voice: "God save the King". His cry was echoed by Baptiste Dubois, a servant.

When the twenty-third victim, the Abbé de Chambertrand, came to bow before Elisabeth, she said to him: "Courage and faith in God's mercy."

Then it was her turn. She refused the executioner's hand and walked firmly up the steps, alone.

At the moment when they were going to tie her to the plank, her neckerchief of Indian lawn slipped down, revealing a silver medal of the Immaculate Conception, which, with a little pocket book, was tied round her neck with a silken cord.

Desmarest, the executioner's assistant, wanted to tear away this neckerchief altogether. "In the name of your mother, Monsieur, cover me . . ." she begged. Those were her last words. (In such wise, Ovid tells us that Lucretia, at the moment of death, took care to fall with modesty.)

"Tunc quoque jam moriens, ne non procumbat honeste," . . . "Even then, when already at the point of death, she took care to sink down decently."

And then, two very strange things happened which were to mark that day with the seal of the supernatural: first, the drum did not sound after her death: before he could give the signal to the drummers, Macé, who had known the princess in the Temple and had shown respect for her, fell down in a dead swoon. A police report says he was carried away by the affrighted guards, paralysed and dying.

There was therefore no cry of "Long live the Republic", as was usual after the drumming.

Secondly, many old French families have long held the tradition, handed down to them from eye-witnesses of the scene, that at the exact moment when Elisabeth died, a delicious perfume of roses filled the Place Louis XV. This is not unknown at the death of saints. To take but one example among hundreds, the body of Saint Dominic exhaled an odour which clung for long after to the hands of all who had touched his bones.

It cannot be explained away by the fact that several people came to the execution carrying bouquets of red roses. The Place Louis XV was very spacious, and the supernatural odour was universally diffused over a wide area, and not localised.

People went away to their homes, downcast and sad.

. . . . . .

Monseigneur Beauchesne writes: "Quite near the guillotine was a cart drawn by two horses, containing two baskets: one for the heads, another for the bodies of the victims. When the executioners had thrown into the basket the twenty-fourth head which was Madame Elisabeth's, they laid out her body, covered with her clothes, on the heap of corpses piled in the other basket; as a result, her clothes were hardly blood-stained, whilst those placed at the bottom of the basket seemed to have been bathed in blood.

"The cart was driven away, escorted by the police. The crowd parted before it. . . .

"The convoy going slowly, followed the rue des Champs-Elysées,[1] rues de la Madeleine, de l'Arcade, de la Pologne, Saint-

[1] Then wooded fields and "terrains vagues", full of pot-holes, dangerous as night.

Lazare and du Rocher. People stopped to see it pass; a few windows slightly open, gave glimpses of the foreheads of several persons, speechless and motionless, perhaps kneeling. The retinue climbed the rue du Rocher very slowly, and stopped a moment (no doubt to give the horses a breather), at the spot where the ground stops rising and where this path, at that epoch, ceased being called rue du Rocher, to be named rue des Errancis, which at that time only existed in outline. It led to the Monceau barrier.

"A hundred yards beyond this barrier, the convoy passed between the only house on this road and a heap of stones facing it, on the right; (this heap) in olden days had served as a pedestal to a Calvary knocked down at the Revolution. It reached the barrier, it crossed it; then, taking a turn to the left, it turned its back to the customs pavilion and halted in front of a door, just large enough for carts, built into the city's enclosure wall. The door opened and the cart went into the enclosure, which for about the last two months, had served as cemetery for the victims of the revolutionary tribunal. The Madeleine cemetery, doubly peopled by the scythe of natural death and the blade of the guillotine, now lacked earth to cover the bones of the departed. Moreover, for a long time past, the inhabitants of the quarter had complained of the fetid miasmas which this cemetery exhaled.

"As soon as the cart had gone into the new enclosure, the door was immediately shut, policemen and idle lookers-on went away; alone, two carters and a police superintendent accompanied the convoy.

"This piece of ground which broadened out as it spread towards the parc de Monceau with which it was contiguous, had before that time been given over to cultivation; one half was still flower-beds, and the other half kept the trace of furrows broken into here and there by open trenches, some of which had been filled in, on preceding days, as was shown by the fact that the earth had been newly turned and very badly levelled in some places, for there were signs of hurry, and the triangle of the guillotine went faster than the mattock of the grave-diggers. This field of rest had been inaugurated on the 4th Germinal, year II (March 24th, 1794). . . .

"Now, the doors of the '*enclos du Christ*', (name given to this piece of territory), have just closed on Madame Elisabeth and her noble escort. The carts stop on the brink of the gaping pit . . . several feet away from the little wall which separates the enclosure from the garden.

"They unload the blood-stained cart. According to the declaration of the eye-witness . . . the body of Madame Elisabeth, recognised by the carters by her clothes and the place it occupied on the summit of the cart, was the first or among the first to be placed on the edge of the pit. All the bodies are successively stripped of their clothes before being thrown into the grave. An inventory is kept of these different items which are destined to be given to the Hôtel-Dieu.

"Occasionally, the grave-diggers go down into the pit to arrange the corpses so that they are not too packed together; . . . The body of Madame Elisabeth—always according to the witness of the grave-digger—must have been laid (face downwards), at the bottom of the pit, on the side nearest the wall. The heads having been placed at random in the cavities, the grave-digger has not been able to indicate where Madame Elisabeth's head could have been buried."[1]

.   .   .   .   .   .

The May night falls. The King's daughter, all glorious within, now sings her Vesper hymn in Paradise. Exactly twenty-four years before, her grandfather, Louis XV, had died of smallpox at Versailles. The horror of his death had spread consternation at court, and his parasites had fled, far and wide, leaving his meagre bier to go practically unattended to St. Denis, where he was buried among the Kings of France. So had been snuffed out, in intolerable stench, the greatest lecher that France had ever known, and one who had left behind him a more disastrous trail of weeping and shame than many men.

The innocent victim expiates for such crimes. Twenty-four years later, to the day, Louis XV's grand-daughter, a spotless lily of France who had filled the court with the sweet odour of her holiness, was sacrificed and thrown into a nameless grave. This friend of the poor was denied even a pauper's burial.

.   .   .   .   .   .

[1] de Beauchesne, op. cit. t.11, p. 235; see also p. 263 *et seq.*—fascinating. Louis XVIII's attempts to locate the tomb were half-hearted and fruitless.

In Paris that day there reigned so deep a stupor, so dismal a silence, that the monsters who had perpetrated the crime, trembled lest their tyrannous popularity should wane. Lord Grenville says that they were astonished at Elisabeth's heroic tranquillity, and forbade the publication of any detailed newspaper reports of her execution.

One tiny touch: Théodore de Lameth tells us in his memoirs that, fleeing just then to Switzerland, he found a red-capped revolutionary in his coach. This man recognised him and said: "My red cap, and all that you heard me say this morning must horrify you: but, like yourself, Monsieur, I'm trying to save my life. What purpose would be served by my death? And I have a family. Why should I have more to fear than others? This is the reason: but my God! Why did I not recognise you at once? I have seen you so often at Versailles, at balls, at the poor Queen's suppers! I was footman of Madame Elisabeth, of that angel!" His features were convulsed, and his tears flowed continuously.

Her footman was the first to weep for one whose untimely death broke many hearts.

Jules Mazé, in *"Visages d'Autrefois"*, tells us that various people, at different times, are said to have glimpsed Madame Elisabeth at nightfall, gliding slowly along the alley of lime trees on the terrace of Montreuil.

Elisabeth had taken into her service, and married to one of the King's kitchen valets, the young girl of the Rue Champ La Garde who had risen from a bed of mortal sickness at her kiss. After her mistress's death, the young woman was inconsolable: whenever she could, she slipped out at dusk to gaze at the château. One evening, she was kneeling behind the house and praying to the princess, when, on one of the steps leading to the garden, there appeared before her a white-clad woman whose face was hidden by a veil. The maid rose and wanted to flee in terror. Then the woman lifted her veil and Louise recognised the smiling princess. "I have not forgotten you, dear little Louise, I am watching over you. . . . Love me always." The vision faded, seeming to melt into the shadows already darkening around the house.

At first, the young woman was rooted to the spot: she trembled like a leaf shaken by the wind. Pulling herself together, she hurried home, where she told her husband what had just happened to her.

The husband believed her, for she was not subject to hallucinations, but he begged her to speak of this to no one—advised her henceforward to pass without stopping in front of the princess's old dwelling. This was wise advice—the Reign of Terror was then at its height, and, at Versailles, as elsewhere, it needed little to open prison doors to the most upright people. Later, when the danger was past, the young woman could not refrain from confiding to several members of her family and to one of her friends about the favour with which this princess had honoured her. Everybody thought Madame Elisabeth was a saint, and she was loved and revered by all who were fortunate enough to have known her. These good folk never doubted that the princess had appeared, and, through them, the story has reached us. Story or legend, we know not. In any case, it seems that Louise never varied in her accounts, even when, one day, the *curé* of Montreuil questioned her very closely.

.   .   .   .   .

If there is any truth in this tradition, it is consoling to think that, even in the bliss of her eternal reward, Elisabeth did not lose her human personality of eighteenth-century châtelaine. She would still think tenderly of the charming château where she had known the "*douceur de vivre*" in park and garden, with her ladies-in-waiting, and she still protected one of the numberless "little folk" on whom she had lavished her overflowing tenderness.

May this short study of the perfect friend, whom Horace Walpole called angelic and a saint, make her known to an ever widening circle, even beyond the confines of her own country, so that she may become the friend and protector of many.

FINIS

APPENDIX

A few dates, giving the chronology of the Revolution
(Selected from "The French Revolution", by J. M. Thompson)

1789

May 5.	Opening session of States-general
June 20.	Tennis Court Oath
July 14.	Fall of Bastille
July 15.	First emigration
Aug. 4	"Abolition of Feudalism"
Aug. 20.	Declaration of Rights begun
Oct. 1.	Versailles banquet
Oct. 5.	Parisians march to Versailles
Nov. 2.	Nationalisation of church property
Nov. 9.	First session of Assembly in King's riding school, near Tuileries. (The States-general are now called Assembly)

1790

June 19.	Abolition of Nobility
July 12.	Civil Constitution of Clergy
July 14.	First Fête of Federation

1791

Feb. 20.	Departure of King's aunts
March 10.	Pope condemns Civil Constitution
April 2.	Death of Mirabeau
June 20–21.	Flight to Varennes
June 25.	Return to Paris
July 14.	Second Fête of Federation
Sept. 14.	King accepts Constitution
Sept. 30.	End of Constituent Assembly
Oct. 1.	First session of Legislative Assembly

Nov. 12.   King vetoes decree v. émigrés
Nov. 14.   Pétion, Mayor of Paris
Dec. 19.   King vetoes decree v. clergy

1792

March 20.   Declaration of war v. Austria
June 20.   Crowd invade Tuileries
July 14.   Third Fête of Federation
July 30.   Arrival of Marseillais
Aug. 10.   Attack on Tuileries
Aug. 13.   Royal family imprisoned in Temple
Sept. 2.   Fall of Verdun. Prison Massacres
Sept. 21.   Abolition of royalty. 1st year of republic
Nov. 20.   Discovery of "iron chest"

1793

Jan. 21.   King's execution
Feb. 1.   Declaration of war v. England and Holland
March 7.   Declaration of war v. Spain
March 16.   Revolt in Vendée
April 6.   Comité de salut public
July 13.   Murder of Marat
Oct. 16.   Queen's execution
Nov. 10.   Feast of Reason in Notre Dame
Nov. 22.   Closing of Paris churches
Dec. 4.   Revolutionary government

1794

May 10.   Execution of Madame Elisabeth
July 28.   Execution of Robespierrists

Footnote. Names of successive forms of government.
1. States-general.
2. Constituent Assembly.
3. Legislative Assembly.
4. Convention.
5. Commune.